Golf Architecture

Golf Architecture

A WORLDWIDE PERSPECTIVE

VOLUME FIVE

COMPILED AND EDITED BY **PAUL DALEY**

First published in 2009
by Full Swing Golf Publishing
PO Box 1187
Glen Waverley
Victoria 3150 Australia

National Library of Australia Cataloguing-in-Publication entry:

   Golf architecture: a worldwide perspective. Vol. 5 / compiled and edited by Paul Daley.

   9780646510101 (hbk.)

   Golf courses–Design and construction.
   Landscape architecture.

   Daley, Paul.

712.5

Cover and text design by Andrew Cunningham – Studio Pazzo.
Typesetting and layout by Andrew Cunningham – Studio Pazzo.
Printed in China by Everbest
Prepress services by Splitting Image, Melbourne

Photograph on p ii: Chambers Bay, Washington, USA: Looking North-west from the
public trail over 'Foxy'—the 404-yard par-4 second hole. The Lone Fir, Puget Sound and
Fox Island present a striking background. (Photograph by Aidan Bradley.)

Contents

DEDICATION

Robert Edwin Labbance:

10 July 1952 : 24 August 2008

Radio presenter, music aficionado, restaurateur, photographer, collector, speaker/presenter, historian, researcher, writer, editor, biographer, son, brother, uncle, husband, father and friend

A courageous, prolific, celebrated and universally admired golf writer,
Bob lost his battle with amyotrophic lateral sclerosis (ALS) on 24 August 2008, dying peacefully at his home on
Northview Road in East Montpelier, Vermont.

Thank you for your offerings

Rest in peace

Acknowledgements

Full Swing Golf Publishing acknowledges the progressive work in business and golfing circles by Kumho Asiana. Mr Hyunil Kim, and others, have been gracious and a pleasure to communicate with, as has Mr H. C. Paik at Weihai Point, located in mid-eastern China.

Neil Crafter, in penning the Foreword, has outlined a succinct, stimulating and highly educational review of the seminal events within the field of golf-course design, especially pertaining to crucial developments within the United Kingdom, the United States and Australia. By according due credence to a series of interrelated endeavours at The Old Course, St Andrews, in the mid-1800s, it helps explain and link many future golf-course design developments.

A warm thank you is extended to the Volume Five contributors. While always pleasing to receive feedback that involvement has been enjoyable, one soon realises it's not quite a carnival atmosphere. And nor could it be, when involving the production of an essay, biography (some authors suggest this element is like pulling teeth), assistance with image captioning, PDF review, recording then providing third-party quotation details, supply of a contributor photograph, essay reviews, and sourcing materials such as plans/drawing/photographs—all set against a series of tight publishing timelines. And while the online time commitment varies among contributors, a single essay can, not uncommonly, be the culmination of up to 150 email exchanges. Less frequently, it's as little as ten. The relationships forged, and the contributors' output, are always greatly appreciated.

Full Swing Golf Publishing is proud of its ongoing association with Toro Australia. While the advertisements produced by its graphic design team are perennially soothing and agreeably subtle, Toro's products, more importantly, are highly reliable and benchmarked for their quality throughout the turf-grass and golf-course architecture industries.

Andrew Cunningham of Studio Pazzo, once again, demonstrated his graphic design, layout and bookmaking skills. His younger brother, Michael, lent great support with his treatment/conversion of images from RGB to CMYK. The use of acronyms, such as these, is more evidence that at one point the world went mad!

It is a sombre duty to acknowledge the fine work of Kevin R. Mendik, who came to the fore in completing a précised account—originally commenced by Bob Labbance—on the life and times of architect Wayne Stiles.

Bob, in spite of experiencing the debilitating effects of amyotrophic lateral sclerosis (ALS), was ever-keen to chisel a 1,500-word essay on Wayne Stiles, who, he maintained, was an under-appreciated master of golf design from the so-called 'Golden Age'. Primarily, Bob's plan was that the published essay would reflect an adaptation from his co-authored Stiles biography (written with Kevin). Pleasingly, the editor failed in his efforts to pare the essay to the standard 'Golf Archie' extent. Indeed, it proved an almost impossible task, given the breadth of absorbing information and level of interest one instinctively knew was contained within the extended version.

My gratitude is extended to Wendy Skilbeck for proofreading the manuscript. Her clear-headed approach, professionalism and friendship over the years, has made her a great ally.

Thank you to the many photographers whose images appear in this volume. Your craft—more than mere 'eye candy'—is greatly admired by readers, authors and publishers. And while singing their praises, I'd like to congratulate my good friend David Scaletti, who, after hovering frustratingly around a ten or eleven handicap for several years—a regular 'bandit'—is rejoicing in his new status as a single-figure handicap golfer. Go Scats!

Jenny Restarick has produced yet another professional index, and continues to play a key role in each volume throughout the series.

Courtesy of the Monterey Peninsula Country Club and Heidi Strantz/*Seventh Heaven*, we are thrilled to make available to a wider audience the coloured renderings by her late-husband, Mike Strantz. Interested parties seeking more information on Mike's sketches and golf-course designs can visit www.MikeStrantzDesign.com

Golf-club management staff, worldwide, confirmed all manner of current and archival course-related details, as did many helpful design staff. While barely detectable by the readership, behind-the-scenes assistance will always play a significant role with this title.

In closing, Full Swing Golf Publishing wishes to acknowledge James Affleck, Michael Beer, Milburn Calhoun, Sally Clark, Michael Clayton, Perry Cho, Martin Chuck, Michael Cocking, Susan G. Drinker, Forrest Fezler, Shannon E. Fisher, Jim Flynn, Kylie Foskett, Bob Grossi, Mary Ann Henker, Kai Hulkkonen, Linda Hurdzan, Jonathan Ireland, Margo James, Mike Keiser, Brad Klein, Bill Kubly, Cindy Marler, Bill McCreadie, Paul Mogford, Jim Nagle, Jeff Nelson, George Philpott, Danielle Rapp, Mitch Scarborough, Matt Schiffer, Roby Seed, Colin Sheehan, Joshua C. F. Smith, Mark Thawley, Tom Ward and George Waters for their valued contributions.

Magenta Shores Golf and Country Club, Central Coast NSW

One great result.
visit www.toro.com

TORO. **Count on it.**

Foreword

Neil Crafter

Golfers are truly fortunate when compared to participants in other sports, in that we partake of our recreation on such a varied collection of playing fields. While every tennis court, apart from differences in surface finish, must look the same to Roger Federer; to Tiger Woods every golf course is a unique and changing canvas that must be studied and learned if he is to master its nuances.

In golf's earliest times, golf courses were more often 'found' than designed. One of the first seminal moments in golf-course architecture was Old Tom Morris's efforts in the mid-1800s to thin out the whins and widen The Old Course at St Andrews, 'so that if one is afraid to face the bunkers he can go around their corners'.[1] He widened the greens and created new tees, setting in place the basic framework of the course that has so influenced generations of architects from Charles Blair Macdonald, Harry Colt, Dr Alister Mackenzie and Tom Simpson, through to those of today. Study of The Old Course, such as Mackenzie did in preparing his famous plan of the links in 1924, is a special reward in itself and a prerequisite to developing the necessary understandings of the principles of golf design in order to become a competent and inspired practitioner.

The establishment of inland golf courses in Britain, particularly in the sandy heathlands near London was, perhaps, the next crucial development in the blossoming progression of golf design from its roots in the coastal linksland of Britain. Early inland courses on unsuitable soil, such as the Coldham Common course at Cambridge that Bernard Darwin played during his time at Trinity, were sadly all too common. 'The ball could be holed on those greens of beaten mud, which at their best rather resembled a head of hair plastered down with brilliantine',[2] lamented Darwin. Architects such as Park Jr, Fowler, Colt and Abercromby led the charge to the heathlands, establishing first-rate courses on land far from the sea. Crucially, the push materialised on land that had the twin attributes of

OPPOSITE **Glenelg Golf Club, South Australia, Australia:** Neil Crafter's remodelled par-3 third hole—at one of Adelaide's Big Four sandbelt clubs—features the sod-revetted bunkering style that was introduced to the course during its 1998–2004 redevelopment. (Photograph courtesy of Glenelg Golf Club.)

undulations suited to golf and sandy soils that allowed for excellent drainage.

In the United States, Macdonald's design for the National Golf Links of America on Long Island was similarly a seminal event. The establishment of this course, utilising the principles of the holes that he had studied and recorded during his time in Scotland and England, set the stage for the ongoing development of golf design in North America through the twentieth century by men such as Albert Tillinghast, Donald Ross, William Flynn, George C. Thomas, Stanley Thompson and Robert Trent Jones.

For golf in Australia, the development of golf-course architecture was kick-started by Scottish immigrant professionals such as Dan Soutar, Carnegie Clark, James Scott and George Lowe (both Sr and Jr), while locals 'Cargie' Rymill in Adelaide and Eric Apperly in Sydney were at the forefront of home-grown design. But the arrival of Dr Mackenzie on these shores in October 1926 set off a chain of events that spread like a nuclear reaction throughout the game in this country that still resonate today. All of a sudden golfers were contemplating their courses and wondering why they didn't measure up and how they might be improved.

One Australian who capitalised on his opportunity of being the right man in the right place at the right time was Royal Melbourne member and 1924 Australian Open champion, Alex Russell. However, Russell was most fortunate to be there at all, considering that while commanding one of the four guns of the Twelfth Heavy Battery of the Royal Garrison Artillery in France in July 1916, an incoming German shell exploded right next to where he was standing. Russell was thrown into a trench by the explosion and was lucky to be alive; a more direct hit would have seen the man who would become Australia's greatest home-grown golf architect laid to rest in the fields of France. Russell was repatriated back to England and ultimately saw action again in France in the last two years of the war as a

battery commander. Russell's experiences in France and Belgium no doubt had a major impact on the rest of his life, as did meeting Dr Mackenzie at Royal Melbourne. The two men, with their similar Cambridge and Army backgrounds, no doubt hit it off, despite the twenty-two-year age difference between the younger Russell and Mackenzie. That Mackenzie took Russell into partnership is well known and, in Russell, Mackenzie could doubtless see a younger version of himself, albeit one who was a more accomplished player. Russell carried on Mackenzie's work after he left Australia; without Russell it is doubtful that Mackenzie's legacy in this country would be as strong.

In recent years, the efforts of golf architecture enthusiasts in Australia have had a positive impact on the world scene, beginning with the Society of Australian Golf Course Architect's (SAGCA) annual publication *Golf Architecture* magazine, and continuing with the similarly named series of fine books *Golf Architecture: A Worldwide*

Perspective conceived and implemented by Melbourne's Paul Daley—and if you are reading this Foreword you are holding the fifth volume of his series in your hands. Paul's masterly flair has been to capture, in a collection of seemingly disparate essays on golf courses and course design by a varied group of contributors that include practicing architects, golf writers and enthusiasts worldwide, a sense of timelessness and interest through the carefully assembled subject matter and wonderful photography he sources for each issue. Paul's books have added considerably to the library of golf-course architecture and long may the series continue.

OPPOSITE **The Hornbill Golf & Jungle Club, Sarawak, Borneo: Designed by Neil Crafter, the golf course at the Borneo Highlands Resort is one of the more unusually named courses in world golf—and one of the more spectacular, too. This view is captured from behind the first green, looking down the fairway towards the clubhouse. (Photograph courtesy of Borneo Highlands Resort.)**

Introduction
Paul Daley

Golf development, via the agency of golf-course design, materialises in a range of models, be it high-end/low-end private, affordable public, resort, residential and non-residential, plus variations on these themes. Seeking a worldwide perspective on golf design, and interrelated golf markets, necessitates a wide-ranging search for suitable material. Pleasingly, even after five volumes, prospecting continues to be an enjoyable aspect of the series.

In the case of a golf membership model, a key marker of a club's exclusivity is its joining fee (sometimes referred to as initiation fee), which may peak as heftily as $650,000 for Sebonack on Long Island, New York. Elsewhere, the amount may be purely nominal. In most cities of the world, the 'going rate' for courses of a particular standard, or locality, holds sway. Due to supply and demand issues (of available golfers), some clubs—approaching or experiencing a dire financial situation—are abolishing joining fees altogether, merely to boost the membership base and stimulate an influx of revenue through other avenues.

Full Swing Golf Publishing is delighted with the quality and breadth of the essays, covering courses in Australia, Canada, China, England, Poland, Scotland, the Netherlands, Uruguay, the USA and Wales. Some essays in Volume Five are specifically related to the discipline and conundrums associated with golf-course architecture, while five essayists have elected to enlighten the readership with restoration/remodelling case studies. The publisher, being of a slightly esoteric nature himself, is pleased to introduce esoteric essays into the mix, along with six change-of-pace Picture Essays.

We welcome twenty-two debutant contributors, and welcome back those contributors who are making a re-appearance in the series. It's always pleasing, too, when a potential contributor—generally, a student of golf-course architecture—acts on his/her intuition and sends an unsolicited essay. More often than not, assuming the basic 'shell' displays potential, this initiative is rewarded by gaining a spot in the currently produced volume, or being earmarked for one of the following two.

A potpourri of diverse talent has been assembled within Volume Five. While the majority of contributors are golf-course architects, other professions and vocations are represented. The line-up includes writers, design panellists, a club archivist, a university lecturer, a director of operations, an historian, an investment management advisor, retirees, past club captains, committee members and a course superintendent. And courtesy of Doug Sobieski, we gain the thoughts of an ex-PGA golf professional turned technology leasing wiz! The common link is that each contributor is clearly passionate and knowledgeable about their chosen subject matter.

Two of the bigger success stories in the golf-design industry are Korea and China—the latter, frequently announced through the prolific twelve-course Mission Hills development (216 holes). Currently there are over 500 Chinese golf-course projects on the books, either in planning, under construction, or completed and due to open.

One of the most exciting, recent Chinese golf developments is this volume's cover club, Weihai Point Golf & Resort, located in Shandong Province in mid-eastern China. Designed by Golfplan – Fream, Dale & Ramsey, the course boldly bites into the Yellow Sea and presents an abundance of spectacular cliff-top vistas and shotmaking challenges.

The city of Weihai, itself—among the most dynamic and fastest growing in China—is but eighteen years old, and is advantageously placed for tourism and commerce, being nearest geographically to both Korea and Japan. It pays due heed to engineering and major infrastructure, with its three first-rate ports, two international airports within short distance, and a rail service that transports cargo and passengers to all points of China.

Weihai does more than pay 'lip service' to having a social conscience, as evidenced by the accolades for its HR and environmental performance: China's first National Hygienic City; China's first National Model City; China's first City Group for Environmental Protection; China's first National Garden City; and twice a winner of the UN-awarded Best Practices for Improving Living Environment. The young city is ticking all the right boxes and is clearly above the practice of 'window dressing' for international eyes. Having a world-class golf course within its environs won't do it any harm, either.

As David Dale alludes to in his Weihai Point essay ... any given project can experience problems. And sometimes, given the right mix of untoward circumstances, they fall over completely. Indeed, golf developments fail to get off the ground with such frequency that rejections rarely attract sustained global attention.

An exception to this rule was the proposed $2.5 billion coastal development at Balmedie Beach on Menie Estate, just north of Aberdeen on Scotland's east coast. The curtain looked set to fall on the project in late November 2007, when the Aberdeenshire Council's Infrastructure Services Committee ruled against the planning application for Trump International Golf Links. And what grandiose plans Donald Trump's team had presented: a 570-hectare resort, including two championship golf courses designed by Martin Hawtree; an eight-storey, five-star hotel; a golf academy; upward of 1,000 holiday homes and 500 private houses. Trump, previously, declared it would house the 'greatest golf course in the world'. In a long-running, public tussle leading up to the council vote, Michael Forbes, a salmon fisherman, simply refused to sell his ten-hectare farm—a not unimportant detail, given its locality in the middle of Hawtree's proposed course.

Feelings on both sides were running high. Trump was moved during one press conference to call Forbes's property 'a disgrace' and 'in total disrepair'. Forbes maintained his line, telling Trump what he could do with his money—rumoured to be an offer in the vicinity of £375,000 to sell. Following these setbacks to Trump's plans, a curious sidebar evolved: being wooed by Northern Ireland's feisty First Minister, Ian Paisley, to transfer the project to Northern Ireland. But there was still a ray of hope in Scotland; namely, intervention by the Scottish Executive, which ordered an independent local planning inquiry. The three inspectors listened to evidence concerning environmental values and damage, a world-class golf course, economics and social benefits of the project to the region. Pivotally, at that point, the momentum swung in favour of Trump's project receiving the green light. And so it transpired. The projected opening of Trump International Golf Links is between the summer of 2011 and springtime, 2012.

Historically, golf-course architecture has evolved in response to any number of influences. Equipment and technology-based advancements have always been a factor, although never, perhaps, as starkly (or as regularly amplified, almost annually) as over the past twenty years. At hand, are four relatively new influences: global water crisis management; land management; the staggering world financial crisis in late 2008; a worsening of the reality where young golfers are struggling to find the time or money (or both) to play. Such is the intensity of contemporary life, coupled to ever-increasing expectations from employers, people are forced into working longer hours—thanks mainly to the unhealthy, umbilical-like reliance on computers. All of this gives rise to the greater need for shorter-than-regulation-size courses (in yards/metres) plus holes: six, twelve, etc., instead of automatically being eighteen. Given these four factors, and other influences that always lurk, it will be interesting to observe the impact on golf development and golf-course design over the coming few years.

I trust you enjoy the fifth volume of *Golf Architecture: A Worldwide Perspective*.

Good golfing ...

Weihai Point Golf & Resort, China

David Dale

I don't think we at Golfplan are much different from most course architects in this respect: we relish original design on a clean slate—and we greatly enjoy the challenge of renovation—but the prospect of blowing up an existing golf course and starting from scratch? That falls into neither conventional category, and it can, frankly, be a peculiar hybrid. Even if given a completely free hand, this sort of course-replacement exercise can be complicated, for reasons both artistic and practical. However, if the site and client are both attractive enough, we're game. In this context, taking on the Weihai Point project was appealing.

Let's start with the property: a peninsula almost two golf holes wide extending some 2,500 metres into the iconic Yellow Sea.

Separating this anything-but-flat piece of terrain from sea level are sheer rock cliffs ranging from ten to thirty metres in height. The climate in mid-eastern China is pleasingly temperate, almost arid, and perfect for bentgrass greens/fairways.

Add to this extraordinary landscape a trusted client, the South Korean-based Kumho Asiana Group, for whom Golfplan had already designed Asiana Country Club in 1989, and Jinju Country Club in 1996. Who could say 'no' on this site to a two-time repeat customer?

In retrospect, I can see that we were destined to work at Weihai Point. I dare say no golf-course firm has done more work in Asia for foreign developers. In China, alone, projects include The Orient GC at Xiamen,

for a Taiwanese developer; Grand Shanghai GC for a Singaporean developer; Grand Dynasty Holein Golf Club in Beijing, opened in 2008; Qiandaohu Country Club which opened near Huangzhou in spring 2008—while some of our finest, more recent work can be found in Korea, where the developers could observe and play the courses: the feted Club at Nine Bridges, the spectacular new Pine Beach Golf Links near Hae Nam, and our thirty-six hole complex at Bear River Resort, new home to the Korean PGA. In short, we couldn't say 'no'.

Accordingly, Golfplan – Fream, Dale & Ramsey said goodbye to the former Pan China Golf Club in March 2007. We welcomed the Weihai Point Golf & Resort in September 2008. The result, as you can see

OPPOSITE **Weihai Point Golf & Resort, Shandong Province, China: The 345-yard second hole, an attractive par-4, features a multi-level green and overlooks the Yellow Sea to the east. (Photograph by Tom Breazeale.)**

OPPOSITE **Weihai Point: An even 500 yards, the par-5 opener provides a panoramic view atop the peninsula from the highest greensite on the course. Weihai's second green is visible in the background. (Photograph by Tom Breazeale.)**

from the pictures here, is pretty special.

A great many things came together on the Weihai Point project to make it so, and some had nothing directly to do with the golf itself, other than enabling its eventual design. I'll get into some of those serendipitous events further down. There's a lot to tell.

But I don't want to complicate the story. For the golf junkie, the appeal of Weihai Point Golf & Resort is completely straight-forward: it hits you square in the forehead when you see the pictures, or the instant you walk through the front door. The clubhouse designers did a wonderful job, because the moment you step into the building, you see through to the other side where picture-windows reveal a panoramic view of the property: 270 degrees of water and peninsula—golf, ocean and sky as far as the eye can see.

We took advantage of this same dynamic on the first hole, a par-5 where the putting surface sits out there, almost starkly, against this same incredible backdrop, on this same wondrous horizon. At the second tee, you're standing on the cliff-edge mesmerised by the

elevation and the crashing surf below. The holes, beginning with the second and through to the eighth, play right along this precipitous coastline, out to the end of the peninsula and back.

With raw material like this, I know what you're thinking: how bad could the Pan China Golf Club have been? Well, it's a situation we've seen before: the original developer ran out of money, and the engineering company—a non-golf concern out of Beijing—ended up owning the course. They designed and built Pan China themselves, operating on the premise that none of the golf holes should come *too* close to the cliff edges. Let's be fair: these were engineers working out of their element. But this was a dubious, strategic-design notion on any seaside property; on this narrow strip, it produced a routing that verged on the surreal.

Suffice to say, we moved the holes down to water's edge, went with an out-and-back routing that any Scottish bus driver could have conceived, then set about blasting away a goodly portion of the rock that ran down the

peninsula's spine, thus creating the width (read: bail-out areas) these dramatic, risk-and-reward, seaside holes demanded.

Without resorting to an exhaustive hole-by-hole dissertation on Weihai, here are a few, designed to provide a fun sample.

The 500-yard, par-5 sixteenth hole requires something approaching a 220-yard forced carry over the roiling sea to the cliff-guarded fairway beyond. The second landing-area on this dogleg left sits some fifty feet below the first, but good players can reach the benched green in two shots. The putting surface sits at cliffside, guarded by an array of pot bunkers—six in all.

The par-3 seventeenth plays from an elevated tee to a very wide putting surface only 145 yards away. Bunkers guard the right and left front corners, and the ocean spreads out behind it. It's no easy matter to stand on the tee here and not think of the seventh hole at Pebble Beach. When the wind is blowing, it's very hard to stand on this tee, full-stop.

And speaking of Pebble, Jack Nicklaus has called the approach to its eighth green the 'greatest second shot in golf'. If there's a 'greatest first-shot' category, I hereby submit for consideration the drive on Weihai Point's twelfth hole. The drive across this stretch of open sea is, if anything, more spectacular than the famous approach to Pebble's eighth hole. It's that grand, and the hole's just getting started, for the approach on this 410-yard par-4 plays uphill to a green complex where the putting surface is its own peninsula in the sky.

The greens at Weihai cannot be easily pegged in a throwaway line. Almost all can be accessed via the bump-and-run shot, but there is no overriding style. Some are gentle; some boldly undulating. Some are long and narrow, while others present enormously wide. Several are raised; several more sit at grade. Many are perched at cliff's edge, while a few are protected by what little 'inland' this narrow peninsula could provide.

Weihai's bunkers are a different matter. We kept the bunker faces steep and the sand low (to keep it from blowing away). It's a great look but eminently practical. For a comparable style: think James Braid at the King's and Queen's courses at Gleneagles, in Scotland. (We've recently undertaken renovation of the Braid-designed Bukit Course at Singapore Island Country Club. We researched that job at Gleneagles itself, where we fell in love with the bunkers.) It wasn't difficult to envisage Braid's bunker style working perfectly here at Weihai.

It's almost cliché to hear an architect ardently praise the client, 'without whose wisdom and perseverance (and cash), this great project would not have been possible'. At Weihai Point, however, a great deal of credit for the final product does indeed go to the chairman of Kumho Asiana, Mr Park Sam-Koo. Let me make the case for his love and respect for the game—and this project—with a single number: 6,235. That's not the amount of South Korean won (in millions) he spent on the project. It's the length of Weihai Point Golf & Resort, in yards.

The golf course never suffers for this lack of so-called 'championship' length. It's a resort course, and it's a thinking-person's course: one hole will require a driver off the tee; the next tee-shot may call for three-iron.

The short par-4 third hole is a good

RIGHT Weihai Point: Preservation of the existing pine trees was a government mandate—not a single tree was removed during construction. The new clubhouse was designed by Harvard graduate, Ken Min Sung Jin. (Photograph by Tom Breazeale.)

BELOW Weihai Point: Fishing beds are prominent in the sea—especially in the western, calmer side of the peninsula. The seventeenth green overlooks this stunning oceanscape. (Photograph by Tom Breazeale.)

OPPOSITE Weihai Point: A short par-5, the nuances of the carefully bunkered tenth hole requires golfers to analyse and execute *all* shots in a strategic manner. (Photograph by Tom Breazeale.)

example of the latter scenario. From an elevated tee exposed to the peninsula's piercing winds, you could get away with driver; but the hole's length, contour and prevailing crosswinds really call for a low-trajectory long-iron. There's nothing wrong with asking the golfer to think strategically, to play a hole's contour, to play the wind. It's exhilarating.

The point is, Chairman Park had no interest in creating a monument to himself, or yet another 7,600-yard, punishing monster in search of a tour event. Yes, there is a lovely clubhouse, a golf hotel and some luxury villas—the development, of which, our new design at Weihai enabled. But the Chairman recognised, as we did, that only a 6,235-yard resort golf course would fit comfortably on this extraordinary property. So, that's what we built.

But this is not to say Chairman Park didn't spend liberally. He did. The bedrock was a real challenge here; we moved some 300,000 cubic metres of it. Without the extra ten to fifteen yards in fairway width afforded by this very necessary (and very expensive) blasting, Weihai Point would have been a veritable 'ball-eater'. Complicating the design and construction processes further were local environmental restrictions that absolutely forbade the uprooting of any trees, even if followed by judicious reforestation.

What's more, every square inch of the playing surface at Weihai Point was sand-capped, with sand imported from Qingdao at great expense. Even with this drainage-friendly measure, we herringbone drained the full length of every fairway and installed more than 300 individual catch basins.

Chairman Park did not build Weihai Point Golf & Resort because he's a golfing saint. He loves the game, unquestionably, but he also runs a busy airline that flies regularly between Seoul and Weihai, the booming heart of Shandong Province. It's an investment, and I'd be shocked if it weren't a successful one. But the man knows the game, appreciates what he found at Weihai, and he never let ambition or ego or profit compromise what I believe to be one of the world's great new golf courses.

As noted previously, Chairman Park, Kumho Asiana and Golfplan go back a long way. We designed two courses for them in Korea, but we also served as site consultants on more than twenty projects that never got built. During one of our many site walks, Chairman Park started talking one day about how much he liked Golfplan's blend of man-made contours and natural contours.

I acknowledged that, as a firm, we do make a practice of taking natural landforms adjacent to a proposed hole and carrying that contour through the golf hole—blending it with contours on the other side or to an adjacent hole. 'Like Mackenzie courses', Chairman Park said casually, and we walked on. Now, I ask you: who could say 'no' to someone who compares your work to Alister Mackenzie's?

OPPOSITE **Weihai Point: One of the most picturesque views found on the golf course—staring down the spine of the peninsula—is encountered along the par-4 third hole. Golfplan's routing then takes golfers to the 'edge of the world' and back, with successive par 3s. This picture shows the third hole (foreground) and fourth hole, beyond. (Photograph by Tom Breazeale.)**

ABOVE RIGHT **Weihai Point:** Ken Min Sung Jin's use of glass and roof lines display a harmony with the natural landforms, serving as an excellent backdrop to the 330-yard ninth hole. (Photograph by Tom Breazeale.)

ABOVE LEFT **Weihai Point:** The bunkering on the eighth hole is visually bold, yet purposeful. Steep, grass-faced hazards can intimidate players, while bunker maintenance is enhanced by keeping the sand low and out of the wind. (Photograph by Tom Breazeale.)

BELOW **Weihai Point:** The location of the seventeenth green was originally slated for condominium development. Now, it's forever preserved in company with the famed seventh hole at Pebble Beach. (Photograph by Tom Breazeale.)

OPPOSITE **Weihai Point:** During the project's planning phase, a short walk to 'the point' revealed a great opportunity to create the spectacular par-3 fifth hole. (Photograph by Tom Breazeale.)

TOP **Weihai Point:**
The eighteenth hole
plays uphill from tee
to green; from the
landing area, a
dramatic view to
the sixteenth hole
creates a lasting
memory of the
Weihai Point
experience.
(Photograph by
Tom Breazeale.)

BOTTOM **Weihai Point:**
From the green of the
par-4 seventh hole,
golfers access views
to the eighth,
fifteenth, sixteenth,
seventeenth and
eighteenth holes.
(Photograph by
Tom Breazeale.)

RIGHT **Weihai Point:**
Customised green
design for each site
condition is utilised
by the contractor and
shaper. (Rendering
by GolfPlan)

OPPOSITE **Weihai Point:**
Note the resemblance
of the illustrative
sketch and the
finished fourth-hole
greensite.
(Photograph by
Tom Breazeale.)

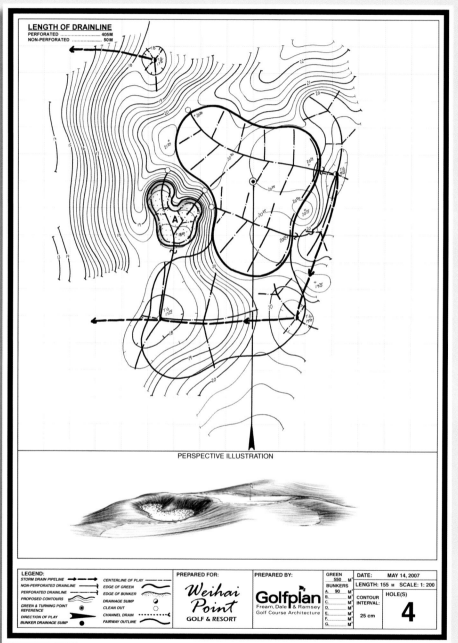

LENGTH OF DRAINLINE
PERFORATED 405M
NON-PERFORATED 50M

PERSPECTIVE ILLUSTRATION

LEGEND:

STORM DRAIN PIPELINE — CENTERLINE OF PLAY
NON-PERFORATED DRAINLINE — EDGE OF GREEN
PERFORATED DRAINLINE — EDGE OF BUNKER
PROPOSED CONTOURS — DRAINAGE SUMP
GREEN & TURNING POINT REFERENCE — CLEAN OUT
DIRECTION OF PLAY — CHANNEL DRAIN
BUNKER DRAINAGE SUMP — FAIRWAY OUTLINE

PREPARED FOR:
Weihai Point
GOLF & RESORT

PREPARED BY:
Golfplan
Fream, Dale & Ramsey
Golf Course Architecture

GREEN 550 M²
BUNKERS
A. 90 M²
B. M²
C. M²
D. M²
E. M²
F. M²
G. M²

DATE: MAY 14, 2007
LENGTH: 155 M   SCALE: 1: 200
CONTOUR INTERVAL: 25 cm
HOLE(S) **4**

Weihai Point: The par-4 sixth hole is terraced atop a coastline composed of pine trees and rugged, rocky outcrops. The existing bedrock had to be blasted to create a playable fairway—albeit, one that is reached by a forced carry from the tee. The 'deception bunker' short of the green is designed to ensnare the unwary or overly casual golfer. (Photograph by Tom Breazeale.)

SAND VALLEY 9TH
AGOLFARCHITECT.COM
21/06/08
PAR-3
150M.

Rescuing Sand Valley, Poland: A critical lesson for investors

Tony Ristola

The value of any experience only comes from knowing the truth. This is the story of Sand Valley.

It started one bright July day with the ceremonial shovel of dirt from the owner; this time, wielding an excavator. The builder participating in the festivities was selected on the strength of previous work within the country. The architect, an architect's association member, provided a neat and tidy set of detailed plans including a specifications book itemising every feature, right down to the type of grading stakes. During his infrequent 'site-visits' he was 'to constantly supervise the construction from the first cleared tree', ensuring the work was carried out according to plan.

After the party ended, construction progressed over the ensuing months. The weather, always a critical element, played a winning hand delivering merely six days of rainfall! 'Site-visits' by the architect were made. According to most theorists, this represents the modern ideal for building a golf course. But contrary to theory, something, more accurately, *most everything* went poorly and culminated with the so-called 'experienced' builder being fired.

I arrived at Sand Valley, Poland, eleven months after construction began. Having taken the project sight unseen, and expecting to clean up the mess, I proceeded to walk the property for five days, making notes and shooting hundreds of photographs to document the state of affairs. It took that long to evaluate the totality of the mess that had been made. It went beyond shoddy work. The site was a confusing jumble of clutter and disarray, and I continually unearthed new surprises as the days and weeks went by.

The five-day walkabout became an eleven-page report for the investors to ponder. With fourteen holes ripped open in some manner, I found it difficult to find anything worth saving. Valuable time, a season's perfect weather, and an untold sum of money were poured down the drain. All this was difficult for the ownership to swallow, so two consulting engineers and a superintendent visited; all confirmed the dismal state of affairs. Though no declaration was made, we all

OPPOSITE **Sand Valley Golf & Country Club, Paslek, Poland: Completed in June 2008, a conceptual sketch of the 150-metre par-3 ninth hole helped guide the 'work-to-be-completed' timetable. (Sketch by Tony Ristola.)**

knew the project had to begin a second time.

As construction commenced anew, only the basic routing was maintained; and here we adjusted greens and tees to garner the best possible holes. Otherwise, the original plans were abandoned, and the course designed in the field.

Sifting through scores of ideas and actively mining opportunities on a daily basis, greens, fairways and features were shaped and adjusted in real-time using continual communication and monitoring—only possible since construction was lead by the architect on an all-day, everyday basis. There were no fancy looking detailed plans, just the vision of the architect leading construction, a variety of conceptual sketches and constant face-to-face communication with the workers.

Unfortunately, the weather, that most critical factor, changed fortunes after the restart. The previous record dry summer was followed by a record wet summer. The rains that brought recurrent floods to England brought Poland wave after wave of rain. Our longest dry spell was a mere ten days.

During the wet summer, the owner came to realise the value of keeping dirt work to a minimum. The standard method of manufacturing new contours from existing terrain means the earth must be moved three times: firstly, to strip away and stockpile the topsoil; secondly, to shape the contours; lastly, to replace the topsoil after the irrigation and drainage are installed. This chews up a lot of time, and, when done to most holes, comes at significant expense.

Had the original concept been to utilise the land largely as found and then use clever dirt-moving solutions, the work would have been significantly simpler and faster. Thousands of construction hours, tons of fuel and headaches could have been spared.

The project is being seeded as I write, and I'm proud of the result. It is the product of a small core of locals who slogged through months of ten- to fifteen-hour days. What we built is a course nonpareil to northern Europe and harkens back to the design ideals of the Golden Age of golf. The holes differ greatly in character. The greens are a variety

of sizes ranging from 350 to 1,600 square metres. They are fairly wild and their fescue-colonial bent surfaces will be maintained at playable speeds. The fairways are wide: 35 to 70 metres with some combined fairways in excess of 130 metres. Because the fairways are wide, bunkers are cut into the fairway or placed centrally and, with the wind in the region blowing seemingly equally from the four points of the compass, play will be fun, varied and interesting.

The property has multiple personalities with holes running along the river, river dunes, and open rolling terrain, over canyons, through forest, along ridges, wetlands and through a sand quarry—a mixture of high and low country. Most holes enjoy expansive views of the region; but what ties this diverse property together is the element of sand—after all it's the main focus of the project's name. We don't have a large collection of formal bunkers, some thirty-eight, but there are several hectares of attention-grabbing, low-maintenance sandy scrub.

Now nearing the project's end, the owner

SAND VALLEY 4TH
AGOLFARCHITECT.COM

06/10/08   PAR-5   2nd shot.
                    (3rd shot.)

SAND

NOTE: WASTE AREA TIES INTO - BLEEDS OUT INTO BUNKER RIDGE BEFORE No. 10 G.

CONCEPTUAL ILLUSTRATION (1)
SAND VALLEY GC. No 10
MEMBER TEES
12/05/07.

WATER

clearly sees how things could have been done simpler, easier and cheaper—and with impressive results, too. Experience is a great teacher and, to his credit, instead of hiding the false start and challenges, he has been very open about it all. His candour and openness is a tremendous gift and benefit to future investors, and to golf development in Poland. Equipped with this knowledge, others can avoid the hard lessons Sand Valley had to endure. If they heed his advice, they will be able to create affordable, first-rate golf, protect their investment and help to grow this great game. Moreover, the owner of Sand Valley will have left a most valuable legacy in this developing golf nation.

Specifically, he clearly sees how daily involvement by the architect is a tremendous driving force, especially in an emerging golf nation and continent where golf-course builders are scarce. He believes an architect leading construction daily provides 'something really valuable for product quality', because continual assessment and improvement of strategic value and the creation of special details makes 'stuff look just stun-

ning, yet does not cost all that much to build; details just not possible on a turn key project'.

Unfortunately, the initial problems Sand Valley encountered have been repeated continually for more than a century, especially in emerging markets. Lack of knowledge and an attitude of 'it won't happen to me because we have highly detailed plans' are prime reasons such mistakes are guaranteed to recur. Even armed with knowledge, investors—especially those in developing golf nations—face huge challenges. With too few truly qualified golf-course construction companies in Europe, leaving builders alone for days or weeks at a time amounts to playing Russian roulette with millions. The only sure-fire and economical way to overcome these risks is for the builder to receive constant monitoring and guidance from the architect. It's simple, powerful and common sense; it was used to rescue Sand Valley.

OPPOSITE **Sand Valley: A conceptual illustration of the tenth hole was produced after a couple weeks on the Polish site. Portrayed from the forward tee; arrows indicate the drainage flow lines. (Sketch by Tony Ristola.)**

Sand Valley: The 200-metre par-3 tenth hole, as it was built, without the wetland to the right or bunkers fronting the green. The forward tee is in line with the front of the green; the back tee, as noted in the illustration, is on a diagonal. (Sketch by Tony Ristola.)

Yarram Golf Club, Australia

Trevor Colvin

Yarram Golf Club celebrated its 100th birthday the very month this book was released.

The township of Yarram is two-and-a-half hours east of Melbourne and its golf club started out like many around the world: in quite a different location, with its course presenting a significantly different golfing experience to what it does today.

Officially formed on 6 May 1909, just nine days later fourteen players took part in Yarram Golf Club's Opening Day at a course known as the 'Aylesbury' course. It was situated in close proximity to the town on private property and owned by the Fleming family.

Like many early golf courses on private property, livestock was a problem. The major work undertaken by the members in the opening year was to net the greens to protect them from cattle and sheep, which were partial to eating the greens and 'pugging' them—so badly during winter that putting was a near impossibility. It must have been difficult enough to putt on rough, mown natural grass at the best of times; contending with hoof marks made good scores a rarity.

The first course record was set by Mr B. P. Johnson, who shot an eighty-eight to defeat his nearest rival, Dr Langley, by ten shots. That it occurred during the first club championship that September showed he had a sense for the big occasion.

During 1910–1911, the course spread, amoeba-like, and parts of it were on five separate private properties.

Many golf courses, such as Yarram's 100 years ago, were constructed along simple lines by comparison to today's courses, essentially being rough fairways in working paddocks, with fenced-greens and a mown, fenced tee at the other end. It wasn't too difficult a task, therefore, to change a course, or build another as the members of Yarram found during the formative years.

All of the farming properties the Yarram course occupied were close to the sea, low-lying and barely above sea-level—the perfect scenario to be inundated by flood. Indeed, the bad floods of 1912 caused part of the course to be unplayable, leading to the members being invited to use the property of the Robertson family for golfing purposes.

OPPOSITE **Yarram Golf Club, Victoria, Australia:** Taken from the outside of the dogleg, an image of the par-4 sixteenth hole typifies the attractive nature of the treed Gippsland property. The green, like many throughout this beautiful layout, is well-guarded by bunkers. The hole's length can be reduced by cutting the dogleg corner, although this strategy raises the odds of driving out of bounds (not pictured, to the left). (Photograph by David Scaletti.)

Early 1913 saw the return of golf at Aylesbury. The first Women's Championship was played that year, with Miss E. Waddington being the inaugural winner. It doesn't bear thinking about how she managed this feat wearing the heavy, long and undoubtedly uncomfortable clothing of the era.

The club recessed during the First World War, but at war's end, organised golf at Yarram took flight. A new nine-hole course was built at yet another site, which remained in play until 1922 when the club moved to a new course built by Mrs Stockwell on her farming property at Port Albert.

By 1931, the club had outgrown this course and finally sought a new venue in its own right. Courtesy of forward-thinking committee members, the club leased a parcel of bush from the government (which the club bought in 1947), leading to an eighteen-hole course laid out by golf-course architect Augustus (Gus) Jackson. Thirteen of those holes are still in play today. Gus Jackson was a highly successful golfer, winning his first tournament at age ten and going on to win the Victorian Open twice and representing Victoria Golf Club in top-grade Melbourne pennant. Jackson also redesigned Orbost Golf Club in the far east of Victoria.

Also in 1947, the club bought an adjoining block, now known as 'The Paddock', which currently houses the tenth through fourteenth holes.

Yarram golf course has many attributes, not the least of these is its abundance of water. When many Australian golf courses are burning in drought, Yarram is always relatively lush and green, and playable all year round, due to the progressive members who had the foresight to drill for water. At a depth of 1,200 feet (equivalent to a reasonable par-4), they struck good water and it has been flowing consistently ever since.

The present layout was completed when grass greens replaced sand-scrapes in 1969, and that is when Yarram became the excellent test of golf that it is today. The greens were artfully designed by a member called Bob Blackwood, prior to him relocating to Swifts Creek. To his eternal credit, Blackwood resisted the temptation to place a conventional green at the end of each hole. Life member Tom Brown played a pivotal role in the co-ordination of the works program, especially of the front nine's greens—laid after, not before, the completion of the back nine's greens.

One of Blackwood's most beguiling green creations is found at the 255-metre par-4 fourteenth hole. This green complex, and its

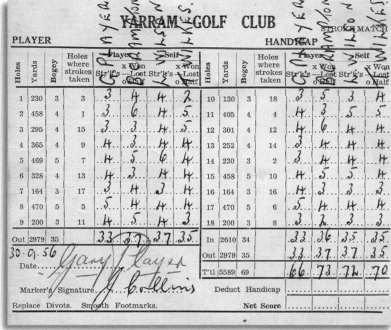

YARRAM GOLF CLUB — STROKE MATCH

PLAYER .... HANDICAP

Holes	Yards	Bogey	Holes where strokes taken	Player Str'k's	x Won o Lost	Self Str'k's	x Won o Half	Holes	Yards	Bogey	Holes where strokes taken	Player Str'k's	x Won o Lost	Self Str'k's	x Won o Half
1	230	3	3	3	4	4	2	10	130	3	18	3	5	3	H
2	458	4	1	3	6	H	5	11	405	4	4	H	3	5	5
3	295	4	15	3	3	H	5	12	301	4	12	4	6	H	H
4	365	4	9	H	3	H	H	13	252	4	14	3	H	H	H
5	469	5	7	H	5	6	H	14	230	4	2	3	H	H	H
6	328	4	13	H	3	3	H	15	458	5	10	H	5	5	3
7	164	3	17	3	H	3	H	16	164	3	16	H	3	3	3
8	470	5	5	5	H	H	H	17	470	5	6	5	H	H	H
9	200	3	11	H	5	H	3	18	200	3	8	3	2	3	3
Out	2979	35		33	37	37	35	In	2610	34		33	36	35	35
								Out	2979	35		33	37	37	35
								T'tl	5589	69		66	73	72	70

Date 30·9·56 ..... Gary Player

Marker's Signature ..... J. Collins ..... Deduct Handicap ....

Replace Divots. Smooth Footmarks. ..... Net Score ....

OPPOSITE ABOVE LEFT Yarram: A view along the par-3 eighteenth hole, from well short of the green on the right-hand side of the fairway. A hearty country welcome waits in the clubhouse, beyond. (Photograph by Trevor Colvin.)

OPPOSITE ABOVE RIGHT Yarram: This image shows the sixth green through the foliage between the fifth and sixth fairways. (Photograph by Trevor Colvin.)

OPPOSITE BELOW LEFT Yarram: A par-3 punctuated by a steep gully, Yarram's tough finishing hole has a bunker cutting into the left side of the heavily sloping green. From the tee, visitors invariably under-club and misjudge the hole's elevation change. (Photograph by David Scaletti.)

OPPOSITE BELOW RIGHT Yarram: When departing the eighth green, golfers take this walkthrough path to the ninth tee. (Photograph by Trevor Colvin.)

ABOVE LEFT Yarram: An exhibition match took place on 30 September 1956 with South African professionals, Gary Player and Trevor Wilkes, alongside Australian amateurs, Bruce Crampton and Les Wilson. Player showed them 'a clean pair of heels' by scoring sixty-six. (Photograph courtesy of Yarram Golf Club.)

ABOVE RIGHT Yarram: Player's scorecard. (Photograph courtesy of Yarram Golf Club.)

BELOW Yarram: Ever the showman, the gallery is fixated upon Gary Player. The picture harks back to an era when gallery ropes were less commonly used. (Photograph courtesy of Yarram Golf Club.)

idiosyncrasies, is typical of what makes Yarram a wonderful golf course. Because of the left-to-right tilted green shape, placement of the tee-shot has to be centre-fairway, or right of centre, in order to lessen the diabolical impact of the sinuous bunker that wraps itself around the front and left side of the green. The bunker receives an enormous workout, as golfers who 'split' the fairway are forced to aim their short approach shots toward it in order to allow for the ball bouncing well to the right upon landing on the green's surface—even crisply struck pitch shots directed at the green's centre (from the incorrect position) can run off the green at the right. Compounding the difficulty of the hole, especially for longer hitting golfers, is the out-of-bounds fence situated twenty metres over the back of the green. In many instances, this makes the choice between a driver and three-wood not quite clear-cut.

The greens and dam were provided for a total cost of $7,000, largely due to volunteer labour. Forty years on, the volunteer ethic is still alive and well. In fact, Yarram is an all-volunteer course, with a complete absence of paid staff. It was recently voted the best volunteer-run course in Australia, and it regularly rates in the top ten public access golf courses in Victoria. The members keep it in immaculate order. The course is so good that it is now part of the Victorian Pro-Am circuit and the golf professionals eagerly look forward to playing it each summer.

Another strength of Yarram golf course is that it is carved out of natural bush and sits on gently undulating sand hills. It is a true sandbelt golf course, where the fairways offer beautiful lies—good enough to tempt you with a driver. But stray barely half-a-metre off the fairways, you may have to pick a ball very cleanly off sand or pay the price for going at the ball a fraction too steeply. By straying a full metre off the fairways, you might also have to contend with, apart from a sandy lie, your ball sitting on bark and having to play around or through one of Yarram's thousands of trees.

At 5,717 metres, Yarram is a relatively short course by contemporary standards. On this fact alone, it reads like a 'walk in the park'. It's anything but. The Yarram layout is a true test of golf in a beautiful natural setting and the members have resisted any temptation to sanitise it. Play the fairways and Yarram is generous. Miss them and suffer a commensurate penalty—isn't that how the game of golf was designed to be played?

At a certain point in time, following a visit by a great Australian golfing identity George Naismith, Yarram's bunkering was heavily rationalised: some of these hazards were removed completely, while many others were reduced in area by thirty to fifty per cent. Others were converted to grassy hollows. It was a master stroke, easing the pressure from this aspect of course management.

Some holes throughout the layout appear mundane on the scorecard, but such a medium is not designed to alert golfers to a hole's inverse camber, or its strategically placed vegetation. Rest assured, there's plenty of intrigue to keep you on your toes. Yarram is a challenge, but it is also a delight.

The opening four holes contain three of

OPPOSITE **Yarram: The par-4 fourth hole is among the most difficult on the course. Calling for an accurate drive that must avoid ferny bracken to the right; a safe drive leaves a lengthy approach to a well-guarded green. And like most of Yarram's greens; this one will keep you 'honest'. (Photograph by David Scaletti.)**

OPPOSITE ABOVE RIGHT **Yarram: The fifth hole, a dogleg par-5, traverses some of the most exciting terrain on the layout and culminates in an elevated green that falls off on the left side. (Photograph by David Scaletti.)**

OPPOSITE BELOW **Yarram: The green of the uphill, medium-length par-3 seventh hole was recently modified. The idea, being, to quell the incidence of 'semi-unplayable' putting that could occur in summertime. Although two-putting is still hardly routine, nor should it be, the measure has proved to be popular. Note the abundantly sandy nature of the course just past the tee. (Photograph by David Scaletti.)**

the most challenging you will encounter, commencing with a 218-metre par-3. The second is a tight, bush-lined par-4 of 431 metres—often mistaken as a par-5—while the fourth hole, a 376-metre par-4, traverses magnificent 'golfing country' bordered by ferns and bracken to the right, complete with a property elevation change around where a good drive finishes.

Respite among the opening quartet is found at the third hole, being a mere 278 metres in length. One point of interest: it features one of the longest tees in Gippsland. Locals are well aware that the first, second and fourth holes face east and, if an easterly breeze is blowing, their length and degree of difficulty become even harder.

Every hole in this undulating bush layout presents its own nuances, while the quality of the final four holes can scarcely be bet-tered by a country golf course. Yarram members are used to hearing such sentiment from visitors. The first of these is the short par-3 fifteenth—Yarram's signature hole—guarded by many bunkers and a steep bank at the rear. Being elevated and at the mercy of 'fluky' winds, club selection is often tricky, even for seasoned members.

The fifteenth is followed by a 373-metre par-4 that doglegs to the left—a beautiful and highly challenging hole, which has an unmistakable 'come hitherto' appearance from its elevated tee. Visitors, in particular, rate it among the best three holes on the layout.

The seventeenth hole looks easy on paper at only 290 metres, but it is a sharp dogleg right. Drive too long, and you are in the bracken at the end of the fairway; too short, and you may not be far enough past the trees strategically located on the right side of the fairway, which block your second shot to the green. It is a difficult tee-shot choice: go for the 'straight enough and long enough' option to have a clear shot to the green, or lay-up the left side and play over the tall gum trees.

Yarram's final hole, a 186-metre par-3, plays over a deep gully and is seemingly longer than its official length. With peering eyes from the clubhouse taking an interest in proceedings, plus a good score on the line, the hole can be a brute!

The climate in and around Yarram is enviable, being not too hot in summer and reasonable in winter. Out on the course, the vegetation and wildlife are simply beautiful to be among. Kangaroos, kookaburras, galahs and other birds of the bush are constant companions. If you are lucky you may get a look at one of the magnificent, large goannas that thrive in the surrounding bush. Much of the bush is native eucalypt and coastal banksia, with ferns, bracken, blackboys and kangaroo tails throughout. The members resist any temptation to thin it, except for a metre or two off the fairway edges.

The publisher of this book, Paul Daley, is a Melbourne-based member of Yarram who enjoys escaping 'the Big Smoke' a few times each year to play the course. He told me during one round in 2008: 'I'm fortunate to have the opportunity to play many golf courses. Yarram, with its subtle intricacies, is a course I could play every day of the week'. We members agree.

Any golfer who takes the trouble to play Yarram will see why it's rated so highly, and why this humble country course was chosen to appear in this publication alongside some of the world's best and most glamorous golf courses. Yarram beckons and welcomes you, any day of the week.

LEFT **Yarram: The par-3 fifteenth hole under construction. (Photograph courtesy of Yarram Golf Club.)**

RIGHT **Yarram: A contemporary view of the brilliant fifteenth hole, with its distinctive ring-bunkering and a depression that hugs the green, beyond. Although, at times, merely a 'flick' from the tee… the hole's compensating factors are the 'fluky' winds experienced, the green's furiously sloping design, and the 'lottery' when pitching from over the green. A favourite of many members; the fifteenth hole marks the start of Yarram's Big Four finish. (Photograph by David Scaletti.)**

The resurrection of A. V. Macan in the Pacific Northwest

Scott Stambaugh

Assemble a group a golf-course architecture enthusiasts, and count the minutes before discussion gravitates to the work of the so-called Golden Age architects. Typically, the conversation revolves around Ross, Tillinghast, Mackenzie, Macdonald, Travis, Thomas, Raynor and Flynn. And then, someone references the work of Macan and the room goes silent. Eyebrows are raised and a question, inevitably, is posed: Who's Macan?

Because the work of golf-course architect A. V. Macan was predominantly regional, most are unaware of his contribution to the game. Mention the possibility of filling in a bunker on a Tillinghast course: rioting in the streets. Mention the need to rebuild a Mackenzie green: petitions circulate for pub-

lic stoning. Mention that Raynor's work may have been overrated: internet discussion forums crash. If clubs on the east coast of the United States were altering the work of their beloved courses at the rate Macan's efforts continue to be disregarded, the Golden Age of architecture would, sadly, be reduced to being enjoyed only through old photographs and words. Unfortunately, the value of restoration is on the 'slow' train from the east coast to the Pacific Northwest.

Arthur Vernon Macan was born in Dublin, Ireland, in 1882, and attended Shrewsbury, one of England's leading private schools for boys. It is thought that while at Shrewsbury, Macan may have picked up his first golf club at the age of nine at the nearby

newly opened Shrewsbury Golf Club.

In 1900, Macan returned to Dublin and enrolled at Trinity College, his father's alma mater. Macan's father, A. V. Macan Sr, graduated from Trinity in 1868 with a degree in medicine. He served as a volunteer in the Prussian army and later was named master of the Rotunda Hospital, the highest calling of the obstetric profession in the United Kingdom.

Macan had little interest in following the career path of his father, so he studied law and became a lawyer. In 1910, Macan met his future wife, Juliet Richards, whose father was a prominent lawyer in Dublin. A year later, Macan married into the family and found himself with a position within his new

OPPOSITE **Overlake Golf & Country Club, Washington, USA: Suffering the curse of 'lost' hole-locations, the back-left portion of the tenth green was expanded by over ten feet to recapture them. (Photograph by Scott Stambaugh.)**

While serving as the Executive Secretary of the Pacific Northwest Golf Association (PNGA) in 1947, Macan donated his 1913 championship trophy to the Association. He wanted it to become the perpetual trophy for the Men's Amateur Championship, provided that it displayed engravings of all past winners from 1899 onward. The trophy was renamed the Macan Cup and continues to serve as a perpetual trophy. (Photograph courtesy of the PNGA.)

father-in-law's firm. After a year working for the Richard Law Firm, Macan came to the realisation that his interest was not in law, but in golf. During the latter part of 1912 he made the decision to relocate to Victoria, British Columbia.

Arriving in Victoria, Macan hit the ground 'swinging,' winning the B.C. Men's Amateur at the Victoria Golf Club, his newly adopted home course. In 1913, Macan won the Washington State Amateur, the PNGA Men's Amateur and a repeat victory at the B.C. Men's Amateur.

Set to defend his title at the 1914 PNGA held at the Seattle Golf Club, Macan suffered a humiliating defeat in the semi-finals to Californian Jack Neville. A second-round defeat in the 1915 PNGA at the Tacoma Country and Golf Club was to be the last tournament Macan would participate in before the onset of the First World War.

Macan enlisted as a volunteer with the Eighty-eighth Victoria Fusiliers in 1916. In early 1917, he participated in the assault on Vimy Ridge in France, where he lost his left foot when struck by an exploded shell-casing.

He was transported to London where he spent a month in recovery. Because of the severity of his injury, it was necessary to amputate his left leg from the knee down. He stayed in a London hospital for the remainder of 1917, returning home to his wife in Dublin, where he remained until 1920. He spent his time reading what little published material was available on golf-course architecture.

The writings of John Low became Macan's biggest influence on his foray into golf-course architecture. *Concerning Golf* (1903), a seminal title by Low, was one of the first books that contained a defined set of principles for golf-course architecture. As chairman of the Green Committee of The Old Course in the early 1900s, and said to have been influential on the placement of the new bunkers on the outward nine, Macan readily adopted Low's architectural principles. Among the most influential figures of the game around the turn of the twentieth century—one of the founders of the Oxford and Cambridge golfing society in 1897 (captain for twenty years); a semi-finalist at the

British Amateur in 1897 and 1898 (runner-up in 1901); an expert on the rules of golf; a twenty-year chairman of the rules committee of the Royal & Ancient Golf Club—Low was hardly lacking in credentials to impress a young architect such as A. V. Macan.

Returning to Victoria in 1919, Macan continued to play competitive golf, now with the added burden of a wooden left leg. Despite this, he was still a contender in the B.C. Men's Amateur and the PNGA Men's Amateur for several years to follow. The venue for the 1922 PNGA Men's Amateur was the Colwood Country Club (since renamed the Royal Colwood Golf Club) just outside Victoria, and it marked Macan's first venture into golf-course architecture. Perhaps the first tactically designed course in the Pacific Northwest, Colwood's wide fairways, strategically placed bunkers and undulating greens were enjoyed by all. Thereafter, Macan was in high demand. As he was one of the only Golden Age architects to be working in the far reaches of the United States and Canada, his services for designing new courses, as well as remodelling work, took

Overlake: The simple act of removing one tree reveals the quality of the sixth hole. (Photograph by Scott Stambaugh.)

him from British Columbia to as far away as Northern California.

Macan was extremely busy throughout the 1920s. In British Columbia he laid out the Marine Drive Golf Club, Gorge Vale Golf Club and Langara. In Washington, he completed the Manito Country Club, Inglewood Golf Club, Fircrest Golf Club, Glen Acres Country Club and Broadmoor Golf Club. In the Golden State, it was the California Golf Club of San Francisco. And in Oregon, he designed the Columbia-Edgewater Country Club, the Colwood National Golf Club, Illahe Hills Country Club and the Alderwood Country Club, which he considered one of his greatest accomplishments. Alderwood hosted the 1937 US Men's Amateur Championship won by 1933 US Open Champion Johnny Goodman—the last person to win the Open as an amateur. Due to an airport expansion in Portland, Alderwood unfortunately was laid to rest in 1953.

Work slowed through most of the 1930s and 1940s, when new openings were few and far between. The 1950s saw a resurgence of new-course construction and Macan's services were in demand yet again. He com-

pleted the Nanaimo Golf Club, Richmond Country Club and a new course for the Shaughnessy Golf and Country Club in British Columbia. In Washington, he finished the Overlake Golf and Country Club, Sun Willows and added nine holes at the Yakima Country Club. He also completed renovation work at esteemed clubs such as Waverley Country Club in Portland, the Victoria Golf Club and the Seattle Golf Club, preparing the latter course for the 1952 US Men's Amateur.

Macan continued working into the 1960s—his *sixth* decade in the game! In 1964, while in the middle of two projects in Washington, he passed away suddenly from a heart attack at the age of eighty-two. In a remarkable career that spanned over fifty years, Macan was once quoted: 'I have worked for every private or semi-private golf course in the Northwest except for the Portland Golf Club.'[3]

A pervasive 'change-will-make-it-better' attitude plagued many golf courses throughout the 1970s, 1980s and early 1990s, leaving most of Macan's work altered beyond recognition or destroyed altogether. Revolving-door

committees and their subsequent marching orders to golf-course architects—most of whom have varying design styles and philosophies—have left a distressing number of Macan's designs suffering from an identity crisis.

Even now, as the golf industry enjoys this current renaissance period of golf-course architecture, both in terms of new design as well as the thriving business of classic golf-course restoration, too few of Macan's original layouts are sharing in the celebration. There could be several reasons for this state of under-appreciation:

- Macan experienced success *only* on a regional level; most of his work has gone unnoticed by the masses on the east coast of the United States. Because he was credited with only two designs outside the Pacific Northwest, his name rarely comes readily to mind to golf enthusiasts outside the region.

- Few clubs that employed Macan to lay out their original design have come to appreciate the significance of his time-

OPPOSITE ABOVE LEFT
Overlake: With the exception of the green, the third hole was completely overhauled in 2007. The removal of nearly sixty trees now affords fabulous territorial views and much-needed sunlight. One additional measure: sand-capping the approach to the green has created a very firm playing surface, allowing for some interesting run-up shots to be played. (Photograph by Scott Stambaugh.)

OPPOSITE ABOVE RIGHT
Overlake: An up-close view of the tenth green. (Photograph by Scott Stambaugh.)

OPPOSITE BELOW
Overlake: This image of the seventeenth hole demonstrates the wonderful contrast between native area and maintained turf. (Photograph by Scott Stambaugh.)

less design qualities, or acknowledge his relevance to the game. The lost opportunity, arising out of this oversight, is that the various golf clubs fail to recognise that restoring and preserving the intent of Macan's original design adds greatly to a club's reputation, appeal and legacy. The Pacific Northwest is full of fine, classical designs, yet most clubs in the region neglect to consider restoration as a viable option.

- The restoration business is distinctive. No matter how fine and ethical the intent, it is sometimes difficult for an architect to avoid the temptation of 'leaving their mark' on a project. Likewise, to comply with the club brief, regardless of one's personal belief's or design traits, takes a special skill. It is a precarious situation, as few architects are in a sufficiently sound financial position to turn away work.

- Restoration work requires that a great amount of education is directed toward the membership, as well as to all personnel directly involved with the project. Many superintendents at older, private clubs have become increasingly educated on the subject of classic golf-course architecture. As a result, they now are one of the main driving forces behind educating memberships on the value of restoration. Revealing the benefits of restoration and a long-term vision for the golf course has to begin with management before it moves outward. Club members, too, have a great responsibility in regards to course preservation, as they ultimately have a big say in determining the direction of their facilities. Few new players to the game, however, have any sort of connection with the historical aspects of a club. If new members need a history lesson in order to learn more about what it is they possess and why they need to embrace it, management has to be driving the process. If a club does not have strong, educated leaders willing to make this effort, Macan restorative-based projects will continue to be all too uncommon.

One golf club in Washington, in particular, is finally according Macan his due respect: the Overlake Golf and Country Club, Medina. Located just outside Seattle, the original east–west design by Frank James opened in 1927, but only survived for eight years. For the next eighteen years, the property was used first as a horse farm and then as a cattle ranch. The club was 'reborn' in 1953, and Macan was hired to design the reincarnation. Macan routed the golf course in a north–south orientation—completely different to the original routing—stating, 'the clientele we would attract wouldn't like climbing hills'.

Through the years, Overlake has endured four different variations of Golf Course Master Plans. Somehow ... it has endured, unscathed. Macan's original routing still exists and the subtle characteristics and nuances of his greens remain on all but a few holes. As a skilled player and artist, he recognised the importance of creating designs that had characteristics capable of challenging golfers of all abilities.

So, with the 'bones' of the golf course still strong, the club's Green Committee defined a set of goals identifying what needed to be accomplished with a new Masterplan. This plan would be the first in the club's history to make a commitment to preserving the heritage of the golf course. Moreover, it would define the guiding principles for all future key decisions. The major components of this Masterplan would be:

The preservation of Macan's original design intent

'The architect must allow the ground to dictate play.'[4] Overlake has a membership that has relinquished the mindset of 'green equals good'. Completely supportive of a return to the firm and fast regimen, players are exploring (and exploiting) the many different options of getting from point A to point B. The original contours Macan created on, and around, Overlake's greens are traits that can be found on all his courses: approachable in the front; slightly elevated; bold contouring—all design elements that demand a well-played shot to manoeuvre the ball close to the hole. In most cases, this involves a shot played close to the ground.

Recapturing lost green surfaces

One of Macan's design philosophies was, in his own words: 'greens should not be flat but hogbacks, undulations and crowns should be incorporated to defy the backspin players'.[5] Robert Trent Jones Sr once said of Macan: 'He was a generation ahead of his time. Players have become so proficient at playing short-irons into greens. Macan's philosophy is now being introduced to combat this skill'.[6]

Many of the interesting perimeter features of the greens had been 'lost' through the years, as mowing the edges of greens encourages a constant inward creep. Because most of the older courses in the Pacific Northwest are predominantly *Poa annua*, if timed correctly, the process of recapturing what has been lost through the years is quite easy: scalp; topdress; then repeat. Lost hole locations have been restored on over half of Overlake's greens.

Tee restoration

This is one component of the Masterplan where consideration of the modern realities

of golf, in relation to equipment, needed to be addressed. An eventual departure from original forward and distant tee locations will be necessary to accommodate the varied abilities of the membership. Once tee complexes are completed, the club will have a set of 'short' tees (resulting in a manageable 5,000-yard layout) and a set of 'long' tees, designed to stretch the course to nearly 7,000 yards. Macan once said, 'I believe that developing golf courses suitable in the main as immense tests of professional skill is not the answer, unless such courses at the same time provide fun, entertainment and relaxation for those who pay the bills'.[7] Variation in course length is the first step toward all-player enjoyment of the course.

Restoration of all bunker features

The reality of a bunker is that it begins its demise the day it is opened for play. The constant blasting of shots, poor raking by players, movement of sand by machine-raking, weather-related washouts and, subsequent contamination, plus improper edging, are just some of the ingredients necessary for

Overlake: Macan's routing of the front-nine at Overlake offers a multitude of possibilities for the membership. Because this private golf club averages just 16,000 rounds per year, it is possible to visit early in the morning, or perhaps late in the day. This enables the luxury of beginning and ending at the clubhouse by playing a variety of hole-combinations. (Routing plan courtesy of Overlake Golf & Country Club.)

Two holes: two different configurations
Three holes: the first through to the third (the most popular)
Four holes: two different configurations
Five holes: four different configurations
Six holes: two different configurations

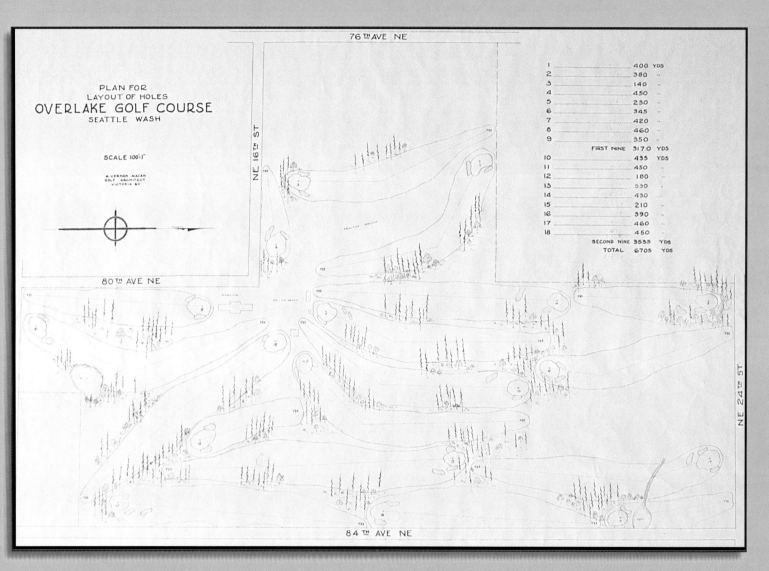

PLAN FOR
LAYOUT OF HOLES
OVERLAKE GOLF COURSE
SEATTLE WASH

SCALE 100:1"

A. VERNON MACAN
GOLF ARCHITECT
VICTORIA B.C.

1	400	YDS
2	380	"
3	140	"
4	450	"
5	230	"
6	345	"
7	420	"
8	460	"
9	350	"
FIRST NINE	3170	YDS
10	435	YDS
11	450	"
12	180	"
13	530	"
14	430	"
15	210	"
16	390	"
17	460	"
18	450	"
SECOND NINE	3535	YDS
TOTAL	6705	YDS

76 TH AVE NE

NE 16 TH ST

80 TH AVE NE

84 TH AVE NE

NE 24 TH ST

Arthur Vernon (Mac) Macan
1882 - 1964

The Colwood Golf Club was the first golf course designed by golf course architect and renowned golfer, A.V. Macan in 1913. Five decades and 55 courses benefited from his wisdom and expertise in the Pacific Northwest. Today, our members are still proud to honour this man, and his legacy lives on. For this, the membership of Royal Colwood Golf Club is eternally grateful.

ABOVE LEFT Royal Colwood Golf Club, Victoria, British Columbia, Canada: The memory of course designer, A.V. Macan, is honoured with this plaque on the seventh tee. (Photograph courtesy of Scott Stambaugh.)

ABOVE MIDDLE Overlake: Typically, an attractive yet understated entrance sign announces the A.V. Macan-designed Overlake Golf and Country Club. (Photograph by Scott Stambaugh.)

ABOVE RIGHT A thoughtful pose by A.V. Macan (circa 1925) while golfing. (Photograph courtesy of Overlake Golf & Country Club.)

BELOW LEFT A.V. Macan (circa 1919) is seen escaping from a bunker, in the middle picture. (Photograph courtesy of Overlake Golf & Country Club.)

BELOW RIGHT Overlake: A mark of respect is paid to A.V. Macan. His signature was 'lifted' from club correspondence between the two entities during construction of the golf course. (Photograph by Scott Stambaugh.)

APRIL 16, 1919.   THE SKETCH.   6.

THE ACTIVE SERVICE GOLF TOURNAMENT : QUALIFIERS.

bunker deterioration. The simple fact is that after fifty years of play, Overlake's bunkers are beyond being worn-out and are in need of repair. Rebuilding the bunkers will return them to their former intended state: bold contours and irregular; rough-hewn; somewhat undefined, with natural looking edges.

Recapturing lost fairway and approach surfaces

Much like the green complexes, fairways and approaches had shrunk to the point where features on the perimeter of the course felt obsolete. And worse, the 'ground' game was no longer a practical method of play. Features such as mounding, preferred landing-areas, fairway bunkers and even some greenside bunkers felt as if they were no longer part of the golf course. Nearly five acres of turf has been recaptured to date, bringing many of the course features back into play. In addition, the introduction of a simple up-and-back pattern of fairway mowing has created a visual impression reminiscent of a bygone era.

Development of a tree management plan

Overlake is in the infancy of addressing one of the biggest issues on the horizon for older golf courses: serious tree issues with no management plan in place. A comprehensive tree management plan will create a permanent, long-term vision for one of the club's most valuable assets. It will also provide guidance for future Green Committees and assist them in making consistent, educated decisions for all tree-related matters. Protecting desirable trees, planning for replacements and, most importantly, removing trees that are having an adverse impact on the design and playability of the course, will preserve the essential character of the golf course for generations to come.

Reintroduction of native areas

The wall-to-wall manicured golf course is quickly becoming a thing of the past. Water restrictions, fuel/energy/fertiliser costs and increased labour costs are having a major impact on the changing nature of golf-course management. There has to be a trade-off for continuing to provide highly manicured playing conditions without absorbing the substantial cost increases of doing so. Reducing maintained turf is the most viable option of accomplishing this state.

And so the resurrection of A. V. Macan begins. It will be a constant journey—fraught with attempted derailment from some quarters, no doubt—and a learning experience at all times. Such is life at a private club. This exercise, though, has left one essential lasting impression on the committee, plainly stated by Macan's mentor, John Low: 'Committees should leave well enough alone, especially when they have a really fine golf course'.[8]

Overlake: A.V. Macan nominated this hole (fifth) as the most interesting one he'd ever built. (Photograph by Scott Stambaugh.)

Barnbougle Dunes, Bridport, Tasmania

One great result.

visit www.toro.com

TORO® **Count on it.**

Scioto, Nicklaus, technology and me

Michael J. Hurdzan

Even after more than fifty years in golf-course design, working on hundreds of projects, worldwide, for all types of clients on all types of sites, there are some experiences that are so special that they stand out. One of my fondest memories had a gestation period of about fifty years, but came together in a matter of days, and only lasted a few weeks. In fact, as that experience started to materialise, I actually thought it was going to be a catastrophic nightmare. You can glean from the title of this article that the experience I am talking about is the total remodelling of Scioto Country Club golf course, and working with Jack Nicklaus on this, his boyhood golf course. To the uninitiated that doesn't sound bad, until you look at it from my per-

spective. Firstly, a little bit about the players involved, both past and present.

Scioto Country Club's golf course was designed by Donald Ross in 1916. Soon after, because of its superb routing, it became recognised as a superior test of golf. In 1926, Scioto hosted the US Open, followed by the 1931 Ryder Cup, then the 1950 PGA Championship. Next was the US Amateur in 1968 and, finally, the US Senior Open in 1986. It was also the place where young Jack Nicklaus learned the game and a need for course management—the latter skill, in particular, that ultimately earned him eighteen professional majors, worldwide fame and the title of the 'greatest golfer ever'.

In the early 1960s, Dick Wilson was hired

by the club, on Nicklaus's recommendation, to completely remodel the golf course—one nine at a time over two years. Wilson, in turn, sent two young associates to handle the design details, Robert Von Hagge on the front nine and Joe Lee on the back nine, both of whom had their own, distinct design concepts for greens.

Von Hagge's inclination was to make the greens small with large, continuous slopes that flattened out near the edge of the putting surface. Lee, on the other hand, designed large greens with flatter areas in the interior and more slope on the outer edges. Both designers followed Wilson's concept of raising greens up in the air four to six feet, as was a common style on flat land such

as in Florida where Wilson was based.

Conversely, Donald Ross's original greens were laid pretty close to existing grade. But the Ross Scioto greens were not 'push-up' greens as was common in those days; they were, instead, the predecessors of today's USGA method of construction. Fortuitously, a very famous soil scientist and professor at nearby Ohio State University by the name of Professor Vivian had taken an interest in the construction of Scioto. The greens were built by creating a cavity like we do today, and then filling that cavity with some sort of rootzone material—not unlike what is done today. Ultimately, Vivian developed a golf green rootzone that he believed would resist compaction, drain well yet hold a great balance of soil, water and air. Extremely fertile, it would be easier to maintain than the standard push-up green. By whom, or why, the decision was made to rebuild these original Ross/Vivian greens remains a mystery. But rebuild them they did, using the Wilson/Von Hagge/Lee concepts.

Another figure of note in the saga of Scioto's greens was the Ohio Governor, James Rhodes, whose political reign spanned from 1963 to 1971, and again from 1975 to 1983. A reasonably proficient golfer, Rhodes was a long-time member at Scioto and, by all accounts, a 'dealmaker extraordinaire'. For Wilson to raise Scioto's greens he needed fill material. As it transpired around that time, there was a new underground parking garage being built at the Ohio State House/Capital building. The story goes that Governor Rhodes arranged to have excess fill from that construction hauled to Scioto—the Wilson greens, therefore, were built on top of, and with, construction debris. This included a mishmash of soils, rock, concrete chunks, huge pieces of asphalt, pipe, wire, bricks, etc.

About this time in the early 1960s, the USGA had just introduced its green construction method. With the benefit of hindsight we can see it was not well understood, with numerous case studies, country-wide, of poorly executed greens and, occasionally, disastrous outcomes—even at places like Scioto. The Scioto greens had suffered from a lack of quality control: of materials used; the depths that those materials were

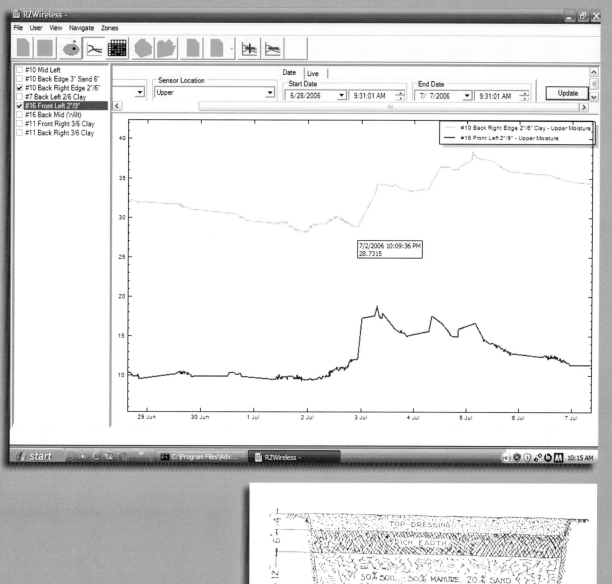

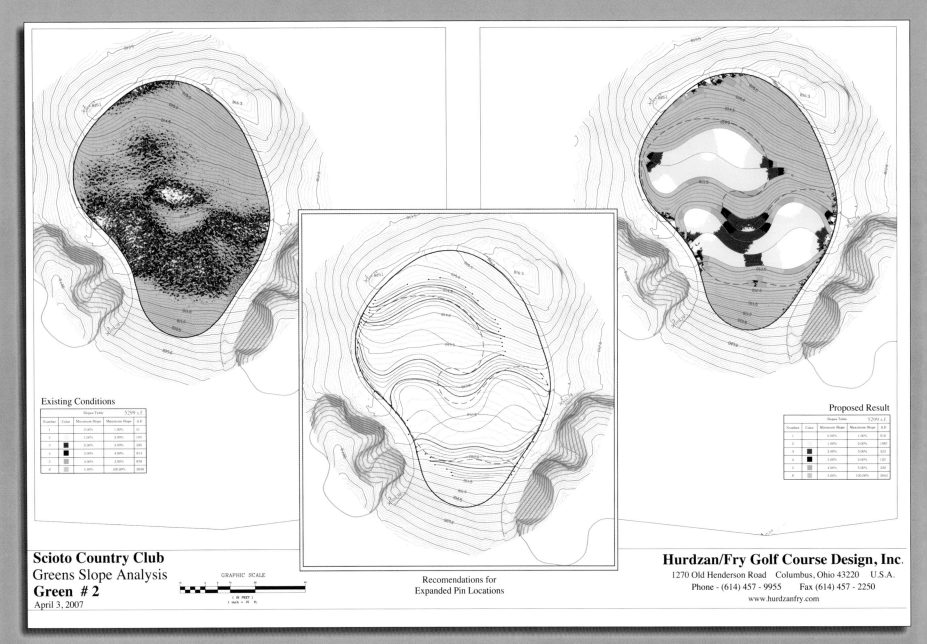

Existing Conditions

Slopes Table		5299 s.f.		
Number	Color	Minimum Slope	Maximum Slope	S.F.
1		0.00%	1.00%	31
2		1.00%	2.00%	193
3		2.00%	3.00%	585
4		3.00%	4.00%	914
5		4.00%	5.00%	938
6		5.00%	100.00%	2638

Proposed Result

Slopes Table		5299 s.f.		
Number	Color	Minimum Slope	Maximum Slope	S.F.
1		0.00%	1.00%	316
2		1.00%	2.00%	1067
3		2.00%	3.00%	323
4		3.00%	4.00%	120
5		4.00%	5.00%	230
6		5.00%	100.00%	3043

Scioto Country Club
Greens Slope Analysis
Green # 2
April 3, 2007

GRAPHIC SCALE

(IN FEET)
1 inch = 10 ft.

Recomendations for
Expanded Pin Locations

Hurdzan/Fry Golf Course Design, Inc.
1270 Old Henderson Road   Columbus, Ohio 43220   U.S.A.
Phone - (614) 457 - 9955   Fax (614) 457 - 2250
www.hurdzanfry.com

Slope analysis of number two green at Scioto Country Club. Left drawing is of Dick Wilson green showing very few hole locations (colored blue and white). Middle drawing is proposed contour changes to create hole locations shown on right drawing (colored blue and white). Wilson green had only 224 square feet of area less than 2% slope, while Hurdzan and Nicklaus green produced almost 1600 square feet of area with less than 2% slope. (Courtesy of Hurdzan/Fry Environmental Golf Design.)

installed; the uniformity of the profiles. Succinctly, the greens were so poorly constructed that it was only through the superior dedication and skill of the golf-course superintendents (especially Mark Yoder for the past twenty-eight years) that the greens were even serviceable all-season long. Everyone knew the greens were a ticking 'time bomb'—destined for failure—but members were not convinced they were sufficiently bad to warrant closing their course for a year to rebuild the greens. Although Scioto has been a *Golf Digest* Top 100 Course, seemingly, forever, the greens were just okay even during the best of times, and a near-embarrassment during bad times.

The 'me' part of this story is that growing up in Columbus, and being from a golfing family, we all considered Scioto Country Club to be the finest course we'd seen or played. Since our family status was blue collar at best, all we could ever do was marvel at Scioto from across the stonewall property fence. It seems like only yesterday that we'd try at every opportunity to gain a spot in the field, regardless of which local golf competition would be held at the venue. To our family members, Scioto was held in such high regard it verged on being our ideal of a golfing Camelot. Even today, we hold it in that same high regard. Indeed, Scioto is the best US country club I have ever visited. So in 2004, when asked to serve as their golf-course architect and consultant, I considered it to be a crowning achievement; a professional validation that I had mastered my craft and earned the right to be trusted with improving what many consider to be a masterpiece. Needless to say I was eager, and flattered, but also slightly intimidated and nervous about measuring up to the task.

As with any major golf course improvement, Hurdzan/Fry does plans that are intended to offer suggested changes in a form that members can understand—and provide opportunities for their critical review. Finally, during the autumn and winter of 2005—after satisfying the critics and getting the approval of the committee and members—all of the greenside bunkers were rebuilt, or modified. Hot on the heels of this important success, we did all of the fairway

ABOVE Jack Nicklaus and Dr Mike Hurdzan collaborated on the redesign of Scioto Country Club greens in 2007. The results were great greens and a strong friendship. (Courtesy of Hurdzan/Fry Environmental Golf Design.)

LEFT Nicklaus and Dr Mike Hurdzan discuss the renovations to Scioto Country Club greens. Fairways were also regrassed while club was closed from July 2007 to April 2008. (Courtesy of Hurdzan/Fry Environmental Golf Design.)

bunkers the following fall and winter of 2006. By now the pressure had eased, somewhat, as we had earned the members' trust and confidence that we were *not* going to mess up their golf course. Even so, they still did not want to rebuild their greens.

Convincing Scioto's membership that it was necessary to rebuild their greens was achieved by utilising technology. The green staff set up a series of tests to demonstrate the effectiveness of possible remedies to the greens—all stopped short of rebuilding. This included various forms of aerification, drill and fill techniques, installing narrow trench tile into the greens, and even vacuum drainage. To measure the effectiveness of these tests, sensors were installed in the rootzones to measure soil moisture, soil temperature and soil salinity. That data was then transmitted, via wireless, back to a computer/data logger in the superintendent's office.

The condition of Scioto's greens at the start of the 2006 summer was flawless. All that changed, however, with several days of slow, prolonged rain followed by very hot,

humid conditions around 4 July. The result: golf was wiped out and, almost immediately, the quality of greens noticeably started going downhill. When members saw how closely the decline of their greens correlated to the soil moisture sensor data gathered and graphed (of the rainy period), it became crystal clear that their greens needed to be rebuilt, even if it meant closing for a year.

Even though the front-nine and back-nine greens were distinctly different in style, and both halves suffered from lack of 'pinnable' hole locations to accommodate ultra-fast putting speeds, the members were reluctant to allow me to change the greens. To guarantee the membership we could reverse engineer the greens back to exactly what they were before, required another new piece of technology called LIDAR (Light Detection and Ranging) mapping. Sensitivity is its strong suit, using laser scanners to map objects within fractions of an inch. A company called Woolpert Engineering mapped all of Scioto's greens in what amounted to one point two (1.2) inch contours or ten contours per foot. Our firm then used a sophisticated slope-calculation program to develop colour-slope maps. The idea, being, that interested parties, upon inspection, could determine immediately whether the greens were too flat or too steep. On some greens, less than five per cent of the playing surface had less than two per cent slopes—the level, which is ideal for hole locations. This proved to be shocking and why, subsequently, I was permitted to slightly alter slopes within six of the greens to create more hole locations.

With all of this technical data and personal observations of the greens by the members, the club voted by an eighty-five per cent margin to close the course on 9 July 2007. The notion of rebuilding the greens to my plans, under strict budgets of time and money, had finally been given the green light! All eighteen greens and practice greens had to be rebuilt for less than $1.2 million and the work done by 1 September, allowing just fifty-five days for construction. Many of my colleagues would say that this amount of budgeted time and money is ridiculous, if not impossibly low. There was no room for error or changes in either consideration.

Five weeks before the green-reconstruction program was due to begin, Jack Nicklaus happened to be in town for the Memorial Tournament, the classic event he created. Hearing on the 'grapevine' that Scioto was closing in order to rebuild its greens, he asked the club if he could visit and provide some input to the process, citing his boyhood memories and experiences, coupled to his knowledge as a professional golfer and golf-course architect. Well ... if you've ever met Jack Nicklaus, you know how hard it is to say 'no' to him, so the club naturally agreed to his request.

Now I have met Jack numerous times, mostly at ASGCA meetings, to say 'hello' and that's about it. We did, however, have a few things in common: we are both about the same age; we went to Ohio State University; and we care a lot about Scioto. Like most of the readership, I'd heard he had an ego of sorts, was pretty opinionated about golf-course architecture and architects, and really didn't care about collaboration. And so when informed: 'Oh ... by the way, Jack Nicklaus would like to stop by and offer

some opinions on the green reconstruction', my initial reaction was this is either a very bad joke, or an ominous setback for the continuation of my tenure at Scioto. I was upset, disappointed and disheartened, for this project meant a lot to me and I thought that Jack would insist that *he* be the golf-course architect. On the other hand, I couldn't fault him, or the club, in the advent that I was dumped in favour of the 'Record Book of Golf'.

What I didn't expect was for the members of the improvement committee to affirm that under no circumstance would I not remain as lead designer; and secondly, that Jack was in favour of that, too. Still, I was quietly sceptical, and remained so, until after the first couple of visits that Jack and I spent together sharing ideas about what could, or could not, be done to the greens. After a while, I really started to like the guy: I got to know Jack the man, and not the myth and legend. Ultimately, over the course of our seven or eight lengthy joint sessions spent at Scioto, I believe a friendship developed that will be ever-lasting. In fact, whatever success we may have achieved at Scioto—enough to earn it the honour of Renovation of the Year 2007 by *Golf Inc* magazine—was the result of melding our ideas and concepts.

One of the most interesting things to me was how Jack and I forged agreement on individual green design, but from two distinctly different approaches. For example, I looked at the green from the agronomic side of how many hole locations were available, surface drainage patterns onto and across the green, traffic patterns, room to turn or operate maintenance equipment, and aesthetics. Jack, too, was concerned with aesthetics, but he was also intensely interested in shot values and target sizes, the kind of break and speed of approach putts to each hole location, and bunker recoverability, to name a few—strictly player issues. Today, evidence abounds that Scioto's greens are agronomically correct, player-friendly and flexible.

Another interesting experience for me was to see how much Jack trusted his eyes, allied to an ability to see subtle grade changes that the rest of us could measure but not see. I relied on the 'smart level' or grade stakes for precise measurements, and we usually agreed within a small fraction of measurement. There's little doubt this attribute has played an important role in him being such a great putter throughout his playing career—even as a senior golfer.

We also agreed on extending putting surfaces closer to water hazards, putting in small undulations within the putting surfaces, and how to mitigate severe grade changes. We disagreed on some bunker placements, the use of trees to shape strategy and some fairway contours. Overall, we enjoyed a most amicable collaboration and the proof is the quality of Scioto's greens that are firm, fast, true, challenging and aesthetically pleasing. We stayed within the financial budget and seeded the green precisely on the projected target date. The grow-in phase was spectacular. I think we both feel that the kindred spirit of Donald Ross would be more appreciative of our greens, than Mr Wilson's, to compliment his splendid and timeless routing.

Remembering the artistry of Mike Strantz

Mike Strantz was a testament to resilience and perseverance. He re-designed and built the Shore course at Monterey while receiving chemotherapy for an aggressive oral cancer. Cutting a striking figure at Monterey, Mike could be observed driving stakes into the dirt while wearing a ski cap to ward off the chill of the brisk peninsula winds. Over a year later, Mike was able to see his dream realised at the opening of the re-designed course.

The re-design was an immense challenge for Mike Strantz; but also the fulfillment of a dream that came true. An excellent golfer, he knew the northern California golf courses well, loving and often enthusing about the dazzling vistas along the Pacific coast. He was inspired and energised by the harsh beauty of the brilliant blue Pacific beating against the ancient, mammoth rock outcroppings. In a bold initiative, Strantz decided to completely re-route the Shore course. This move, he sensed, would best-utilise Monterey's incredible natural resources.

Alas, in 2005, he lost his courageous fight against cancer. Today, a plaque at the fifteenth green honors Strantz's passion and dedication to his craft and his art.

Monterey Peninsula Country Club (Shore Course), California, USA: Strantz used the crashing Pacific Ocean shoreline to create the dramatic, almost 600-yard par-5 twelfth hole—the longest on the course. Lengthy sand bunkers, natural wetlands, a native creek and sharp ocean winds all make for a challenging hole, especially when a golfer can hear barking sea lions not far from shore. (Drawing by Mike Strantz.)

OPPOSITE **Monterey Peninsula:** With its appearance of rough and rocky outcroppings, the windswept par-3 seventh hole conjures up thoughts of golfing in the United Kingdom. Making the hole even more interesting, the left to right wind challenges the tee-shot 'carry' over coyote bushes. Like only yesterday, Forrest Fezler recalls when the small, four-inch coyote bushes were planted. He says, 'The thing about those bushes is that they grow fast and the wind shapes them while they are growing. They are just beautiful.' The hole finishes amid one of the highest points on the golf course. (Drawing by Mike Strantz.)

Monterey Peninsula: Creating a 'moody' uphill shot near the end of the course, Strantz's seventeenth hole was one of his few attempts at adaptation from the original layout. In the process he molded an elegant, rolling fairway to accompany the gentle, old streambed on the right. (Drawing by Mike Strantz.)

BELOW Monterey Peninsula: Monterey's majestic, tree-lined finishing hole has an uphill second shot that teases golfers—only the green's 'false' front is visible. But this par-4's robust green can be forgiving, especially since the clubhouse is not far away. (Drawing by Mike Strantz.)

OPPOSITE Monterey Peninsula: The fifteenth-hole vista inspired Mike Strantz to re-route the entire Shore course. Uppermost in his mind was extracting full advantage of the powerful scenes along the Pacific coast. Now, the fifteenth green shares centre stage with a resilient and stubborn ancient cypress, growing out of rock and sand. (Drawing by Mike Strantz.)

Monterey Peninsula: This hole, the eleventh, was the last one that Mike Strantz designed. How fitting that he employed all the textures of nature—the dark green cypresses, the bold rocks, the angled walking paths, the rough-edged shrubs in the waste bunkers—to complete his final canvas. All these discordant shapes work in harmony to the curving lines of the manicured fairway. And then in the background, a booming Pacific Ocean is omnipresent.
'It's a touching hole for me,' said Forrest Fezler. 'I remember standing on the tee with Mike— we'd run out of room and were wondering how we'd make it work. "I think I've run out of golf holes," Mike said to me. That was the last hole Mike designed. You have to wonder if he knew.' (Drawing by Mike Strantz.)

ABOVE Monterey Peninsula: With time-worn rocks edging the two-tiered tenth green, Strantz unveiled a golf hole that may be unique. In typical Strantz-style, a strong left-bend in the fairway honours a bunker of hand planted native plants; namely, coyote bush, California sage, wild fescue, and tufted deschampsia grass. Thereafter, the incline to the green brings all forces together: sea, sky, wind, rock, grass, and sand. (Drawing by Mike Strantz.)

BELOW Monterey Peninsula: Tough, tight, and daunting, the ninth hole doglegs sharply to the right, tempting long-hitters to go straight for the green. The spectacular tee is set high enough to spy the green and also the surrounding ocean. On a clear day, Strantz instinctively knew an observant golfer might catch a glimpse of a water spout from a distant whale. (Drawing by Mike Strantz.)

Royal New Kent, Virginia, USA: Reflecting the wide-open tract that was formerly forested for lumber, Strantz utilised the swaths of open land to create a wide and long course, reflective of a British Isles course—complete with deep bunkers, doglegs and rolling fairways. The second hole, featuring a 'horseshoe' fairway, is interrupted by a large natural ravine that the golfer must either swing hard (and carry), or take the long, but safe route around—a typical risk/reward design option favoured by Strantz. Forrest Fezler, a former touring professional who worked with Strantz on Royal New Kent, opines that the first two holes at Royal New Kent are rather tough. He states: 'Most architects start out their courses with easy, friendly holes. Not Mike. He seemed to say, "Here it is ladies and gentlemen... now you know what you're in for." ' (Drawing by Mike Strantz.)

Silver Creek Valley, California, USA: Remarkably, the course was renovated and rejuvenated by Mike Strantz in 2002 while commuting between Charleston and San Jose—an impressive feat, given he was recovering at the time from radiation treatment for oral cancer. Forrest Fezler, his friend and his design associate, was instrumental in maintaining the momentum of the design and construction at Silver Creek Valley. 'The layout stayed the same,' said Forrest Fezler, 'but we took out what I call "chocolate kisses" all over the golf course'—weak moguls that distracted rather than added to the golf course. Fezler and Strantz instead created a more aesthetic golf course that was visually exciting, sculpting all new bunkers and tee complexes, plus major overhauls on three holes. Best of all, they added visual impact to the greens, but did not interrupt the green's surface, allowing the course to stay open throughout the entire renovation. On the second green, Strantz added a large waste bunker in front (eight feet at its deepest), and a smaller bunker on the right-hand side, along with dramatic touches and undulations to the edges of the green. (Drawing by Mike Strantz.)

TRUE BLUE PLANTATION

detailed grading
and
shaping plans
for
hole no. FOURTEEN

14

scale

True Blue Plantation, South Carolina, USA: A 'wild' golf design, the course lies across the street from Mike Strantz's first solo design venture, Caledonia Golf and Fish Club. While the tight and charming Caledonia was built on stunning marsh vistas and sweeping rice fields, the True Blue tract was inland, with fewer elegant trees and was void of vistas, marsh and sea-island charm. Meeting the challenge, Strantz created a 'rough-and-tumble' golf course—a counter-weight to the refined Caledonia. The lucky find, though, was when the clearing crew hit sand. Inspired by this natural resource, Strantz fine-tuned True Blue with Pine Valley in his mind, creating wide fairways to balance the sand hazards. A bonus at the fourteenth hole—with its nearly 'horseshoe' shaped tee that allows golfers to play the par-3 from a variety of angles—is how the two-tiered green supports a novel shot, offering landing areas from different directions. Strantz was proud of True Blue. To him, making a stunning golf course out of downtrodden lowland was an achievement. (Drawing by Mike Strantz.)

Royal Queensland Golf Club, Australia

Ian Lynagh

Contrary to what the old French proverb says about 'change and staying the same', I often observe, as a golf club archivist, that with heritage issues it can be quite the reverse: 'The more things change; the more things change'. This appears particularly so when it comes to the golf course itself. Tinker with it over time, and before you know it, the course you once had is but a past memory. Sometimes this is for the betterment of the layout; sometimes not.

As living entities, golf courses are subject to many ongoing agents of change. Nature's elements exert their influence on landforms and vegetation. Persistent plantings, zealous watering and constant nurturing produce varied environments and introduce new ecosystems. Most significantly though, piecemeal tinkering at the edges by well-meaning committees, enthusiastic amateurs and even sometimes by professional designers, can impact markedly over time on how a course presents and how it plays. One can only wonder just how many of our club courses have evolved simply by club authorities attending to the pressing issues of the day, without any real reference to yesterday, the course's heritage, or tomorrow, the course's future.

Over its eighty-eight-year history, the course at Brisbane's Royal Queensland Golf Club (RQ) has not escaped the influence of such change agents. The original 1920s layout was a links-style course on reclaimed tidal flats near the mouth of the Brisbane River. It was virtually treeless with naturally undulating fairways bordered by tidal flats and indigenous vegetation. Some eighty-eight years later, this layout had become a sub-tropical parkland course, being spectacularly treed and featuring manicured fairways, trimmed bunkers and flat perched greens. A search of the club's archives reveal no real evidence of intent to produce such a monumental change—this appears to support the assertion that when 'things are just changed; things really do change'.

In 2004, this river parkland course was seriously challenged by the government's

OPPOSITE **Royal Queensland Golf Club, Queensland, Australia: The 'dinky' 125-metre par-3 eighth hole is a reworked Mackenzie original. Its relocated tee exposes golfers to a challenging angle, especially as the green is seriously perched and undulating. The sandy wasteland is new; the 'wind' factor is the same. (Photograph by Kimbal Baker.)**

plan to duplicate the massive Gateway Bridge already straddling a narrow section of the course. To the then RQ board, making adjustments to the layout around the proposed location of this intrusion just did not seem a satisfactory response to cope with such a gross assault—one bridge was disturbing enough, but two was two too many. Rebuilding a new eighteen-hole course away from the bridges was seen as the only viable option. Michael Clayton Golf Designs (MCGD) was engaged to carry out this major and challenging task. This time it was a matter of change 'by design' with a vision of the outcome, and not just an adjustment to address a pressing issue.

Michael harbours fond memories of RQ, having won the Australian Amateur Championship there in 1978. However, it was not just this fond memory for the course that landed his firm the contract. Clearly, Michael's keen interest in golf history, respect for traditional club courses and, in particular, his adherence to the design philosophies that underpin such layouts, were the compelling factors in his appointment.

While RQ's original 1920s course was laid out by Carnegie Clark, it was the famed Alister Mackenzie who established its character direction in 1926. This being the case, it followed that the brief presented to MCGD envisaging a traditional championship members' course, should be based on Mackenzie's thirteen design principles and constructed in a style sympathetic with its natural environment.

Complicating matters was the fact that the designer's canvass was hardly 'blank'. The existing course was one of championship quality with a noted elegance and charm, as reflected by the staging of three Australian Opens in the club's impressive CV. The challenge facing MCGD appeared one of designing and constructing a traditional club course—perhaps, even, one having playing characteristics not unlike those of the original layout—on grounds that housed an admired river parkland course.

It appears relevant to note what the original course was like. Photographic and print records indicate a links-style course of natural landforms and vegetation, open and wind-affected with undulating fairways and in-situ sandy loam bunkers. Mackenzie's observations of the course following his 1926 visit, as reported in the next few paragraphs, are recorded in the club's archives and shed some light on the subject:

This ground is excellently adapted for the construction of a golf course which might even compare favourably with some British Championship courses ... Although the ground at first sight appears flat, yet it is full of minor undulations of somewhat similar character to the famous seaside courses like St Andrews ... the subsoil consists entirely of sand... (And the area is) full of very fine golfing features ...9

Mackenzie's recommended directions for the development of the course included:

There should be as little rough grass as possible and the fairways should be widened considerably in irregular lines. There should be alternative routes at

OPPOSITE ABOVE
Royal Queensland: A
natural wasteland cuts
diagonally across the 208-
metre par-3 seventeenth
hole; with the series of
bunkers defending the left
side, Michael Clayton has
created a hole that is both
interesting to play and has
strategic merit.
(Photograph by Kimbal
Baker.)

OPPOSITE BELOW LEFT
Royal Queensland: The
bunker-less seventh
green, one of two on the
course, is defended by its
seriously sloping
'shoulders', along with a
definitive swale through
its centre. (Gary Lynagh
Photography.)

OPPOSITE BELOW RIGHT
Royal Queensland: The
open design of the new
layout is evident in holes
such as the sixteenth, a
519-metre par-5.
Extensive wetlands,
fairway undulations and
strategic bunkering,
provide the challenge.
(Gary Lynagh
Photography.)

every hole, and the bunkers should be placed near the centre of the fairways, but care should be taken that they do not block out the view of the green in the direction it is desired that the player should take ... The regular banks across the fairways should be converted into hillocks and bunkers of a more natural appearance ... all banks and hummocks should be made with graduated slopes ... and should be varied as possible ... in their natural positions ... I think it would be desirable if some scrub were removed bordering the river ... (leaving) irregular islands of bushes.[10]

In summing up Mackenzie concluded: 'The course at Hamilton should have a very great future and not only be an excellent test of golf but extremely popular to all classes of players ...'[11]

The responsibility for the implementation of these design concepts was passed to the club's greenkeeper, R. S. Black, who reputedly had a thorough grasp of Mackenzie's philosophies and principles, enabling him to proceed in developing the course along such character-laden lines. What happened in the ensuing eighty years that lead to it evolving as a meticulously groomed river parkland course, may very well be just another example of: 'the more things change; the more things change'.

From this perspective, the challenge MCGD faced could be seen as one in which the differing worlds of these two courses merge—that is, to redesign an existing parkland course into a layout with more traditional Mackenzie-like features, typical of its origins. The question, from a design viewpoint, was how to best meet that challenge. Observing from the sideline, the essence of MCGD's modus operandi involved:

- 'opening-up' the course by the selective removal of numerous, mostly nondescript trees, while retaining all species and specimens of significance in locations that have minimal strategic impact on play;

- enhancing the influence of the wind on play by this opening-up, and configuring holes (particularly the par 3s) in a manner that on any one day the wind variability is maximised around the course;

- constructing wide fairways and shaping them in a manner that emphasised the natural contours of the ground, thus creating undulations, rises and falls, particularly around greens, which impinge significantly on the play;

- constructing bunkers utilising the sand in-situ with a natural look as if they have been present for ever, and strategically locating them to present challenges to all levels of golfers from varying tee and fairway positions;

- constructing greens of varying size, shape and orientation. Some would be heavily bunkered, some bunkerless, but all with marked undulations, slopes and swales, and including a few with a definite 'quirkiness' about them;

ABOVE Royal Queensland: The twelfth hole, a 405-metre par-4, epitomises the course's wide-fairway design. With bunkers to the left, and sandy wasteland (not visible) on the entire right side, the generous fairway is welcoming. (Photograph by Kimbal Baker.)

BELOW Royal Queensland: The Brisbane River runs the full length of the 411-metre par-4 fourteenth hole, and is noted for the strategic challenge its bunkers and fairway undulations provide. (Gary Lynagh Photography.)

OPPOSITE Royal Queensland: As a lone sentinel in a vast, open space, this traditional pot-bunker guards the left side of the 353-metre par-4 fifteenth hole—and is to be avoided. (Gary Lynagh Photography.)

- emphasising the course's location and its natural estuarine environment, allowing tidal flats and wetlands to intrude (in places) onto the fairways; and

- developing massive sandy wastelands in the natural waterways and gullies—all in play.

Subsequently, in November 2007, Royal Queensland Golf Club opened its 'New Course', an eighteen-hole, 6,550-metre championship members' layout. It did so with heightened expectations and much enthusiasm.

On examination, clearly this is a course of strong character. It has a definitive identity, a harmonious sense of belonging and shows marked Mackenzien features, particularly in its playing characteristics. It is a course that sits comfortably within its natural environment. It utilises those natural features—the undulations and slopes, the wet and wastelands, the strategically placed bunkers—as the main defences of its greens. Most significantly, RQ's generous fairways provide the golfer with options on almost every shot from tee to green. It is, indeed, a strategic golf course. Its natural simplicity belies its playing complexity.

Michael Clayton illustrates the strategic nature of the course by the inclusion of two exciting short par-4s in his design, especially that of the third hole. He comments:

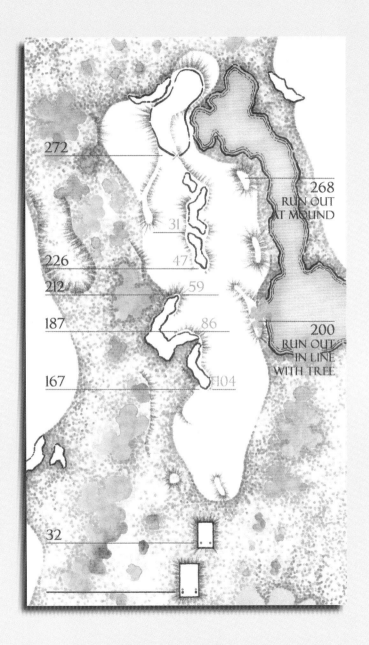

272

268
RUN OUT
AT MOUND

31

226

47

212

59

187

86

200
RUN OUT
IN LINE
WITH TREE

167

104

32

Some of the finest holes in Australia are our par-4s under 300 metres, and a course is not seen as complete until it boasts a confounding driveable par-4! The famed tenth on the West Course at Royal Melbourne is, perhaps, the finest example in Australia of a hole under 300 yards that continues to confound the best players in the world, along with the members.

Mackenzie, of course, delighted in designing holes on the borderline of par. Our aim at Royal Queensland's third hole was to build a hole where the tee-shot could be legitimately played with five or six clubs; anything from a driver to a mid-iron.

This is the question posed by three of the finest short par-4s in the country—the fifteenth at Victoria and the third holes at Royal Adelaide and Kingston Heath. RQ's third hole has bunkers littering the fairway, and it is quite easy to find the short grass by playing a four- or five-iron to the wide expanse of fairway (to the right), but that will leave the player with a long pitch to a difficult, dangerous and undulating green. The further right one flies, the more difficult the angle into the green.

The longer the tee-shot, the more the player is forced to deal with the bunkers and the less short grass there is to hit.

Taking the driver is not really the 'right' shot, but it is awfully tempting to take a 'fly' at the green. No one really wants to take a three-iron when the perfect long tee-shot offers the likelihood of a birdie.

There are multiple ways to play Royal Queensland's third hole, and there is no right or wrong way to play the hole. That is the essence of making a golf course constantly stimulating and interesting to play.

There's ample evidence that Clayton's design philosophy, and the actualisation of it in RQ's new course, reflects much of the original 1920s layout—certainly in its playing characteristics. Clearly, however, it differs markedly in its visual presentation. The new layout, while prominently featuring elements of the natural terrain, is set in a somewhat more ordered and softer environment than the original. An impressive array of magnificent trees—a gift from the parkland days—remains, albeit almost totally sidelined from play.

Royal Queensland's 'New Course' has successfully materialised as a meeting of two worlds—two courses from different eras. Michael Clayton and his design team have achieved their brief in a most skilful and sensitive manner. Undoubtedly, the new course at RQ makes a statement: a statement about its natural environment; a statement about its origins and the club's heritage; and a statement most certainly about a traditional strategic approach to playing the game of golf.

Contrary to my opening assertion about change, Michael Clayton Golf Design's change 'by design' in the Royal Queensland's layout may very well be a case of, as the French say: *'Plus ça change, plus c'est la même chose'*—the more things change; the more they stay the same!

ABOVE **Royal Queensland: Tee-shot options abound on the third hole, a 292-metre par-4. Golfers can lay-up either long or short, right or left, or 'fly' the bunkers to the treachery ahead. (Photograph by Kimbal Baker.)**

BELOW **Royal Queensland: The third green-complex presents several challenges: a 'beach' and water to the right; a deep, off-green swale to the left; a tough back bunker; and a severe ridge running up the green. (Gary Lynagh Photography.)**

OPPOSITE: **Royal Queensland: A stylish Course Guide has been produced for the benefit of the membership and visitors. In this instance, the intricacies of the short, teasing par-4 third hole can be surveyed. (Graphic by Michael Cocking, Michael Clayton Golf Design.)**

Less is more: The Dunes Club, USA

Charles S. James

In 1985, Chicago businessman Mike Keiser purchased sixty-eight acres of land in New Buffalo, Michigan. Located in the heart of 'Harbor Country', New Buffalo is one of a string of small beach communities along Lake Michigan's south-eastern shore. Keiser's motivation was to prevent condominium development from having an impact on the charm and character of the area near his family's summer home. For several years the property lay dormant, serving primarily as nature sanctuary and outdoor activity refuge for the Keiser family on their regular weekend visits to the resort community. Soon, however, Keiser began to envisage the land, located just beyond the reach of the bluffs, as amenable to golf.

Specifically, the sandy, rolling, wooded duneland—filled with scrub, oaks, juniper and pines—struck him as offering a similar landform to the pine barrens of southern New Jersey, home to Pine Valley Golf Club.

Following his muse, Keiser contacted Dick Nugent in 1988 and asked the Chicago-based golf architect to make the short drive to visit his property. At the time, Keiser could hardly have imagined he'd just begun a highly improbable journey: from greeting card entrepreneur to leading figure of the late-twentieth century revival of US golf-course architecture.

Keiser's Bandon Dunes Golf Resort, of course, introduced the golf world to David McLay Kidd while propelling the career of

Tom Doak and burnishing the reputation of the design duo Coore & Crenshaw. Each of the Bandon courses, set amid the rugged southern Oregon coastline, vigorously embraces Keiser's belief that golf should be enjoyed in a natural setting and, preferably, walked in the company of a caddy. Beyond this, the Dunes Club and Bandon Dunes are the manifestation of Keiser's entrepreneurial modus operandi: create that which fully satisfies a personal vision and aspiration, employing an uncompromising standard of excellence, and success—internally defined—is achieved. Validation of this ethic, however, is evident in the unqualified commercial and artistic success of Bandon Dunes, as well as in the distinct and profound aesthetic Keiser

OPPOSITE **The Dunes Club, Michigan, USA:** The versatility of the nine-hole layout is exemplified by the par-3 second hole. Here, two sets of teeing areas are separated by eighty-five yards of dense woods, offering an angle of approach that deviates by sixty degrees. The 'short' tee on the right-hand side of the photograph presents the hole from 115 yards to 175 yards. A 'long' tee, shown on the left, extends its length from 145 yards to 220 yards. (Photograph by Walt Bukva, Bukva Imaging Group Inc. © 2002-2008.)

OPPOSITE The Dunes: The approach shot into the green on the par-5 third hole must navigate a rugged duneland waste area of sand, fescue, scrub and pines. The right-hand side of the picture shows the landing area for the tee-shot on the par-4 fourth hole. (Photograph by Walt Bukva, Bukva Imaging Group Inc. © 2002-2008.)

was able to create at the Dunes Club. The enthusiasm with which his creations have been received by golfers from around the world clearly illustrates Keiser's dictum that golf 'as it was meant to be'—that is, afoot among 'nature perfected'—resonates deeply in the hearts of golfers everywhere.

Unlike its Oregon cousins, the private Dunes Club lies largely out of the public view. Among golf-course architecture enthusiasts, however, it has achieved a certain mystique. This, it can be argued, emanates from the delightful simplicity and seclusion of the club, its 'walking-only' policy, and the natural beauty of the course, which is only enhanced by the absence of cart paths. Says Fred Muller, long-time head professional at Crystal Downs Country Club: 'Playing the Dunes Club is like playing golf in a garden. Even the walks from the greens to the tees are a delight'. More significantly, the stature with which aficionados hold the Dunes derives from the look and quality of the US parkland course, and the fact that it's a nine-hole layout. The influence that Pine Valley would come to have on the design is evident

in the Dunes' wide, rolling, pristinely manicured fairways, which are dramatically bound by fescue, scrub and expansive sandy waste areas.

The merit of the layout has been recognised by the golfing press: *Golf Magazine*'s 'Top 100 Courses in the US' panel ranked the Dunes Club as high as seventy-six,[12] while *Golfweek* named it the twenty-ninth best 'Modern' course in the country. No other US nine-hole course has ever been so highly ranked. And *Sports Illustrated* declared the Dunes the best nine-hole course in United States in a 1997 feature article titled 'Small Wonder'.[13]

While nine-hole courses are frequently regarded as unusual, they are, in fact, surprisingly common. Of the 17,000 or so courses in the United States, 4,800 are nine-hole layouts. Included among these are such renowned gems as Donald Ross's Whitinsville Golf Course and George Thomas's Marion Golf Course, both in Massachusetts. Not included are former nine-hole masterpieces that have been subsequently expanded, such as Ross's Rolling

Rock Club in Pennsylvania and Perry Maxwell's original nine-hole layout at Prairie Dunes. It's worth noting that many of the great golf-course architects who practised in the United in the early twentieth century—Alister Mackenzie, Charles Blair Macdonald and Seth Raynor, to name a few—built nine-hole courses.

Keiser first met Dick Nugent over breakfast at a roadside diner during the winter of 1988. Nugent, along with Ken Killian had co-designed Kemper Lakes—site of the 1997 PGA Championship—and had done restoration work at Medinah Country Club and Butler National. He came recommended by superintendent Paul Voykin of Briarwood Country Club, a suburban Chicago course designed in 1921 by H. S. Colt and C. H. Alison.

Joining Keiser and Nugent that morning was Pete Sinnott, founder of ServiScape Golf Management, an Indiana-based golf-course maintenance and consulting firm. Also present was John Cotter, a principal at the renowned Wadsworth Golf Construction Company. Cotter was widely acknowledged

for his skills in green siting and construction. Following breakfast, the men drove the two miles to Keiser's property and spent several hours wandering the snow-covered site, gathering ideas and sharing thoughts.

It was clear that the small parcel of land would prove insufficient to house an eighteen-hole golf course. Keiser's acreage was roughly two-thirds of the 104 acres available to Donald Ross in 1914 when he created Wannamoisett Country Club in Rhode Island—a par sixty-nine layout and the archetype of land-constrained golf design. Keiser, however, was philosophically at ease with the unconventional. After all, he'd built a small, quirky recycled paper greeting card maker that had long-prospered in the shadow of two industry giants. If his land was better suited to nine holes—or seven, ten or twelve holes for that matter—well, then so be it.

In their preparations, Keiser and his colleagues made several trips to Pine Valley to study George Crump's famous design and to discuss maintenance issues with then-superintendent Eb Steiniger. Back in Michigan, the division of labour called for Nugent, with Keiser's input, to perform the routing. Mass grading and green construction duties were awarded to Wadsworth. Lastly, Sinnott would be responsible for the final grading, irrigation, seeding, plantings and grow-in. Reflective of Keiser's penchant for collaborative engagement, the group's overall design plan was free-flowing and informal. While a topographical map was produced, aerials were dispensed with and the routing plan was routinely tweaked in the field. No formal grading or drainage plans were prepared, just Nugent and Keiser's basic routing diagram.

A key aspect of the routing proved the need for parallel holes. Although Keiser resisted the prospect, Nugent convincingly argued that the limited acreage mandated that a certain number of holes run adjacent to one another. A major attribute of the finished design is that while six holes run parallel, the golfer is largely unaware of the fact. Separation, achieved via natural waves of tall dune mounds, deep fescue and select plantings of assorted pines, makes this possible. The net effect is that each hole provides a desired sense of privacy and isolation.

A second critical aspect of the design was versatility. Recognising that many golfers would opt for a 'round trip', Nugent and Keiser astutely determined that the player's interest on the second nine would be best captured by offering a multitude of tee complexes. This allows the golfer to vary each hole by length, tee angle and elevation. In deference to this stratagem, the Dunes Club has no tee markers; rather, local custom dictates that the winner of the prior hole chooses the tee location for the subsequent hole. In combination with a mid-morning cup change, the nine-hole layout, in effect, approximates eighteen different holes. Nugent and Keiser further recognised the importance of having challenging and generally expansive green complexes to engage the golfer. Par at the 3,125 to 3,492-yard layout is well-defended by the subtle and difficult-to-read slopes of its putting surfaces. Every pin location dictates a preferred region of the green to land the approach shot.

The final key aspect of the routing was

utilising a tall, expansive ridge that traverses the eastern portion of the property. From its peak, the ridge offers dramatic vistas, while its eastern wall forms the perimeter of a rugged valley to the west. Ultimately, this ridge has served as a key aesthetic on several of the Dunes Club's more iconic holes.

Construction began in the spring of 1988 when Wadsworth began clearing the centre lines to a twenty-foot width. The snowmelt allowed the design team to better visualise their nascent golf course, and minor revisions were adopted along the way. Within three months, Wadsworth's mass grading was complete, allowing Sinnott to design and install the irrigation system over the summer. Fine grading and seeding began in mid-August, and by late autumn the Penncross bentgrass fairways and greens, along with the sheep fescue rough, had taken root. (Note: in 2007, under the supervision of superintendent Alan Southward, the club restored its putting surfaces to Penn A4 bentgrass.)

In the spring of 1989, the Dunes Club opened for play. Its sole member was Mike Keiser. Early on, a handful of Keiser's friends were admitted as members. As word of the nine-hole layout spread throughout the region, the membership grew to include a few dozen individuals, primarily Chicagoans with summer homes in the area. To oversee the evolving operation, in 1991 Keiser hired a retired Michigan state trooper named Dave Hettinga as head golf professional. Hettinga has been at the Dunes Club ever since. Today, the club has a membership base of about ninety members, but Keiser states that the annual number of rounds played has remained consistently in the vicinity of 3,500.

The Dunes exudes simplicity. Indeed, the club is so modest that it's hard to find unless you know the address. The entrance is an unmarked, grey cinder path that winds past the gate of a chain link fence and into the woods. A small, white cedar shake clubhouse overlooks the practice putting green, and an attached bluestone terrace scans a portion of the ninth fairway. The tiny clubhouse offers the essentials, nothing more. The simplicity of the club is underscored by the absence of a formal practice range; there is, however, a modest netted practice area beyond the caddy house, as well as a small 'batting cage' near the practice green.

The club's walking-only policy is reinforced by a commitment to a strong caddy program. Over the years, Hettinga has consistently staffed a corps of skilled caddies—no small feat in a region where good 'loopers' are hard to find. The bond between members and caddies is evidenced by the common sight of a post-round drink shared on the terrace. Caddy Appreciation Day is always a well-subscribed event.

The Dunes' challenge is evidenced by its slope, which ranges from 143 to 149. No two consecutive holes run in the same direction. There is a harmonious flow, and an array of shots must be contemplated and executed: draws and fades; aerial and ground-hugging; strategic and heroic.

The par-3 second hole exemplifies the versatility of Nugent and Keiser's design. Both teeing areas are separated by eighty-five yards of dense woods, and offer an angle of approach that deviates by sixty degrees. The 'short' tee, to the east, can make the hole play from 115 yards to 175 yards to a green that is angled from front-right to back-left, and is roughly as wide as it is deep. In contrast, the 'long' tee, to the west, presents the hole from 145 yards to 220 yards to a green that is more deep than wide. From either tee, any shot that misses the green will leave the golfer's ball in a vast depression of low-lying sandy waste. From there, par can only be saved by a well-executed wedge to an elevated, tilted green that is crowned in the middle-back portion. As much as any, the Dunes' second hole evokes the style and look of Pine Valley.

Following a brisk, uphill walk through the woods to the top of the ridge at the highest point on the property, the golfer encounters the visually stunning par-3 sixth hole. There, eight different teeing areas provide remarkable variety. From the tee areas sitting atop the ridgeline, the hole plays as short as 125 yards. On the valley floor below lie four different tee areas, from where the sixth plays as long as 195 yards. And on the opposite side of the valley resides three, mid-distance tee areas. When playing from this region, a tall oak tree guards the left side of the green, so golfers require either a right-to-left play or a delicate shot to the right side of the green. Adoption of the latter, conservative option is not without reward: a facing bank will kick the ball back toward the frontward-sloping, tiered, narrow green. Errant shots to the right of the twelve-yard width green, however, are thrust down a lumpy, tree-laden embankment shrouded in fescue. Shots to the left either find a craggy, sprawling bunker on the face of a steep slope, or fall to the valley floor below requiring a 'blind', lofted wedge up to the slender green. In short, the sixth hole can be an easy par or a hard bogey.

Playing strategy on the 515-yard par-5 eighth hole—proclaimed by golf writer Dan Jenkins as the premier eighth hole in the country[14]—is dictated by a tall oak tree guarding the green some 435 yards from the tee. In years past, the oak stretched across the entire left half of the fairway. However, in 2009, the most expansive branch was trimmed, creating a somewhat less imposing approach to the tiny, elevated, punchbowl green. Nonetheless, strategy still dictates that the third shot approach is best accommodated by a second shot coming to rest on the right half of the fairway no more than 130 yards out. Back on the tee atop the ridgeline, the first shot appears easy enough as the fairway, which lies beyond an irrigation pond and some forty-feet below, stretches seventy-five generous yards wide. However, only the plateau on the middle one-third of the crowned landing-area will readily accommodate the required second shot to the far right-hand side of the fairway. Off-line drives, meanwhile, are kicked to the side, resulting in the need for a shaped shot, in either direction, around the trees flanking both sides of a Sahara bunker bisecting the fairway. Failure to place the second shot in the optimal far-right region has a consequence: the only other way to reach the green in regulation is to execute a hard-hit punch shot with a right-to-left trajectory into, and then over, the face of the narrow, steeply sloped thirty-foot runway that fronts the kettle-shaped putting surface perched above. Having found the green, there is still much to do; the diminutive putting surface is one of the toughest to read on the course due to its subtle bumps and breaks.

The Dunes: A view of the par-3 sixth hole, as viewed from atop the property's ridgeline. With its green perched between a craggy, sloping bunker on the left and mounds of thick fescue to the right, the hole is far from straightforward. (Photograph by Walt Bukva, Bukva Imaging Group Inc. © 2002-2008.)

The fact that the Dunes Club offers only nine holes is viewed by the membership as a distinct positive—there's pride in being able to enjoy the best of its kind. Amid its summer resort locale, a nine-hole layout offers the benefit of better accommodating vacation weekends: a two-hour round allows for plenty of time to retreat to the beach with the family. Other aspects of the club are prized: business is not conducted on the course, and the governance structure frees members from the inconveniences of typical club administration. Children are not only tolerated, they are welcomed. And all members are provided a gate key and encouraged to enjoy the natural beauty of the property during the off-season. Says Fred Muller: 'There is a certain charm and mystique to the Dunes Club being only nine holes. But frankly, the experience is so cool that at times I wish it were twenty-seven holes'.

The Dunes: The par-5 eighth hole, featuring the bunker-laden ridge in the distance. Beyond, golfers encounter a tiny, punchbowl green that is full of character. (Photograph by Walt Bukva, Bukva Imaging Group Inc. © 2002-2008.)

In an era when everyone else was building big, gaudy expensive courses designed to register on the public's imagination, Mike Keiser went to an obscure corner of Michigan where he cobbled a modest little place. The Dunes Club has all of the charm and aesthetics of Pine Valley and with no pretense or worldly aspirations at all—other than to be an intimate golf club, with a modest clubhouse to match.

Bradley S. Klein, Architecture Editor, *Golfweek*

The Dunes: The eighth hole's 'punchbowl' green, as viewed from behind. In the distance the 'sentinel' oak can be seen; historically, it dictated playing strategy on both the first and second shots. (Photograph by Walt Bukva, Bukva Imaging Group Inc. © 2002-2008.)

OPPOSITE ABOVE LEFT
The Dunes: A preview of things to come is evident from the first hole. (Photograph by Walt Bukva, Bukva Imaging Group Inc. © 2002-2008.)

OPPOSITE ABOVE RIGHT
The Dunes: A view from behind the green on the par-4 first hole. (Photograph by Walt Bukva, Bukva Imaging Group Inc. © 2002-2008.)

OPPOSITE BELOW
The Dunes: The strategic placement of fescue-laden dune mounds and select tree plantings effectively separate the incoming par-4 fifth hole (to the left) from the outbound par-5 eighth hole (on the right). The 'camouflaging' of parallel holes is a major attribute of Dick Nugent's small-parcel design. This image was taken from one of the three ridgeline tee-boxes on the par-5 eighth hole; two of these tee boxes also serve the par-3 sixth hole. (Photograph by Walt Bukva, Bukva Imaging Group Inc. © 2002-2008.)

Chambers Bay, USA

Jay Blasi and Bruce Charlton

'The golf course must be good enough to host the US Open the day we open it!' Those bold words—uttered by Pierce County Executive, John Ladenburg—kicked off our first ever design team meeting.

John's dream was to create a golf experience that would bring people from around the world to showcase all of the wonderful assets of Pierce County: Puget Sound; the revitalised city of Tacoma; Mt Rainer, just to name a few. He envisaged creating a public open space that would be enjoyed by the citizens of Pierce County for centuries to come.

The Robert Trent Jones II team dreamed of creating a pure links golf course—one that was true to the traditions of the game. It was a course unlike any we had ever created before, and one unlike any other in the world.

Fortuitously, for both Pierce County and our design firm, an exquisite site would allow us both to realise our dreams.

Pierce County, Washington, had acquired a sand and gravel mine on the shores of Puget Sound in the 1990s. A preliminary Masterplan and feasibility study had been prepared outlining what could be achieved throughout the 930-acre parcel. One major component of the plan was a golf course, which would generate revenue and help utilise the by-products from the adjacent wastewater treatment facility. John Ladenburg, having watched the 2002 US Open at Bethpage Black, inspired his team to 'not just create "any old" golf course; but we should mould a course that could host a major, attract people from all over the world

and stimulate economic development in the area'. He expended every ounce of his political capital and boldly accelerated the process of creating this glorious vision.

The interview

In the fall of 2003, Pierce County initiated a Request for Qualifications (RFQ) and Request for Proposals (RFP) to design a twenty-seven-hole golf course, a public trail and public parks near Chambers Creek. The golf-course architect was to serve as the lead consultant on an assembled team of professionals to design all aspects of the project. In total, fifty-six firms submitted formal proposals.

After careful review of the proposals, five firms were identified and invited to present their plans to the selection committee. As part of the process, firms were welcomed to a guided tour of the site prior to their interview.

Our tour was conducted on 23 December 2003: a profound day where we knew this site and project were both extraordinary.

In order to help the committee members understand our intense passion for the project and enormous belief in its potential, we produced bag tags that read '2030 US Open—Chambers Creek' and presented them to each committee member to close our interview. Fortuitously, in early 2004, our team was commissioned to design Chambers Creek.

The design

Our brief at Chambers Creek was to deliver the best eighteen holes possible. As we do on any project, we performed site analysis while understanding the Pierce County project goals and then seized opportunities among site constraints.

Our passionate vision to create a pure links golf experience would not be deterred. This would require no water hazards, no trees, plenty of width and firm-and-fast play-ing conditions throughout. We wanted imaginative players to relish the experience via use of the 'ground game'. In some instances: to force everyone to utilise the ground game. We set about creating a US Open course, so we studied all elements integral to conducting such an event. We measured tents, bleachers, roadways etc. so that we could spatially accommodate all these items in the design. Thankfully, we were able to utilise an active mining permit, allowing us to move as much sand as needed to completely transform the landscape.

It was our contention, beyond the sandy soils, that Puget Sound was the shining star of the property. And we made every effort to highlight the water. We strived to locate as many holes as possible to appear as if they touched Puget Sound. We suggested that the clubhouse be located detached from the Puget Sound to allow more space for golf adjacent to the water.

In addition to maximising holes 'on the water', we strived to produce holes with as much variety as possible in their length, angle, elevation and direction. This would ensure that golfers would experience different wind and sunlight conditions throughout their memorable round. Very wide fairways throughout would offer numerous angles of attack to each hole location. The out-of-play areas were intended to be 'thin and wispy' where a player could always locate ball and advance it.

Pierce County provided a key luxury: in excess of twelve months for the golf-course design process. This afforded us dozens of site walks to study the potential routing options carefully. As we honed our routing, we staked and cleared the centrelines. This minor clearing led to the only real change in the routing of the course. After clearing some shrub vegetation exposed a natural cove in the dunes, we transformed the sixth hole from a par-3 into a dogleg par-4 (to the right) that played into the dunes. This thoughtful, steady process ensured that there would be few changes to the course in construction.

Midway through the design process we became aware that members of the team were assuming the County would require golf carts on the course. During a meeting to

name the golf course, we made an impassioned plea to John Ladenburg to designate the course as 'walking only'. We simply stated that allowing carts and cart paths would significantly alter the golf holes for the worse. Additionally, we would be prohibited from utilising the grass types that supply firm, fast links golf conditions.

John listened to both sides of the debate, including financial projections with and without carts, and proclaimed: 'We will call it Chambers Bay; and we will walk in 2007'.

Construction

Construction was to begin in the fall of 2005 and be completed by fall of 2006. The construction took part in three phases:

1 mass earth-moving/sand excavation;
2 feature shaping/sand capping; and
3 finishing/grow-in.

The mass earth-moving phase was critical because we had wonderful sands in certain locations and poor soils in others. Our grading plan called for the harvesting of good sand through big cuts while capping the poor materials with large fills. Luckily, the areas we wanted to cut strategically for great golf had excellent sources of sand and our designated fill-areas had poor materials. Once the sand was harvested, this material was screened and then uniformly spread on the playable areas at a depth of twelve inches.

Once mass earth-moving was complete, we crafted the sand into dune landforms. We discovered that if constructing the landforms extremely steep, we could then place the sand and let Mother Nature take over. Over time, the swirling winds would give the dunes the windswept and 'blown-out' appearance we desired.

The entire playable turf at Chambers Bay is the mix of 95 per cent fine fescues and five per cent Colonial bents. The out-of-play areas were hydro-seeded with a fescue mix at half-a-normal seeding rate, in order to ensure that these areas were 'thin and wispy'.

The US Open

In late 2005, we invited the United States Golf Association (USGA), led by Mike Davis, to visit Chambers Bay. On its first visit, in the spring of 2006, Mike was enthusiastic regarding the potential for Chambers Bay to host the US Open. He left this monumental visit by saying something along the lines of: 'It has everything we could ever want; just don't screw up the course'. We took his words to heart!

Between 2006 and the fall of 2007, we had many members of the USGA Executive Committee visit and play the course. The following great news was delivered on 8 February 2008: Chambers Bay was selected to host the 2010 US Amateur and 2015 US Open—making it the first new course since the 1970s to host our national title.

ABOVE LEFT **Chambers Bay:** Taken above the tee, a picture of the 534-yard par-5 thirteenth hole (Eagle Eye), just after grassing and while looking east. The public trail sits just below the fir trees in the background. (Photograph by Dick Durrance II.)

ABOVE RIGHT **Chambers Bay:** A highly challenging par-4, the 500-yard eleventh hole (Shadows) is rated among the toughest holes on the layout. Photographed from behind the green looking south-west, this image depicts the dunescape that was created. (Photograph by Dick Durrance II.)

BELOW **Chambers Bay:** The fifth hole (Free Fall) is a demanding 490-yard par-4, and it has been captured from the right side of the hole. The small 'lions mouth' bunker penetrates the green, forcing players to play over it, or use the ground contours to the right or left. The tall grasses in the foreground were seeded at one-half of the normal rate—a measure to ensure its 'thin and whispy' consistency, allowing golfers to find and hit their ball. This measure was enhanced by the tall grass being deprived of irrigation and fertiliser. (Photograph by Aidan Bradley.)

OPPOSITE **Chambers Bay:** The seventeenth hole (Derailed) is a lengthy par-3 of 218 yards. Photographed from the upper tee, the image shows relic mining structures known as 'Sorting Bins' in the background. (Photograph by Aidan Bradley.)

Pictorial transformation at Chambers Bay

Chambers Bay: Taking in the view of the 521-yard par-5 fourteenth hole (Cape Fear) from the back tee. The large waste area in the foreground is just over seven acres, and entirely created. This was one of the areas of 'good' sand that was mined. The thought being: to cap the entire course in the wish of providing firm and fast playing conditions year round. The large dune to the right of the green was preserved throughout construction, having first been identified during the design firm's initial walk-throughs. (Photograph by Taliferro Jones.)

OPPOSITE Chambers Bay: A view from the tee of the first (Puget Sound), tenth (High Dunes), fourteenth (Cape Fear) and sixteenth (Beached) holes at three stages: prior to construction; during construction; then again just after grassing. These images depict the amount of earthwork that was necessary to create Chambers Bay. For example, the fairway on the tenth hole is now forty feet lower than when started. The progression chart also shows how the right side of the sixteenth hole was a large berm, and how it blocked views to Puget Sound. The finished shot depicts a hole that tips towards Puget Sound, suggestive of it 'hanging over the water'. (Progression photographs by Jay Blasi.)

Machrihanish Dunes, Scotland: Walking in famous footsteps

Paul C. Kimber

Hot on the heels of completing the Castle Course, the latest addition to the 'Home of Golf', I packed my bags and headed west to organise yet another home—the fortieth in my relatively short life. As we established the Machrihanish Dunes site, I was struck by a thought that first presented three years earlier: Old Tom, himself, also had the honour and privilege to both design and build a course at St Andrews, and then do the same on the West coast on the remote peninsula at Machrihanish on the southern tip of the Mull of Kintyre.

The incredibly natural site is located adjacent to the existing Machrihanish course on the Atlantic coast, with the nearest populous being Campbeltown some five miles away. It is only sixty-two miles from Glasgow 'as the crow flies' and can be accessed by twice-daily flights to the old military base at Machrihanish. For us it became a 150-mile, two-and-a-half hour drive from Glasgow through some of the most scenic countryside in Scotland. The route takes in Loch Lomond on up around the top of Loch Long, over the pass called 'Rest and be Thankful', around the banks of Loch Fyne, down past Inveraray, Lochgilphead, Tarbert and, finally, over to the breathtaking Atlantic coast past the islands of Islay and Gigha before reaching Campbeltown—a 'long and winding road' made famous by Sir Paul McCartney's song.

The magnificent scenery encountered en route, directly contrasts with the shock of arrival in Campbeltown. The town that was once a thriving tourist resort for Glasgow's 'well to do'—where many had second homes and the harbour could be found several boats deep in fishing vessels—is now the faintest of shadows of its former self. Campbeltown exists in a state of disrepair, which is the kindest description for the town's buildings.

Those hardy visitors who came to Machrihanish previously played the course, but didn't extend their stay. The vision, therefore, was to create a second course of at least the same standard of Old Tom's links that people would want to sample, creating the need to stay the night to eat, drink and rest. Hotels would benefit, as should all their suppliers. Taxi drivers would do well, ferrying

OPPOSITE **Machrihanish Dunes, Argyll, Scotland:** Looking back from the thirteenth tee over the 194-yard par-3 twelfth hole, golfers enjoy an awe-inspiring panorama of links terrain. (Photograph by Aidan Bradley.)

of the room. In spite of the 'atmospheric' surroundings, the overriding driving force and inspiration during the visits was the quality of the Machrihanish Dunes property: pristine dunes of the right scale for golf; a mile of Atlantic coastline; awe-inspiring views to Islay and Jura. Much of the site was covered in tightly knitted vegetation that would never pass the agronomists view of a perfect sward. To us, however, it was perfectly playable as it was.

Further investigation revealed just enough depth to allow the length of a par-4 and, in other areas, four holes to be played side by side. This would allow flexibility in routings and added the possibility of a less-common links aspect: returning nines. Topographically, the site was very similar to Old Tom's adjoining, existing course, so we knew huge potential existed to create something special.

With fondness I recall a trip in July 2004, around the time of the British Open at Troon, when one of our interns and I hired a car in Glasgow and started on the long drive to Machrihanish. A stunning drive at any

the golfers between the courses; caddies would appreciate the additional workload; greenkeeping staff, too—each sector contributing to an increasing spiral of prosperity for the area. Clearly, this project has the potential to have a far wider impact than just the golfing world. If successful it should be the catalyst to regenerate the entire region.

Site visitations by David McLay Kidd and I were an intriguing affair; they involved staying in the disused Royal Hotel owned by the developer. It was here that we sketched routings in the former great hall of the hotel most recently used as the local nightclub with the glitterball still hanging in the centre

time, the long summer's day provided an opportunity not to be missed. With my golf clubs in the back, I only had a pressing engagement in mind: I was going to play the entire course before it was built—something precious few in my line of work could have done, previously! At 7.18 pm we stood on the proposed first tee and, at 10.20 pm, I teed up on the final hole having only lost four balls. That is how good the site is!

We set up the Machrihanish Dunes site with no more than one excavator, twenty guys and a budget of just £1.2 million, forcing the purchase of old and second-hand equipment. Okay ... it wasn't a horse and cart, but this resource level provided insight to how the 'Great Grandfather' of the game must have felt as he went about his business. Personally, the project was a refreshing change after the full-scale, cauldron-like, intense atmosphere we had at the Castle Course—but certainly no less of a challenge.

With the DMK team busier than ever, I needed to juggle responsibilities of being full time on-site at Machrihanish, overseeing the 'grow-in' phase at the Castle and managing the new construction at G West located immediately west of Braid's Gleneagles. In essence, I was looking after the UK projects. David, meanwhile, was concentrating efforts on the other side of the Atlantic at Stonebrae (California), Tetherow (Oregon) and Huntsman Springs (Idaho).

By way of a background note, how we even progressed to this point at Machrihanish Dunes is a story just on its own: ninety-five per cent of the site was as protected as land can be in Scotland. Following four years of extensive and protracted negotiations with Scottish Natural Heritage (SNH), our own ecologist eventually gained the all-important permissions, albeit with some incredibly strict conditions attached. One stipulation was the constant supervision of our ecologist. We turned this to our advantage.

The combination of environmental restrictions and our knowledge of the site drove the concept of the course evolving to, or possibly returning to 'The Way Golf Began'. This became the tagline for the project; we would create, rather than build, the course and it would be modern golf played over an old-fashioned links—the very essence of minimalism, with the huge advantage of a property that was more than capable of accommodating these goals.

In his capacity as my number two shaper at St Andrews, Conor Walsh had proved himself to be a valuable operator on both excavator and the dozer. He was primed to step up to the plate and become the 'main man'. By shaping the greens and tees at Machrihanish, he did just that!

The process of building the course was relatively simple. The first task, in fact, was attending to the only part of what we would normally call 'shaping' on a golf course. An area of what was destined to become the first fairway had been used for many years as a feeding area for cattle; as such, the natural vegetation and landform had been destroyed. After presenting a cogent ecological argument, we were permitted to shape this area to resemble the rest of the course.

OPPOSITE **Machrihanish Dunes: The revised 329-yard fourteenth hole called for extreme caution during the planning and construction phases. (Photograph by Aidan Bradley.)**

As each area to be constructed was prepared, I would mark out a green or tee and seek agreement by the ecologist—sometimes, after fractious negotiations. The turf would be cut by hand and transplanted—initially, to reinstate any local rabbit damage. Surplus turf was moved (again by hand) to the area prepared on the opening hole.

Supervised by our ecologist, each green site was given a specific location within that area that best-matched slope, exposure and elevation to try to ensure the survival of the plant species in question. It was an involved and deliberate process requiring untold patience.

Once the turf was lifted, the remaining soil and sand was mixed together with the

teeth of the excavator; thereafter, the area was shaped to make it useable as a green. Being limited to working only on the green surface itself meant that the edges were tied into the existing landforms. Little or no sand would be moved. As the greens feature a pure fescue sward, they're not expected to be too fast, and this allowed us to retain some 'interest'

in the putting surfaces. It was a source of professional pride to our team that many of the original bold contours could be retained.

The only areas allowed to be used for bunkers were those areas affected by severe rabbit damage; and they were simply 'ragged' out of the existing land. Maintaining the theme of 'The Way Golf Began' ... old pic-tures of Cheape's bunker at St Andrews were part of the inspiration, as were the existing sandy hollows found on-site.

Gradually the course evolved, and it stayed reasonably faithful to the original plan until we got to the fourth and fifth holes. At this point, a few realisations became apparent. Increasingly, I managed to play more golf, locally, and so became accustomed to experi-encing the windy conditions. It became obvi-ous that the original length of the course—even accounting for its five sets of tees—was too long. There was also an issue, whereby the view of the stunning approach to the fifth green was only really achievable from a cou-ple of parts on the fairway. Compounding

Machrihanish Dunes: A view from the dune above the sixth-hole tees, back over the fifth hole. Old Tom's creation is visible in the background. (Photograph by Paul Kimber.)

the problem, the view was also accessible from an area that was designated as being particularly environmentally sensitive, yet it would entail being trampled upon by the golfers' insistence on walking in straight lines. In order for all golfers to experience the view, I changed the fourth hole from a par-3 to a driveable par-4, and the fifth to a par-3. Thereafter, everyone gained a view from the tee. The consequence, however, would be a layout that presented consecutive par-3s at the fifth and sixth holes. After talking the concept through with David over the phone, he readily agreed to the plan. I was also able to gain some valuable environmental 'points' and so invited SNH to come to the site and agree to the change. It was success all round.

The results at Machrihanish Dunes can only be judged by the masses over the coming years. For now, our work at Machrihanish Dunes has come to a close and we confidently leave the virgin course in the hands of a world renowned owner and operator in Southworth Europe. Southworth has been integral in ensuring that our vision for Machrihanish Dunes will be preserved and enjoyed for years to come.

We are incredibly proud of what we achieved on both coasts of Scotland. As a young architect who gained the opportunity to follow in the footsteps of the game's most famous and historical figure, I can only hope that our firm's footsteps will be held in similar regard over the long haul. I await calls from the East Coast of Ireland to continue the links journey.

There is no greatest golf course: Only greatest golf courses

Mike Nuzzo

Not long after golf began, so did the debate between players as to what was the better golf course in the village. Over the last century this has evolved into a global argument as to what are the greatest courses in the world. Every golf and resort magazine, seemingly, prints its own periodic definitive rankings. The deliberations continue and no one agrees completely with the lists or with each other. Some courses have universal appeal, but even they are rarely seen identically. Everyone has a slightly different definition of the ultimate golf course. This aspect is just one of the many great pleasures of the game. Why do so many players' opinions differ? Howard Moskowitz is a noted expert in the

field of psychophysics—the study of human preferences and their detection ability. His studies have made revolutionary discoveries about colas, coffee, spaghetti sauce and pickles. According to Malcolm Gladwell:

Initially, Pepsi wanted him to identify the perfect amount of sweetener for Diet Pepsi. Moskowitz did the logical thing by making up experimental batches with every conceivable degree of sweetness and gave them to hundreds of people, and looked for the concentration that people liked the most. But the data was a mess—there wasn't a pattern— Moskowitz realized that they had been

asking the wrong question. There was no such thing as the perfect Diet Pepsi; they should have been looking for the perfect Diet Pepsis.[15]

Moskowitz found several other food taste categories that are also segmented. One famous, extensive study was with spaghetti sauce. He determined that everyone had a slightly different definition of what a perfect spaghetti sauce tasted like. He discovered that most people's preferences fell into one of three broad groups: plain; spicy; extra-chunky. This was an especially important finding: there was no extra-chunky spaghetti sauce in the market at that time!

OPPOSITE **The par-5 fourteenth hole has the smallest green at Wolf Point Club, Texas—also the wildest. (Photograph by Mike Nuzzo)**

As with eating, golf is also biologically enjoyable—some even prefer playing golf to eating! Recently, the National Golf Foundation (NGF) published a survey on what the player seeks in enjoyment of the game. It reported that conditioning, camaraderie, design and scoring were among the greatest factors contributing to a player's enjoyment of the game. Trying to remove some of these universals to determine what defines course preferences is a very challenging psychophysics investigation. How is the current golf-course industry segmented? Today, when someone is developing a new course or ranking existing ones, the divisions are almost always limited to public, private, municipal, cost, resort, modern or old. But is that really the best way to typify a golfer? If you were to recommend a course to a friend it is doubtful that any of those descriptors would sway his/her opinion. What you would be more likely to describe are the aspects you most admire about a course.

Are there different categories of courses that suit segments of golfers? I believe golfers can be subdivided into three types or groupings: those who relish the playing challenge; those who revere the course's environment; and those who place the enjoyment-factor above all else. Compounding the confusion is that most golfers want the experience to overlap all three endpoints—but they seek them to different degrees. According to Moskowitz, 'The mind knows not what the tongue wants'.[16] In Moskowitz's spaghetti sauce study, he determined that when he optimised for each individual preference, it would yield the greatest appreciation only by that specific group. When optimising for everyone, the results of each individual preference group were substantially less. It became apparent to Moskowitz that when he made one group happier, he disenfranchised another group. He says:

> We did this for coffee, and we found that if you try and target all segments the best you can score is above average. But if I design for specific tastes or sensory segmentations, I can get an order of magnitude higher, and with coffee that is something you'd die for.[17]

So happiness, in one sense, is a function of how closely our world conforms to the infinite variety of human preference.

I suggest ranking courses based on the type of player by categorising the greatest courses in the world. Try to place each course in the respective category where it naturally best fits—challenging; pretty; or fun. This works even better with the less-vaunted courses, and it wouldn't be much of a leap to describe architects in this same manner. The following few paragraphs provide identifiers of each segment.

The challenge-centric golfer wants every facet of his/her game tested, and for the hole and its required strategy to be clearly visible. They want to be rewarded for a well-struck shot down the middle of the fairway and hate missing putts, either of their own volition, or not. They want the course to be presented fairly and the greens to be nearly flat. They prefer stroke-play events, and I place the typical golf professional in this grouping. Famed courses such as Pine Valley, Oakmont and Shinnecock Hills fit this player to a tee.

The environment-based golfer loves great

OPPOSITE **Draped against a natural drainage swale, the closer you get to Wolf Point's par-3 fifteenth green the more serpent-like it appears. (Photograph by Mike Nuzzo)**

maintenance, pretty views, and lots of flowers, waterfalls and fountains. The stereotypical player of this persuasion could be an executive out hitting a few shots on the course, with or without a cart, enjoying the all-pervading scenery, or merely indulging in relaxing chit-chat. This type of golfer might not even keep score, know all the rules or care less. It doesn't hurt to be reminded that a percentage of the market segment who prefer a pretty course don't even play golf. They utilise a golf course in a whole different way: by choosing to live on the periphery. Cypress Point, Pebble Beach and Augusta National are the poster courses for this type of consumer.

The fun-influenced golfer, like the others, loves the game, but is usually more interested in the course or the history and is certainly more whimsical. They can laugh loudest when hitting into a 'hidden' bunker, and enjoy a subtle strategy. They want their golf ball to stay 'in play' when missing a shot, and prefer more contour to the greens. The returned score is a low priority, as match play is often *their game*. The Old Course at St Andrews and National Golf Links of America (NGLA) are the two standouts that fit this segment.

I'm sure you've noticed how the best debates about golf courses are often heated. Is there a hierarchy of taste? Is one type of player (or course) a higher ideal to aspire to? Many believe their particular flavour is the evolution of the highest order. Did you ever hear a club professional comment that a course is no good because it's too easy? Or that the course is 'tricked-up', or way too long? My answer is an absolute 'no' to a hierarchy of taste. There are just different tastes in the same way that someone may prefer spicy, plain or extra-chunky spaghetti sauce.

The six million dollar question is: what should a new course developer build? A typical business plan would be to have as many rounds as possible. So, traditionally, they would build the course that can meet the objectives of as many players as possible. And like coffee when that is the goal, everyone usually enjoys the course (in part) because everyone enjoys the game—but, at best, everyone enjoys it a little bit less. Why not develop to one particular taste, and then the fun-influenced golfers might flock to your course. There's no guesswork involved; we know this for it coincides closest to their preference.

If in charge of a city developing three new courses, I'd create one of each kind to market to each segment. But because it's very expensive to build just one golf course, most developers try to cater to all, when it's surely more effective to develop for one segment. The challenge is to identify the under-serviced market segment. Such a philosophy makes sense on economic grounds, too. When you think about it, if building a fun or pretty course is your goal, you wouldn't have to make it long and could save a lot of capital and annual maintenance. This, automatically, makes it quicker to play, because the demographic you are catering to doesn't even care about it being 500 yards less than other courses. The occasional challenge-player might play and tell his buddies that the layout isn't as good as Shinnecock; but it wasn't created for this segment ... so that's okay.

Bobby Jones, famously, felt that Augusta National was an ideal course. It appealed to

The eighth and eighteenth holes at Wolf Point culminate in a large, beautifully designed double-green, where golfers experience an array of enjoyable shotmaking options. (Photograph by Mike Nuzzo)

the challenge-golfer and the fun-influenced golfer at the same time. It is also considered one of the best-maintained and prettiest inland courses in the world. Today, however, Augusta National has been evolving and changing on this spectrum, with equipment technological advancements leading the way in order to test the best players in the world. Augusta had to leave its heritage of 'fun' behind, as challenge and fun are often in opposition because 'length of shots' is one of the greater golfing challenges and, at the same time, one of the least-fun aspects of the game.

Maybe someday instead of saying that the new 'Towny Links Golf Course' is a par seventy-two championship test with eighteen signature holes, it will announce itself, first and foremost, as being either challenging, pretty or fun. Until that time, all we can do is cut through the marketing 'fluff' and decide for ourselves. Given all of the above: what type of course is your home course? And while you're considering: what type of golfer are you?

Blackstone Golf and Country Club, South Korea

One great result. **TORO**® Count on it.

visit www.toro.com

The story of Ballyhack Golf Club, USA

Lester George

Several years ago, I was meeting with a client interested in building a First Tee facility in the Roanoke, Virginia area. After viewing several sites, he asked if I had a few more minutes to see a piece of land he had considered for a private club. We crossed the Blue Ridge Parkway on a five-minute drive to an area called Mt Pleasant to encounter one of the most awe-inspiring pieces of mountain property in Virginia.

Astounded by the tremendous rolling grassy terrain, I asked why he hadn't purchased the land. 'A group of us have already tried, and it's not likely you'll be able to buy that farm in your lifetime, Lester', he said. That comment piqued my interest, and I decided to do some digging into the land's history.

Mt Pleasant was once known as Ballyhack. While there is no official documentation regarding this farming community's prior moniker, there are indeed historical references to it. The oldest known schoolhouse in the area was tagged the 'Ballyhack School' on some century-old maps. A later reference—a police report from 1927—states that a Deputy Sheriff was killed while conducting a liquor raid on a home in Ballyhack, Virginia.

This specific property was known as the Saul Farm. The property had been used as a dairy farm and pasture, and there were two brick silos (still standing today) built in 1939. There had been several attempts to develop this land, both by the government and private investors, but an intersection of Interstate Seventy-three was slated for the Saul Farm in the early 2000s, rendering it useless for development.

The Saul Farm kept creeping into my mind.

Since it didn't appear that golf development was possible, I tried to push thoughts of it out of my mind.

Some three years later, I met a man, who upon finding out I was a golf-course architect, told me he owned the best piece of land in the Roanoke area for a golf course. I challenged him, saying, 'I've seen the best piece of land in the Roanoke area for a golf course, and I don't believe it's yours'. He described the property, and it sounded eerily familiar. I still couldn't believe it was the same property, but felt compelled to visit Roanoke and look. Lo and behold, it was indeed the Saul Farm!

The very next morning, as if by design, the front page of the Roanoke paper declared that Interstate Seventy-three was to be rerouted and would not pass through the Saul Farm. After

OPPOSITE **Ballyhack Golf Club, Virginia, USA: The 350-yard par-4 eleventh hole. (Photograph by Shannon E. Fisher.)**

OPPOSITE ABOVE **Ballyhack: The par-5 fifteenth hole features a double-green it shares with the thirteenth hole. (Photograph by Shannon E. Fisher.)**

OPPOSITE BELOW **Ballyhack: The par-5 tenth hole, captured looking down 'Windy Gap'. (Photograph by Shannon E. Fisher.)**

reading the article, and thanking the powers that be that I happened to be in Roanoke on the very day this article was published, I immediately called the owner and asked him to sell me the property. He had two full-price offers from residential real-estate developers, but he agreed to take a contract from me, as well.

Two days later, he called to let me know he had a contract from another party for more than the asking price. I could not raise my offer, but I implored him to reconsider, stating a golf course was the perfect use for that land. He agreed that the property should be something greater than a subdivision, but said he had to take the higher offer. As I hung up the phone, I faced the realisation that my dream of building a golf course on this land was simply not to be.

Two hours later, I received a phone call from the landowner, who stated, 'I think you're right. It should be a golf course, and your plan will keep the land relatively rural'. He said he would have my contract signed before I returned to Richmond.

Pinching myself to validate this stroke of luck (or fate), I applied for rezoning of the land and started routing the golf course. The first thing I did in the zoning process was to meet with the Mt Pleasant neighbours, who welcomed my plan for the land. Previously, ideas floated for the farm had included a landfill, a sewage-treatment facility and a subdivision. After several meetings with this group, they unanimously supported the golf course at the county zoning hearings.

Now that the zoning was approved, I contacted Bill Kubly of Landscapes Unlimited. We've had great success working together on many projects—most notably, Kinloch Golf Club, which is the highest rated course in Virginia history. I wanted Bill to build this golf course; after about twenty minutes on the farm, Bill was convinced that I had found something special.

Having been involved in the construction of Sand Hills, Nebraska, and being a principal in Sutton Bay, Bill recommended we adopt a similar model. Cleverly, he probed:

Why not create a remote-destination private golf club with guest housing and limited residential lots? People are tired of having to buy residential lots in remote destinations with courses that are real-estate driven, but they do want to belong to a getaway club. Overnight lodging is ideal for those folks.

We agreed that the topography of the land was perfect for a links-style course; I was initially attracted to the land largely because of its native grass, rolling hills and 'brave' terrain that look very much like Scottish highlands. We wanted, unashamedly, a highly exclusive destination golf club with only fifty local members and 250 national members. Within an hour, Bill and I had charted a mental map for a low-impact golf course, Ballyhack Golf Club, based largely on the Sutton Bay model.

We knew, instinctively, that we'd need to bring other partners into the mix to help finance Ballyhack. After interviewing several, I was approached in Richmond one evening by Tommy Balzer, an owner of a prominent architecture and engineering firm called Balzer & Associates. I told Tommy I was seeking a partner who shared the vision Bill and I had for Ballyhack; one, too, who had the fortitude and passion to carry out that vision. Tommy

ABOVE Ballyhack: The seventh hole.
(Photograph by Shannon E. Fisher.)

RIGHT Ballyhack: The ninth hole and its distinctive
barn. (Photograph by Shannon E. Fisher.)

OPPOSITE ABOVE Ballyhack: The sixth hole.
(Photograph by Shannon E. Fisher.)

OPPOSITE BELOW LEFT Looking back towards the tee,
from the 20,000 square foot eighteenth green.
(Photograph by Shannon E. Fisher.)

OPPOSITE BELOW RIGHT Ballyhack: The twelfth hole.
(Photograph by Shannon E. Fisher.)

OPPOSITE ABOVE **Ballyhack: The first hole, as shown from behind the green. (Photograph by Shannon E. Fisher.)**

OPPOSITE BELOW **Ballyhack: The seventeenth hole requires golfers to traverse a cavernous ravine. (Photograph by Shannon E. Fisher.)**

responded, 'We have the passion and the guts to pull it off!' After a meeting of the owners of Balzer & Associates, the Balzers were on board and the Ballyhack team was formed. Construction started in July 2007 and was completed in September 2008. Ballyhack Golf Club was unveiled in May 2009.

Ballyhack is one of the most balanced and rhythmic designs of my entire career. I am honoured to have had the opportunity to design a true, links-style golf course on a property with such naturally bold and domineering features and a panoramic view of Blue Ridge Mountains. The natural elevations of the golf course run from about 950 feet to 1,150 feet, featuring prominent elevation changes. I included a myriad of strategies into my design, all created to take the fullest advantage of the existing terrain. Incorporating the dramatic topography, I designed boldly contoured greens. The golf course can measure anywhere from 7,350 yards (from the back tees), to 5,000 yards (from the front tees), with rolling links-style fairways as wide as 120 yards.

Ballyhack's front-nine is routed around, and between, several major ridges, creating the 'high-dune' look. Between the ridges, there is a beautiful moor that we used as a prominent feature to accentuate the first, sixth, seventh and eighth holes. The second hole is a 530-yard par-5 that plays from a high dune to a natural ridge, encompassing the entire ridge. In places, the second fairway is over 100 yards wide. Although the green is 10,000 square feet, it is perched precariously on the ridge-top and surrounded by falloff. Another interesting aspect of the front nine is the sixth hole, a 320-yard par-4, which defiantly tempts the player to drive over the moor, toward the green. Playing into the prevailing wind, such a notion will challenge even the boldest of golfers.

The back nine features a double green for the thirteenth and fifteenth holes. Players will recognise this feature from the old country. At approximately 25,000 square feet, and separated by a seven-foot deep swale, this feature fits into the landscape so well I couldn't pass up the opportunity to build it. The final hole at Ballyhack, a 480-yard par-4, plays through the middle of the ravine into a natural punchbowl green that is approximately 21,000 square feet. The finishing touch of the design is the use of all cool-season grasses with native grass dunes, featuring a variety of grasses on wind-blown, ragged bunker faces.

This property fell into my lap not once, but three times: when my client led me to it; when I had a chance encounter with the landowner; and, lastly—even though I could not afford to match a higher offer—when the owner called back and agreed to sell it to me. Purchasing and zoning the property before I had even a whiff of an interested partner was a gamble I felt compelled to make; I did not want to let 370 acres of developable, pristine rolling grassland in the Blue Ridge Mountains slip away.

Ballyhack Golf Club delivers time-honoured, traditional European golf to golfers on US soil. It also brings me a great sense of personal satisfaction, because—even though the project took a meandering path—this golf course has been in my head and heart for years. It is with gratitude and humility to nature that I have the opportunity to unveil this breathtaking property to the world with my signature on the landscape.

The Barwon Heads Golf Club, Australia: A New Par-3 Course

The Barwon Heads Golf Club is truly a revered golfing destination in Australia. Its old-world charm extends from its glorious clubhouse (circa 1924) to its classic links, which is regarded by many as one of Australia's finest. While the architectural work of Crafter and Mogford Golf Strategies continues on the 'enhancement' of the championship course, the firm has enjoyed the delightful distraction of re-designing the club's nine-hole par-3 course, first laid out by Legh Winser in 1961.

While it is recalled that Legh was a talented cricketer and 'kept' wicket to an ageing W. G. Grace, it was at golf that he excelled. Born in England in 1884, Legh has an accomplished golfing record: being crowned Australian Amateur Champion in 1921 and an eight-time winner of the South Australian State Amateur title, among his many achievements. By the age of ninety-six, Legh is said to have broken his age no less that 200 times—outrageously, at the same age, he returned a score of seventy-nine at Barwon Heads!

The par-3 course has contributed much to the soul of the club, bringing together its youth through to its most elderly members, as evidenced by the fulfilling sight of 'eighty somethings' and pre-teens sharing the course. Importantly, the course provides a relaxed environment for those new to the game, unencumbered by the grandeur of the main course,

free to discover the joys of golf as well as to learn etiquette and the subtleties of links play. Junior Week is a highlight of the January golfing calendar and enjoys ever-increasing popularity.

The catalyst for the redesign was the creation of a flood-detention basin, providing a much-needed additional irrigation source. The greatest challenge faced by Crafter and Mogford was to create holes that would essentially disguise the construction of the basin wall and the basin itself. Three holes fall within its clutches, with the second and third holes built across the top of the wall. The seventh hole, meanwhile, materialised along its northern bank. The remainder of the holes were re-routed (as a consequence), factoring-in the need for the course to expand its footprint into unused land to the north. A wetland, while still maturing, serves as the centrepiece, with the additional benefit of being an 'in-play' hazard on the second and third holes.

Considerable care was taken to minimise the disruption of the remaining natural contour. The northern 'Murt' holes—fourth, fifth and sixth—are adjacent to Murtnagurt Swamp and have been 'inserted' into the landscape ... rather than imposed. Shaping was limited to the greens and their surrounds.

Purposely bunkerless to maintain ease of play, the designers paid much attention to the use of

'contour hazards' on the course, relying on the golfing interest born out of the intricate, unearthed terrain that was subtly enhanced.

Couch grass fairways and greens ensure minimum inputs are required to maintain the course. The wintergreen couch on the greens provides slower putting speeds than bentgrass—an important aspect; it allowed Crafter and Mogford the freedom to accentuate green undulations and recreate green speeds that golfers would have enjoyed back in 1924.

Reportedly, the fourth hole is a favourite of the design firm, with its tee nestled among time-eternal moonah trees. The sloping green sweeps across the terrain and features a bold depression immediately short of the green. It gathers and slews golf balls at will.

The fifth hole is played across the tail-end of Murtnagurt Swamp to a green slung across a diagonal embankment. On account of the 'short-grass' that lies in front of the green—beyond the reeds and rushes of the swamp and cannot be seen readily—the hole's appearance from the tee is deceptive.

Two holes further on, at the seventh, are where Crafter and Mogford unleashed their most creative work at Barwon Heads par-3 course. They did so by building a most attractive green amid an area almost bereft of natural advantages.

By contrast, the existing features encountered at the proposed eighth and ninth holes were bold, character-laden and provided interesting architectural opportunities for the two designers. A change to the course's character is quickly noted by newcomers to the layout. The eighth hole pays homage to Lahinch's famous 'Dell' hole, and ranks highly among the favourite holes of local golfers at Barwon Heads.

The ninth hole utilises a bold, foreground ridge to deceive golfers with depth-perception. Tee-shots are directed to a wickedly undulating green, where a two-putt will be a good result. A statement followed by a question is often made by players after walking off the ninth green: 'It's only taken us an hour; how about we whip around again?' Now isn't that refreshing in this day and age!

ABOVE **The Barwon Heads Golf Club/Par-3 Course, Victoria, Australia:** The view looking back towards the fifth tee, from behind the green. The sixth green is to the left; Murtnagurt Swamp to the right; the fourth hole lies beyond. (Photograph by Kimbal Baker.)

BELOW **Barwon Heads:** The short eighth hole pays homage to Lahinch's famous 'Dell' hole, although this version is only semi-'blind' when compared to the Irish original. (Photograph by Kimbal Baker.)

Barwon Heads: Looking south over the ephemeral wetland, from the seventh tee. The second hole lies further on, while to the horizon the sixteenth green and seventeenth tees of the Championship course can be seen. (Photograph by Kimbal Baker.)

OPPOSITE **Barwon Heads:** The view across the sixth green highlights the bold contouring of both the approach and the putting surface. (Photograph by Kimbal Baker.)

Barwon Heads: A deep swale eats into the right side of the first green. As the layout makes do without bunkers, contour-hazards such as this swale form an important part of the course's defences. (Photograph by Kimbal Baker.)

BELOW Barwon Heads: The first hole, as seen from the left side, punctuated by its deep green-side swale. (Photograph by Kimbal Baker.)

OPPOSITE Barwon Heads: An image from front-left of the elevated first hole's green site. The walk-off provides a panoramic vista of the second, third and seventh holes. (Photograph by Kimbal Baker.)

The Hotchkin Course, Woodhall Spa, UK: Conserving a heathland course

Richard A. Latham

Little has been published regarding the evolution of the Hotchkin Course at Woodhall Spa. In spite of this classic British heathland course having been rated highly in course ranking lists for the past sixty years, it could be argued that it is not that widely known to the golfing public. Through choice, it has not played host to a major televised professional event and, until the relatively recent acquisition by the English Golf Union, neither has it been widely promoted or advertised.

So, what has made this course so special that *Golf World* magazine has recently rated it as the best inland course in the United Kingdom? Studying its evolution provides a number of key issues that are common to other leading courses: there were a few strong-willed figures who influenced the development in tandem with advancements in equipment; opinions were sought from leading players and architects of the day, but only implemented after careful consideration; the land was nurtured and refined by making the best of what nature provided; and major championships—in Woodhall Spa's case, amateur—were welcomed on a regular basis, which ensured that the challenge of the course was continually reviewed.

Golf was introduced to Woodhall Spa as an additional attraction to the spa town activities in the latter-half of the nineteenth century. By 1890, nearly 50,000 visitors annually came to this small Lincolnshire town by train from London to enjoy the spa waters, which offered relief to some ailments of the day. A nine-hole course was introduced and Woodhall Spa Golf Club was formally instituted in 1891. Four years later, the land that the course occupied was required for town expansion, so another nine-hole course was laid out a short distance away. Golf flourished there for the next seven years until a similar situation regarding land usage arose again.

Stafford Vere Hotchkin, a prominent member and competent single-figure golfer, owned a significant amount of land in and around Woodhall Spa. He offered some of this land—a sandy tract to the north of the town—to the club in order that a permanent home for an eighteen-hole course could be

OPPOSITE **Woodhall Spa, Lincolnshire, England: A view of the third hole on 'The Hotchkin'—the course that was voted by *Golf World* as the best inland golf course in the United Kingdom. Hotchkin Tower, the symbol of the club, is prominent behind the green. (Photograph by Richard Latham.)**

built. Harry Vardon was approached to lay out the holes and he visited in January 1903. Surprisingly, the course took two years to construct, which was due to a drought one year and incessant rain in the other. The site was of poor soil quality and it is reported that some 50,000 cartloads of topsoil had to be brought in. However, one positive feature was that virtually the whole area was covered with a thick layer of sand, which provided excellent drainage. John H. Taylor advised on bunker placements for the new layout and the course opened for play in April 1905.

Hotchkin showed a great deal of interest in the construction and, over the next few years, helped to finance adjustments to the course. By 1911, it was considered that the course needed to be significantly altered and lengthened if it was to keep pace with changes in equipment. Harry Colt was engaged to review the layout; he made a number of suggestions that took two winter periods to fully implement. This work included some new greens, new bunkers and mounding. Most significantly, perhaps,

the par-3 twelfth hole was created at this time. The hole, deservedly, features as one of the great par-3s in the world ranking lists. After Colt's changes, the course measured 6,400 yards and the routing of the course, as it is played today, can be attributed to him.

During the First World War, Hotchkin served in the Leicestershire Yeomanry where he reached the rank of Major, and was to become an Honorary Colonel of the Sixtieth Field Regiment RATA after the war. He also became acquainted with Major Cecil K. Hutchinson and Major Guy Campbell at this time. They were both accomplished golfers and had an interest in golf-course design; he later formed a golf architectural partnership with them. The club was struggling financially at the end of the war and, in 1919, it was reported that 'the landlord, Colonel S. V. Hotchkin, would take over the club as a proprietary one'.

From this time onwards, Hotchkin set about transforming each hole into a true championship test. He had a strong desire to make his course into one of the best and he

lengthened some of the holes by moving greens and incorporating new tees. Hotchkin had obviously amassed a great deal of knowledge from the time Vardon visited, through course construction and the numerous alterations that had been made. He was now applying this knowledge, not just at Woodhall Spa, but to other courses in the area.

Hotchkin wanted the course to look as natural as possible, which is not always so easy to achieve on flat ground. He spent the next twenty years achieving this aim and as the course matured he refined various aspects. By the late 1920s, he visited South Africa and made a huge impact on the modernisation of course there. He also was the sole designer of Humewood, near Port Elizabeth, and this course remained virtually intact to the original design until two years ago when some alterations were made. He formed a partnership with Hutchinson and Campbell at the end of the 1920s; they produced a number of courses, which included West Sussex and Ashridge.

During the Second World War, Hotchkin

Hotchkin Course
3rd Hole

Typical Example of S V Hotchkin's Improvements

Hotchkin's new green built on a raised plateau, completed in the late 1920s

Original green site

Woodhall Spa: Schematic of the present third green site, showing its original location prior to being moved by Hotchkin. He did this type of work on many holes. (Drawing by Richard Latham.)

Woodhall Spa: An archival view of the original third green, with Hotchkin Tower in the background. (Photograph courtesy of Woodhall Spa.)

virtually kept the Woodhall Spa course open on his own by involving himself in green-keeping duties. His ethic of attention to detail and complete devotion to the course was passed on to his son, Neil, who took over the reins in 1953. Neil was not such an expert as his father on course matters, but set out with a determination to embrace his father's architectural principles.

Neil Hotchkin made few changes to the course, other than to lengthen some of the holes to combat equipment advancement. When he decided to make a change he invariably consulted an architect. He invited Cotton (C. K.), Pennink, Lawrie & Partners Ltd to advise in the 1960s and 1970s and then, more recently, Donald Steel made suggestions on bunkering. However, one significant point can be attributed to Neil: the development of the renowned Woodhall Spa bunkers. His father believed that hazards, in particular bunkers, should be bold. Neil wished to continue this principle, but his interpretation of 'bold' appears to have materialised as 'depth'. When studying old photo-graphs, there is no doubt that the bunkers were larger but shallower when the Colonel was responsible for the course. Over the past fifty years they have become smaller and much deeper. In fact, there are few courses in the world that can boast so many deep bunkers, particularly as the site is so unusu-ally level. This depth has only been achieved because of the amount of natural sand under the surface. Refurbishing some of the large, deeper bunkers is labour intensive and can, on occasions, seem like a major civil engi-neering project! Revetting the bunker faces was trialled, but the theme looked hopelessly out of character. Instead, a rolling turf face was eventually decided upon. Some of the challenges of the current management team are to maintain a natural look at the same time as satisfying daily maintenance activi-ties as well as health and safety issues—for both staff and golfers.

The layout of the course is such that lengthening holes has not been too much of an issue. This has allowed the 'drive' haz-ards, including the carries to the fairway, to remain a challenge and retain their impor-tant strategic qualities. All of the four par-5s have been lengthened and, although most of the fairways are generous, heather and gorse presents an immediate visual penalty for a misdirected shot. There are only three par-3s, but the penalties for missing the greens are most severe.

The course is now designated a Site of Special Scientific Interest (SSSI) and a com-prehensive management plan for the non-playing surfaces has been agreed between the company and the government-funded organisation, Natural England. When course alterations or refurbishments are planned, Natural England is included in the consider-ations—such is the ecological importance of the site. Tree management is a particular issue at the present time, with a high num-ber already removed.

In order to safeguard the future, Neil Hotchkin sold the course and additional land to the English Golf Union, the governing body of men's amateur golf. It did so in 1995. The National Golf Centre was created and a

ABOVE LEFT AND RIGHT Woodhall Spa: A study of concentrated precision is shown with the refurbishment to the fifth hole's greenside bunkers, both left and right sides. The scale of the task is self-explanatory, but it's worth noting that the 'rolling grass face' style of bunkering, so clearly shown, can be credited to Hotchkin's son, Neil. (Photographs by Richard Latham.)

second course was designed by Donald Steel (The Bracken), which opened for play in 1998. At this point, the original course was named 'The Hotchkin' in memory of the family and its contribution to golf. A training academy was also built, which includes a four-acre short-game practice area, arguably one of the best facilities in Europe. The academy is used to train not only the elite players in England but also golfers of all standards who wish to improve their game. They also have the opportunity to play on the courses, which are open all-year round to visitors.

In summary, Woodhall Spa has achieved its reputation through the determination of a few to create a true championship course. The land on which the course was built, arguably, was most unsuitable at the outset; only a dogged attitude—at that time when Mother Nature played 'hardball'—made it possible. Having one knowledgeable person solely responsible for development over long periods of time has, undoubtedly, made the difference. Careful monitoring of how the course played in major championships and then making small adjustments, almost on

an ongoing basis, kept the course in tune with advancements in skill and technology. Nurturing the site over a long period has improved the vistas and the general appearance. Such important lessons can be learned from history. Moreover, they can provide those who are responsible for operating and maintaining classic golf courses with a sound basis for planning future development.

Woodhall Spa: Once the National Golf Centre was created, it gave rise to a second course called 'The Bracken'. Designed by Donald Steel, it opened for play in 1998 and presented the opportunity to coin the championship course, 'The Hotchkin'. This image shows the third hole on Steel's creation. (Photograph by Richard Latham.)

Wayne Stiles: An under-appreciated master from the Golden Age of design

Bob Labbance and Kevin R. Mendik

From the time he was a young man, Wayne Stiles enjoyed playing golf as a hobby while manipulating landforms to create towns, estates and parks as a profession.

Stiles joined the architectural firm of Brett and Hall in 1902 as an office boy at age eighteen. As his architectural skills matured professionally and he became a draftsman, so too did his golf skills improve in his leisure time. In 1905, shortly after Brae Burn Country Club established an eighteen-hole course, Stiles became a member. For the next decade he represented the club in Boston team matches, as well as competing in the Massachusetts Amateur, Interclub and state events.

Most golf-course design work in the United States from 1900 to 1916 was performed by golf professionals such as Robert White, Tom Bendelow, Donald Ross, William Tucker, Seymour Dunn, George Low, Robert Pryde, James Foulis and Willie Watson. Stiles, who wished to compete on an amateur level, had decided against entering the golf-course design field until 1916. Given his background in landscape design, which included working for several prestigious clients—Edward Harkness at Eolia in Connecticut and collaboration with the Olmsted Brothers on a private estate subdivision's golf course in Massachusetts, to name a couple—Stiles was poised to bring his well-rounded golfing knowledge to market.

But first, briefly, some background information, explaining the conditions that made it possible. A storm erupted in 1915 after the USGA revoked Francis Ouimet's amateur status, citing his work for a sporting goods firm called Wright & Ditson. When the matter came to a head at the annual meeting in 1916, new rules were drafted that allowed profits to be made from writing upon the game and the profession of golf architecture. This opened the door to the golf-course architecture career of Wayne Stiles.

His first contract was an eighteen-hole layout for the Nashua Country Club. Golf had been played in Nashua since 1896, but the move to a new site in 1916 allowed Stiles to plan a modern layout. Stiles used a steam roller and teams of horses to manipulate the former farmlands, leaving natural hazards in many places.

Donald Ross redesigned Brae Burn in 1912. Given that Stiles had been a member at

OPPOSITE **Oak Hill Country Club, Massachusetts, USA:** Wayne Stiles's background as a landscape architect and draftsman added much to the quality of his course-renderings. (Rendering courtesy of Oak Hill Country Club)

Brae Burn for seven years, was working in the field of landscape architecture and was one of the best players at the club, it is likely that the two met, and perhaps interacted during this time. From then on, the two men's careers would be intertwined, as they competed for jobs, remodelled each other's work and were, at times, improperly credited for the other's design efforts. Many say Stiles was influenced by the work of his contemporary; whether it worked the other way is open to debate.

By 1919—following the cessation of hostilities in foreign lands—Stiles was again seeking golf-course design work. He landed a job for nine holes at Oak Hill Country Club in Fitchburg, Massachusetts, and a nine-hole expansion of the existing eighteen at Bethlehem in New Hampshire. In both cases his work was intertwined with Donald Ross. His contemporary had laid out eighteen holes for Bethlehem in 1910 and, at the behest of the club, Stiles planned an additional nine for a wooded property north of the existing layout. For reasons that are unclear, the loop was never built.

At Oak Hill, Stiles designed nine holes that opened in 1920. The course was expanded to eighteen holes six years later by Donald Ross. In discussion with a club official, there is a degree of uncertainty as to the extent of original Stiles's design work left on the opening nine, other than the routing. It is believed, however, that most, if not all, of the greens were reworked by Ross. The third, fifth, seventh and eighth were subsequently redesigned by Cornish & Robinson. Later still, the third green was redesigned by Tom Doak. The eighth green has twice been redone: once by Brian Silva, and later by Doak.

By 1920, there was finally an expansion in golf development substantial enough to keep both Stiles and Ross busy—and out of each other's way. Stiles landed contracts at Boothbay in Maine, and four jobs in New Hampshire at Laconia, Dover, Franklin and Jackson. His work at Laconia Country Club, Cochecho, Mojalaki and Gray's Inn would all debut in 1921. He lost a job to Ross at the Manchester Country Club in New Hampshire on 5 October 1921.

With most of his work centred in New England it is a mystery how Stiles landed a job in St Louis. In 1929, he employed a nationwide clipping service to locate clubs seeking architects, but in 1921 there must have been a personal connection that led him to Norwood Hills in the gateway to the West.

Originally named North Hills Country Club, the forty-five-hole complex was one of the finest facilities in the Midwest, and eighty-seven years later remains one of Stiles's greatest architectural achievements. The nine-hole short course for ladies and beginners has been eliminated, but the thirty-six holes that remain are mostly original and have been treated with respect throughout their architectural life—today, still reflecting an authenticity and adherence to

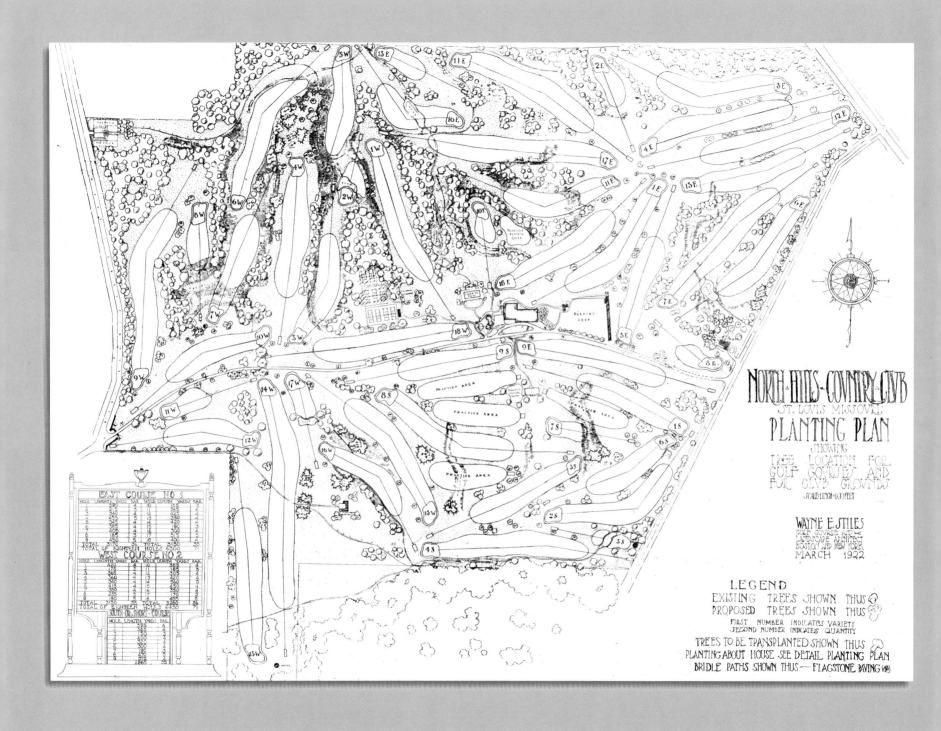

NORTH HILLS COUNTRY CLUB
ST. LOUIS MISSOURI
PLANTING PLAN
SHOWING
TREE LOCATION FOR
GOLF COURSES AND
FOR CLUB GROUNDS
SCALE 1 INCH = 100 FEET

WAYNE E. STILES
GOLF COURSE ARCHITECT
LANDSCAPE ARCHITECT
BOSTON AND NEW YORK
MARCH 1922

LEGEND
EXISTING TREES SHOWN THUS
PROPOSED TREES SHOWN THUS
FIRST NUMBER INDICATES VARIETY
SECOND NUMBER INDICATES QUANTITY

TREES TO BE TRANSPLANTED SHOWN THUS
PLANTING ABOUT HOUSE SEE DETAIL PLANTING PLAN
BRIDLE PATHS SHOWN THUS — FLAGSTONE PAVING

Mink Meadows Golf Club, Massachusetts, USA: Stiles worked within the rectangular confines of an existing firebreak to lay out this course. (Photograph by Kevin Mendik)

OPPOSITE Norwood Hills Country Club, Missouri, USA: Stiles's knowledge of the future growth patterns of large trees has enabled the grandeur of today's park-like property. The thirty-six-hole club was originally known as North Hills Country Club. (Plan courtesy of Norwood Hills Country Club)

Stiles's design principles that has been lost at many of his other courses.

By 1922, his workload in New England had increased substantially. That year saw the completion of projects from northern New Hampshire (Wentworth Resort in Jackson) to southern New Jersey (Wildwood). Six courses opened in 1922, adding to the six that opened the previous year. Suddenly, Stiles was busy enough as a golf-course architect to add staff and consider a design associate.

According to Geoffrey Cornish, who met Wayne in the early 1950s, 'Stiles worked in a very traditional manner. He would visit the site, endlessly walk over the property, sometimes spending two weeks going over the ground. He would lay out the course with his eyes first, and then make detailed drawings of each hole and a complete set of plans'.

Stiles didn't desire projects that he couldn't supervise personally, but the course construction boom of the 1920s provided him with numerous opportunities.

His fees were well in line with other architects of the time and, in many cases, he offered additional landscape design services as part of his contract. A letter dated 10 March 1923 to John Van Arsdale regarding the Hamburg Country Club in western New

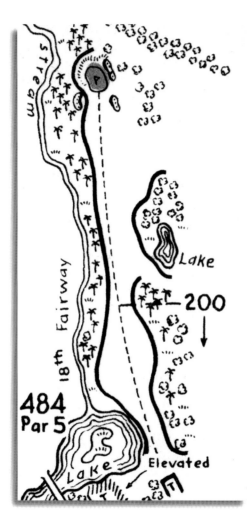

York (known today as South Shore Country Club), authenticates that Stiles agreed to plan the eighteen-hole golf course, and also the location of the club house, driveways, parking areas, tennis courts, swimming pool or other features that might be desired.

By 1923, Stiles had established an office at 103 Park Avenue in New York City, in addition to his Boston office at 97 Oliver Street. Associate W. Hammond Sadler headed the office at the start, adding Arthur Hadden Alexander later in the year. Sadler was a landscape architect who later moved to Palos Verdes, California; Alexander was an etcher and landscape painter who became a printmaker and graphic artist.

It is unclear how or exactly when Stiles met John Van Kleek, who was an accomplished landscape architect by the time Stiles took him on as an associate in 1923.

Reflecting a measured approach to the partnership's output, by 1926 the firm could lay claim to only six courses in Florida— Pasadena Yacht and Country Club with Walter Hagen, Holly Hill in Davenport, Jovita in San Antonio, Palmetto Country Club, Highland Park in Lake Wales and Tarpon Springs Municipal. Yet by August 1929, the list had swelled to seventeen projects that were either completed or under construction.

In February 1931, shortly before the dissolution of the partnership, there were more than forty projects for which plans had been drawn, work was underway or layouts had been finished and opened. Although Van Kleek and his staff were primarily responsible for the work, documentation exists of Stiles making numerous trips to Florida during this timeframe. In addition to Florida contracts, work was ongoing in Alabama, Georgia, North Carolina and elsewhere throughout the South.

Meanwhile, business was booming back in the Northeast. In 1923, before his partnership with Van Kleek, four new Stiles designs in Massachusetts opened: Powder Hill in Amesbury, Needham Country Club, Stony Brae in Wollaston and Haverhill Country Club. In addition he finished remodelling work at Mountain View in Whitefield, New Hampshire. There is no evidence that Van

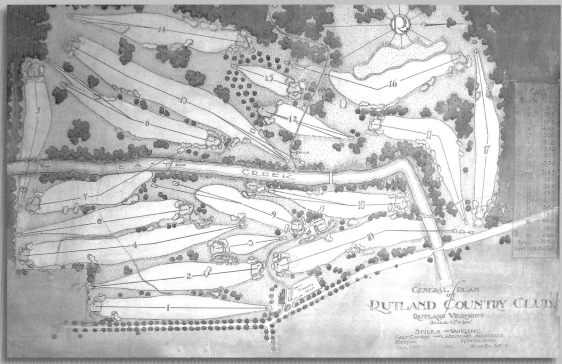

ABOVE LEFT **Rutland Country Club, Vermont, USA:** The classy, 223-yard par-3 fifth hole remains a strong test for golfers of any standard. (Photograph by Bob Labbance)

ABOVE RIGHT **Rutland:** A full color 'as built' plan. (Plan courtesy of Rutland Country Club)

LEFT **Rutland:** The par-4 twelfth hole is as challenging as it is beautiful. (Photograph by Bob Labbance)

Taconic Golf Club, Massachusetts, USA: Probably Stiles's best-known course; it underwent a complete restoration in the fall of 2008 based on original blueprints. (Plan courtesy of Taconic Golf Club)

OPPOSITE LEFT AND RIGHT Taconic: This course continues to maintain high levels of course conditioning, and provides many challenges and visual treats. (Photographs by Bob Labbance)

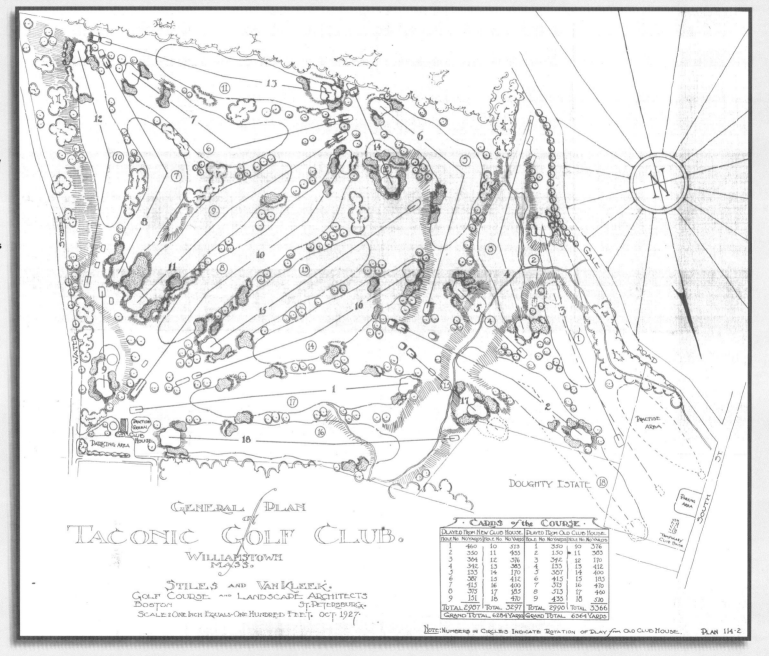

GENERAL PLAN of

TACONIC GOLF CLUB.

WILLIAMSTOWN MASS.

STILES AND VAN KLEEK.
GOLF COURSE AND LANDSCAPE ARCHITECTS
BOSTON   ST. PETERSBURG.
SCALE: ONE INCH EQUALS ONE HUNDRED FEET. OCT. 1927.

· CARDS of the COURSE ·

PLAYED FROM NEW CLUB HOUSE		PLAYED FROM OLD CLUB HOUSE	
HOLE No. No YARDS	HOLE No. No YARDS	HOLE No. No YARDS	HOLE No. No YARDS
1 460	10 513	1 350	10 376
2 350	11 433	2 150	11 383
3 364	12 376	3 342	12 170
4 342	13 383	4 133	13 412
5 133	14 170	5 387	14 400
6 387	15 412	6 415	15 183
7 415	16 400	7 375	16 470
8 375	17 185	8 513	17 460
9 151	18 470	9 433	18 510
Total 2957	Total 3297	Total 2998	Total 3366
GRAND TOTAL 6254 YARDS		GRAND TOTAL 6364 YARDS	

NOTE: NUMBERS IN CIRCLES INDICATE ROTATION OF PLAY from OLD CLUB HOUSE.

PLAN 114·2

Kleek participated in the northern projects, especially in light of the workload he was juggling in the South. In no instance can a Van Kleek site visit, plan drawing or consultation be found from a northern course during the 1920s.

For Stiles, 1924 proved to be his busiest year. Pine Brook in Weston, Monoosnock in Leominster and Unicorn in Stoneham were opened in Massachusetts; Prouts Neck debuted in Scarborough, Maine; the Country Club of Barre and Brandon Country Club were completed in Vermont; Keene Country Club and Kearsarge in North Conway opened in New Hampshire. South Shore in Hamburg, New York, completed an amazing body of work to add to the growing course list.

In addition to the northern work, their first Florida course opened: Pasadena Yacht and Country Club. This collaboration with Van Kleek also included input from Walter Hagen, and the course became a showcase for the firm, leading to a raft of Florida contracts. Hagen acknowledged the association in his 1956 book, *The Walter Hagen Story*, writing: 'During that first season most of my time was spent with Wayne Stiles of Boston, the golf architect, as we planned the design and construction of the championship golf course'.[18]

From 1924 to 1928, at least thirty-seven courses designed by the firm opened in the Eastern United States. Many were nine-hole layouts, some were renovations and quite a few involved remodelling nine existing holes and adding nine more. Some were built by the clubs themselves, some were constructed by local contractors, but a good number were built by a crew that Stiles assembled. In all cases the workers were paid by the club, as expenses for construction were never included in a design contract.

At the completion of Rutland Country Club, Vermont, various items were shipped to Taconic—Stiles's next workplace. Although the Taconic Golf Club layout was not perceived any differently than many of the other courses built from 1923 to 1928, it turned out to be the highest profile project the firm completed. A talented shaper called Bruce Matthews was brought to Williamstown, Massachusetts, due to a lull in golf-course construction in Florida, and he served as construction superintendent for the layout.

Bruce's son, Gerry Matthews, has designed many courses in the upper Midwest and, during research for the Stiles biography, Labbance and Mendik visited him at his offices near Detroit in the summer of 2005. Gerry had a considerable amount of papers, old photos and several dozen individual blueprints of holes that belonged to his father. Taconic was without copies of some materials, although the club possessed a handful and an original eighteen-hole plan. The blueprints were digitised and a full-blown Taconic restoration effort commenced in August of 2008, overseen by Gil Hanse. A bunker between the eighth and eleventh greens had been shown on plans, but not built. During restoration, it was discovered why: a large boulder sat precisely where the bunker would have been. It has been removed and the feature recovered.

In a 1990 interview, Matthews talked in a noticeably respectful manner about Stiles. 'He was a naturalist', said Matthews. 'He'd go through an area and look things over. Then he'd pick green sites and arrange it from

Prouts Neck, Maine, USA: Wayne Stiles laid out an eighteen-hole 'links-style' course at a favorite seaside location of his. Pleasingly, the course is largely intact. (Photograph by Kevin Mendik)

there. Other architects of the time didn't spend a lot of time at their courses. Wayne Stiles made the plans and then would go to the site and construct it.'

Matthews appreciated the way Stiles interacted with his construction crew. 'He would rely on the people who worked for him, with success', notes Matthew. 'He was very solid and happy with what he did—always on the up and up. He only charged cost plus ten per cent for construction. He was very casual, but careful to get his money. He kept up with his clients and asked for payments as he went along.'

While comparisons of Stiles with Donald Ross are common, Matthews felt there was similarity with another noteworthy architect. 'Tillinghast's designs remind me of Wayne's work', he said.

Van Kleek concentrated on other areas of the South, finding work for the firm in North Carolina, Alabama and Georgia. Although many projects were discussed and more than a dozen plans were drawn, Glen Arven in

Georgia and Starmount Forest in North Carolina were the last two layouts to come to fruition. Both opened in 1930, but as the effects of the 1929 stock-market crash rippled through the South, no new work could be found. Van Kleek slowly reduced the Florida staff. The partners engaged a clipping service starting in 1928, seeking jobs across the United States and Canada. Any leads produced were followed up with letters and visits, but none of the work panned out.

The northern portfolio continued to expand in the latter half of the 1920s. From 1926 to 1930, Stiles design work had an influence on playing opportunities throughout the Northeast. Twelve new courses opened in Massachusetts; three in New Hampshire; three in Vermont; as well as clubs in New Jersey and Rhode Island.

In March 1930, Van Kleek reported to the Cornell Alumni Association that he was still engaged in landscape and golf-course architecture work. He wrote that he was, 'Building golf courses and doing landscape work in the south with my partner doing the northern work from our Boston office. About ten courses under construction'.

The Stiles–Van Kleek partnership continued for at least another year. The last project list generated by the Boston office was dated 1 February 1931, and it included fifty-eight northern courses, forty-three Florida layouts and nineteen contracts for courses in North Carolina, Alabama, Georgia, New Mexico, Texas and Mississippi.

Many of the southern courses were never finished, victims of the declining financial situation throughout the country. The list also noted six 'Minature Courses' [sic] usually built in conjunction with a full-sized layout. The miniature courses were not simply 'putting courses' as were the Tom Thumb courses that swept the urban areas of the United States.

It is unclear exactly what circumstances led to the dissolution of the Stiles–Van Kleek partnership in 1931. Unlike many architects who simply closed up shop or entered other professions during the 1930s, Stiles continued to find local work, though his dreams of planning dozens of layouts throughout the country were shattered. However, he did find relatively more work than most others architects of that time.

Putterham Meadows, a municipal course for Brookline, Massachusetts, was a major project that took several years to complete, eventually opening in 1933. A panel of expert advisors, including Francis Ouimet, chose Stiles over Donald Ross and William Flynn for the project, and later praised his work in a series of walking critiques at the property. Stiles also completed Olde Salem Greens, a nine-hole municipal course for the City of Salem, Massachusetts. That course opened in the fall of 1933. His final golf design was for an eighteen-hole private course known as Mink Meadows on the island of Martha's Vineyard. Only nine holes were built, opening in 1936.

Nearly thirty years after meeting Donald Ross, Stiles's last known design work was to remove Ross bunkers from Gulph Mills Country Club outside of Philadelphia. The 'top-shot' bunkers provided direction and decoration on the classy layout, but Stiles felt they penalised the poor player. And so, in a nine-page report, he suggested their removal. In addition, Stiles planned new tees, adjusted mowing patterns, suggested distinct borders between waterways and dry ground, planned paths for better traffic flow, enlarged sections of greens for additional pin placements and offered locations for new trees on the golf course. The report is the most comprehensive found from any of Stiles's remodelling work, although not all of it was implemented.

In the late 1930s, Stiles became friends with William Mitchell of Lake Sunapee, New Hampshire. Mitchell started as a greenkeeper when he was nineteen years old in 1931, later establishing a bentgrass turf farm in North Sutton, New Hampshire. Working with architect Orrin Smith, Mitchell remodelled several Stiles courses, including Augusta in Maine and Needham and Unicorn in Massachusetts. After serving as a navy pilot in the Second World War, Mitchell assumed the superintendent position at Charles River Country Club near Boston. He and Stiles became firm friends.

After the Second World War, Mitchell continued to remodel some of Stiles's courses, apparently with his blessing and, perhaps, even with his help. That included Riverside in Maine (1948); Brattleboro in Vermont (1948); and three Massachusetts courses— Furnace Brook (1947), Franklin (1949) and Duxbury (1951).

Wayne Stiles was invited to join as a charter member of the American Society of Golf Course Architects (ASGCA) when Donald Ross hosted the initial gathering in December 1947, but he decided not to travel to Pinehurst for the meeting. 'By the end of World War II, Wayne was in poor health, although he had once been a very dynamic person', notes Geoffrey Cornish. 'He was not able to attend the early meetings in 1947–48; I think that was because of poor health', Cornish relates.

In the last few years of his life, living along the fourth fairway at Wellesley Country Club, Stiles became friends with Al Zikorus, the club's young superintendent. The two discussed architecture and course maintenance,

and Zikorus went on to become an accomplished architect in his own right. Says Cornish, 'Al Zikorus told me that in the early 1950s that "Wayne was exceedingly interested in advances in turfgrass science and maintenance including new grass varieties and the abundance of chemicals"'.

Wayne Stiles was one who felt the chemical age would eventually answer all our problems; sadly, he never lived to see that future, passing away on 8 February 1953. In his obituary in *Landscape Architecture* magazine, Edward Clark Whiting wrote, 'Wayne Stiles was a congenial companion and a sound advisor in technical professional matters. He was adept at handling clients, even the difficult kind, and he always succeeded in building up that confidence which is essential to good and satisfying work'.

An innovative six-hole design solution: Foxfield, USA

Ian Scott-Taylor

The phone call sounded like a novel from Alistair MacLean, but when I got the phone call from the client it was, indeed, something much more.

In recounting the story of the Foxfield project I feel like Dr Watson writing one of Holmes's famous case studies. And so ... it all started one October morning in 2006. I received a call from Mr George Hyjurick, a softly spoken gentleman, who informed me that he was the Vice-President of Development for the McKee Group. One thing you find working here in the United States, everyone seems to possess a title.

The McKee Group is a high-end housing developer in the Pennsylvania area. They had recently bought a property in that state, on which a nine-hole golf course had to be designed and constructed.

In the conversation, George started to give the background to the predicament he found himself in: 'Well,' he said, 'it's like this: when we purchased this property, we inherited a design for a golf course. And as it's an "Over Fifty-five Active Age Group" project we have to build it as part of our permitting for the over all site.'

Cutting to the chase, they wanted me to look at it and give an opinion. Soon after, an appointment was arranged to meet at the project to view drawings, permits and the site.

On the morning of the visit, I packed my Land Rover and set off for Pennsylvania with a mug of tea and Roxy Music playing in my ear—it's funny what one recalls. When I got to the site, most of the housing and infrastructure was in place.

In keeping with many US housing projects: you have to pass the 'main' gate—as though you're entering a castle portcullis. Once through the gate, the drive dipped to a bridge. Over the bridge, the road rose to the estates; on the left-hand side I noted the land was barren, hilly and foreboding. The pit of my stomach dropped; intuitively, I knew this was where the golf course was destined to be.

As I turned into the car park, or car lot (as is the US convention), a large 'mock' Tudor clubhouse came into view. Two gentlemen stood at the door—one, a big six foot-plus guy, with John Wayne looks and the physique

OPPOSITE **Foxfield Links, Pennsylvania, USA: The course architect, Ian Scott-Taylor—usually, not one to sit down on the job—looks over his handiwork on the sixth hole. Foxfield, a six-hole course, is located twenty miles outside of Philadelphia and includes a 9,200-square-foot clubhouse, a pool and tennis facilities. (Photograph courtesy of Foxfield Links.)**

OPPOSITE BELOW **Foxfield: A concept watercolour of the third hole. During the construction phase, over 25,000 cubic yards of earth were moved in shaping Foxfield. (Watercolour by Ian Scott-Taylor.)**

of a football star. This was George Hyjurick, and not really what I had expected judging from his voice during our telephone conversation.

The other was a man more of my stature—about five foot eight inches, a fine-looking stately gent. This was George's second in command, Gene Mclaughlin. On alighting from the car and the stretch after two-and-a-half hours in the 'old bus', I walked toward the two gentlemen. In a booming voice Gene announced himself and shook hands. George smiled and greeted me with a vice-like grip. After the niceties were observed we entered the clubhouse and shuffled into a room with a long table covered in plans.

George started to explain that the golf-course site of twelve acres sat squarely on top of underground oil storage tanks, and that the site originally was owned by a large oil company called Sunoco, which had used it for storage and a staging area for distribution of its products. The golf-course site was capped with twenty feet of fill, which could not be dug into or contoured in any way, as per agreement with the oil company and the department of environmental protection (EPA). I could fill and shape as much on top as I liked; as long as it was in the budget.

The architect of the golf course had, literally, packed nine holes into eight acres of land. If you shanked a ball on the first tee, you'd kill someone on either the sixth green, fourth tee or fifth green. It was the biggest joke in the design world I'd yet encountered.

With the site plans in hand I set off home to burn the midnight oil on the design, wondering what type of fiasco I had been roped into. With kettle boiling and digestive tea biscuits in the jar, I set to work on the design. After a tilt of around forty-eight hours, with few breaks or sleep, paper was strewn right across the floor. About 3.00 am on the third day I simply couldn't sleep, so I paced the kitchen and walked around the garden. And then it suddenly hit me: six holes at Foxfield instead of nine holes! The nine-hole concept couldn't work with any assurance of safety, plus there just wasn't enough room. Six holes, however, would work perfectly.

The other more important factor was the cost: all earth movement, seeding, growing-in and everything else needed to be completed in a set budget $500,000. Most importantly, the golf course had to be maintenance-friendly. Country club maintenance practices are costly, and this course was to be turned over to a Housing Operating Authority (HOA).

Also it could not be too demanding, as the golfers were of retirement age. It had to be accessible.

After walking the site many times, it became apparent that the course routing could only go one way: clockwise. This was due to a wetlands area, access road and walking path through the site.

The next step was to convince the client, and the HOA, that a six-hole layout was safer than having three extra ones. I felt like Winston Churchill getting ready for one of those famous war speeches, rehearsing like a broken record while driving from Maryland. After much debate, and the explanation of the water colours and scheme design, the six-hole concept was sold. Arthur Daley: look out!

Then George called me in to his office—a 'bombshell' was about to be dropped: 'Ian we're not going to employ a golf-course builder. Additionally, we want to use artificial greens and tees. But we're going to need a wall-to-wall irrigation system'. My heart sunk and missed a beat, worrying about how on earth it could be done properly within the budget.

Well it was a challenge, no question ... but a lot of fun, too. I contacted every synthetic turf manufacturer in the directory, wading through samples galore. George Cowan, owner of Targa Pro, Inc. Synthetic turf—the company selected to supply and install the tees and greens carpet—did a fantastic job. We designed old-fashioned greens to fit into the surrounds, which was treatment George had never done before.

The greens, in fact, looked so natural from a distance that you had to look twice to be convinced they were artificial. I sloped the greens with no contour greater than two per cent, and they fall from the back to the front. The tees were simple gun platforms, which harmonised with the theme of a turn-of-the-twentieth-century golf course. The Rain Bird irrigation company through Atlantic

Irrigation stepped up to the plate; they designed and installed a state of the art irrigation system with maximum water efficiency. My thanks go to Fred Rapp of Atlantic and Scott Killian of Killian Irrigation.

Twenty-five-thousand cubic yards of earth were moved to shape an old-world, early 1900s-style golf course. Given the earth-moving company had experience in golf-course bulk earth-moving—but had never shaped a course before—the outcome would have satisfied Old Tom Morris. With sketch-book, earth models in the dirt, I managed to get the shaper to do what I wanted. To be honest, he turned out better than many experienced shapers I have used before; he was incredible once he got the idea.

Working over twelve hours a day on occasions—with trucks rolling, a bulldozer, hand- and arm-waving by me—we shaped, drained, irrigated, installed tees and greens, and seeded grass on the golf course in just six weeks. For sheer mental examination and on-the-minute improvisation, I've not had as much fun on a golf project since Abu Dhabi in 1997. The product was most satisfying.

I found some large stones on the site that the McKee Group were going to bury. Well ... I hijacked them in transit and built a standing stone circle—the druids of Wales and Ireland would have been impressed! With some of the stones I created a chair and table that was coined the Leprechauns Chair. All this was done with a D4 bulldozer, my own labour and the assistance of one poor soul who I cornered before he could say no. The comments after we finished where well received and certainly added to the old country feel of the golf course. The McKee Group has set the tone for future projects and gained a great deal of publicity from golf magazines and television stations.

I know we all want to have our Augusta Nationals, but for me this six-hole golf course may well be my greatest achievement in design innovation. For the sheer fun of golf-course design and construction, I now know how Old Tom Morris must have felt throughout his life. It's a feeling worth chasing.

California Golf Club of San Francisco, USA

Allan Jamieson

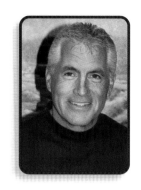

Incorporated in 1918, the California Golf Club of San Francisco is located within the city and county of San Francisco on land leased from the Spring Valley water company. Opting for the long-term benefits of ownership, the founders wisely purchased some 450 acres of farm land at Baden crossing in San Mateo County, approximately ten miles south of the original location.

William Locke completed the original routing, yet when construction was due to begin he was let go and replaced by Arthur Vernon Macan, an Irishman who worked primarily in the Northwest, Oregon, Washington and Vancouver, British Colombia. The Macan routing was an interesting mix: the front nine was a counterclockwise links around a natural landform that rose to an elevation of 260 feet; the back nine was more of a parkland layout with six of the holes being contiguous. The new course opened in 1925. For reasons that have been lost to club history, Alister Mackenzie and his US partner, Robert Hunter, were hired in 1928 to accomplish what Mackenzie characterised in a 1933 essay as a 'reconstruction' of the course. While the routing remained the same, the bunkering was clearly Mackenzie.

In the ensuing years, which saw depression, world war and post-war real estate activity, the club's 450 acres were pared down to approximately 185. The most serious intrusion on the course occurred in 1965 when several acres, including parts of the first five holes, were claimed by the State for a freeway off-ramp and a new street. Robert Trent Jones Sr was called in to adjust the first five holes only, resulting in a rather pinched, straight-line routing that was incongruous with the remaining thirteen holes.

In 2005, the course, and its neighbours, constantly struggled with nematode infestation of the mostly Poa annua greens. Further, the ageing infrastructure caused the course to be extremely wet, given an environment that only receives annual rainfall of seventeen to twenty inches. Most of the neighbouring clubs had, or would soon, embark upon projects of varying scope to modernise agronomically, and/or restore the classic architectural features that had been lost.

OPPOSITE **California Golf Club of San Francisco, California, USA:** This view from behind the new second green. (Photograph by Joshua C.F. Smith.)

Following an extensive search process, the club engaged Kyle Phillips. Phillips made an exhaustive search of the club's history, which turned up photographs of the Mackenzie work in the archives of the University of California library at Berkeley. And as it transpired, Mackenzie's partner in the American Golf Company, Robert Hunter, taught at Berkeley in his later years.

Sean Tulley, the assistant superintendent at the Meadow Club in Marin County, California—the site of Mackenzie's first North American commission—was a valu-

able contributor to the process at California Golf Club of San Francisco. A keen golf historian and instrumental in the Mackenzie Society, Sean was responsible for unearthing early photos of the club (none of us were aware of these), which enabled Kyle Phillips to authentically replicate many of the green and bunker complexes.

As Phillips analysed the possibilities within the club's modern boundaries, he was pleased to discover that the club had approximately twenty acres in the heart of the property not being utilised for golf. This land, he

cited, was the key to alleviating the claustrophobic effect of the 1966–1967 modifications. As is the case with any club embarking on such a monumental task, there was much debate and high emotion about Phillips's final proposal. The plan placed only four holes of golf on acreage that previously contained five holes (and the driving range) .

He proposed a new par-4 along the ridgeline of the unused acreage, thus abandoning another par-4 that would be converted to a self-contained range in the middle of the front nine. The conversion would not impact upon

ABOVE California Club: Approach to the restored ninth hole. (Photograph by Joshua C.F. Smith.)

BELOW California Club: An image of the fifteenth hole's new green-complex, as captured from the nearby trees. (Photograph by Joshua C.F. Smith.)

OPPOSITE California Club: A glimpse of the seventh hole's fairway tilt; golfer's face this approach shot to the restored hole. (Photograph by Joshua C.F. Smith.)

One of the recently reconstructed greens at the California Golf Club—the tenth—showing some effective trapping by
Mackenzie & Hunter

Built by

American Golf Course Construction Co.

1702 Tribune Tower
Oakland

{ Now Building }
Cypress Point Golf Club near Pebble Beach

{ Remodeling at }
California Golf Club · Claremont Country Club

A. D. Mills photo

A rear view of the California Golf Club's beautiful colonial clubhouse taken from the eighteenth fairway, with the remodeled eighteenth green in the foreground.—A. D. Mills.

ABOVE LEFT California Club: Alister Mackenzie took out an advertisement in 1928; it featured the newly bunkered tenth green. (Photograph courtesy of the California Club.)

ABOVE RIGHT California Club: An image taken in 1940 of the original par-3 seventh hole; it is currently the par-3 sixth hole. (Photograph courtesy of the California Club.)

BELOW LEFT California Club: The approach to the eighteenth green, circa 1928, following Mackenzie's work. (Photograph courtesy of the California Club.)

BELOW RIGHT California Club: Approaching the eighteenth green in 1940. (Photograph courtesy of the California Club.)

play. Essentially, Phillips proposed to restore thirteen holes to the 1920s look and feel, while creating five holes that would be compatible with that classic design.

The course had three water hazards: one from the Jones work; and two installed in 1991 with little professional architectural input. They, too, would be removed under the new works. Water storage would be placed in its previous location at the highest point on the property.

Ken Venturi, the 1964 US Open Champion and CBS television golf analyst for thirty-five years, has been a member of the club since 1949. During the club's deliberations, he and Kyle addressed the members one evening. While almost all members agreed that the greens needed replacement, many questioned the scope of the proposal, understandably fearful of the change and the expense. Ken's advice to the members was simple yet profound: 'You only get one chance in a lifetime at this, and you don't get a mulligan'. The message was clear: do the job right; and do it once without having to go back (at higher cost) every few years with a piecemeal approach. Fortunately, the majority of mem-

California Club: A close-up of the second green, with a view to the clubhouse. (Photograph by Mark Thawley.)

bers concurred with this approach and the project commenced in April 2007.

The general contractor was the highly able Olliphant Company, which has also done extensive work for the Pebble Beach Company, including the new fifth hole at this famous course. It is significant, and a point of pride, to mention that nearly forty per cent of the construction contract was assumed by the club's existing staff led by Thomas Bastis and his assistants, Grant Johnson and Josh Smith. The clubhouse and short game area remained available to the members during construction. Many of the club's staff were cross-trained and deployed to assist in preparing the clubhouse for a new coat of paint and other refurbishments prior to reopening day. The club is proud that it retained all of its loyal employees during the fifteen months that no golf was played.

The entire golf course was completely torn up and rebuilt, starting at six feet underground with massive drainage trenches that would 'honeycomb' the property. The goal was to recreate what Macan had started and Mackenzie perfected. That meant, among other attributes, laying the groundwork for a fast, firm course that would bring the 'ground' game back into play. To that end, extensive drain lines were installed at two different depths, while over 100,000 tons of sand was imported to be tilled in with the existing loam.

The Mackenzie-inspired bunkers would number 144, most of which are almost identical to those shown in the 1928 reference photographs. In fact, prior to opening, a prominent golf architecture author toured the course and pronounced Kyle Phillips's work as the most authentic Mackenzie bunkering he had seen. For irrigation, the Toro decoder system was chosen, and is truly state-of-the-art.

On 7 June 2008, a grand reopening ceremony was held, with Ken Venturi acting as host and commentator. Fittingly, he was selected to hit the first drive. Club and PGA Tour member, Aaron Oberholser, would play a six-hole exhibition with past and present club professionals, Bill Ver Brugge and Mark Doss, along with seven-time club champion, Dan Young. A grand party followed and, in the next few weeks, the members would start to enjoy their long-awaited improvements. Most have opined that it was worth the wait. While some had feared that the course might be too difficult, the opposite has been the case. Phillips has made provision for a course that can be stretched to a maximum of 7,240 yards. This won't suit every occasion, so there are three other sets of tees that allow for a course as short as 5,400 yards. Additionally, forward tees are positioned so that the less-skilful golfer is not forced to carry bunkers designed to challenge the more-skilled player. Arthur Vernon Macan was quoted as saying, 'I design a course for the man who pays the bills'. He'd be happy with the result, as this Kyle Phillips renovation/restoration provides an enjoyable golf experience for every golfer from novice to professional.

The California Golf Club of San Francisco was clearly among the elite courses in California in the 1920s, 1930s and even 1940s. No doubt it lost its way for a time, thereafter, but having undertaken the necessary steps, it's ready to enjoy its esteemed position, yet again.

The most important aspect of the renovation was that we took a comprehensive approach as opposed to a 'band-aid' approach. By completely starting over from six feet underground, future generations will be spared inconvenience and the cost that accompanies serial fixes. Members, being members, will argue to the grave about the subjective aspects of golf-course architecture. What is indisputable, however, is that the club has a twenty-first-century infrastructure that will serve it well for many years. One of the basic tenets of the game is to leave the course better than you found it.

California Club: The restored eleventh hole, with its green in the mid-ground. The Cal Club's restored eighteenth green is shown beyond and to the right. (Photograph by Joshua C.F. Smith.)

BELOW California Club: The new fifteenth green, with particular emphasis on the greenside bunkering. (Photograph by George Waters.)

OPPOSITE California Club: An image of the downhill approach to the new par-5 first hole. (Photograph by George Waters.)

California Club: The restored fourteenth hole, showing the harmony attained with its sparse yet classic tree arrangement, and bunkering. (Photograph by George Waters.)

Fuji Classic, Yamanashi Japan

One great result.

TORO Count on it.

visit www.toro.com

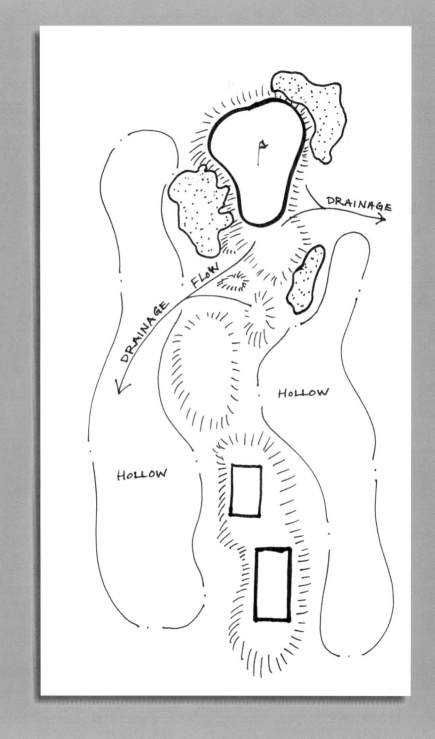

Moving dirt: The philosophy of economical and environmental earth-moving

Mike DeVries

What makes for efficient dirt-moving on a golf-course project? Golf is played on turf, and grass needs a good agronomic environment of sunlight, air movement, water and nutrients to thrive and produce quality turf playing conditions. Construction of a golf course can disrupt the ability of a site to provide these essential ingredients, with the 'dirt work' of a project having a major impact on these main agronomic components. Cutting and filling of material changes the soil composition, which can alter the compaction of materials, the ability to absorb and percolate water, and may change the nutritional value of the soil by mixing topsoil with poorer quality subsoils. Sunlight and air movement may be improved where extensive dirt-moving takes place, as vegetation is removed to allow for the cutting and filling of material.

Understanding the hydrology of the site—knowing where the water was originally, is currently and where it wants to go—is critical in making choices about where and how to move dirt. Aim to keep the water flowing as innately as possible, either with creeks, ditches, drainage pipe, sheet flow or surface drainage, to where there is less play and traffic. Recognising the hydrologic components with regard to the dirt-moving will help the site and golf course function better in the long run.

To move dirt efficiently requires a response to the intricacies and smaller movements in the ground in order to help preserve their natural processes and qualities. Recognition of the unique characteristics of a parcel of land, and feeding off them to create a site that will function correctly, is the most important ele-

ment to consider when building a golf course. Localised cutting and filling of areas allow the design to respond to the natural lay of the land, while also considering the design strategy and playability of the golf course. Instead of thinking only in terms of filling or cutting, the combination of the two can be used simultaneously to double your efforts and create more relief in a flat section of ground or reduce the severity of a steep slope.

Studying the older courses that were built by horses and pan scrapers illuminates this concept. During the construction of these older courses, they did not have the ability (economically) to move dirt long distances. This required thoughtful use of the dirt available around a green site. Material dug from bunkers around a green was used to prop up the putting surface so water would drain off

OPPOSITE **Localised cut-and-fill to create a par-3 hole from existing material. Build the centre-ridge formation from broad cuts from bunkers and hollows to create subtle features and surface drainage away from playing areas. For bigger features, spread cuts out further. (Sketch by Mike DeVries)**

to the lower surrounding terrain. When land was flat or had minimal natural drainage, accentuating a swale to do so was a judicious use of grading to create playing interest and improve agronomic conditions. A fine example of this technique is evidenced at Essex Country Club in Windsor, Ontario, where Donald Ross had a very flat piece of ground and poor-to-average draining soils.

Having a site with good, well-draining, sandy soils is the best way to start moving dirt in the most economical way possible. Frequently, however, a site has poorly draining soils, flat terrain or environmentally sensitive areas that are difficult or impossible to build upon. Winged Foot Golf Club has hard granite just underneath its surface, but A. W. Tillinghast was able to scrape off the good dirt to build up the bold green contours and create relief to the low areas. On the other hand, Pinehurst has pure sandy soil and relief throughout the property, so Donald Ross was able to easily mould the land into whatever feature he desired without concern for difficult materials.

Good soils allow for less 'topping' of poor fill material, which means less stockpiling of material to move to another location. When better material must be stripped off before the bulk dirt-moving takes place, good scheduling can allow for the stockpiling of the first area to be worked for the bulk dirt move, with topsoil from the second area then stripped to top the first area, and so on. This sequence permits a single moving of the dirt for most of the project.

A common construction problem involves what to do with poor or inappropriate building materials, such as stumps, rocks, really bad soil or other debris. Frequently, bury holes are developed in out-of-the-way locations to accommodate these by-products, but what do we do with the dirt that is dug up to create space for the buried material? With modern excavators and off-road trucks, we can move material easily from one location to another; the 'excess' dirt is often carted to spots to build up and fortify teeing areas, or for mounds. What this often fails to consider is how this dirt 'ties-in' with the existing landforms and environmental structure, leaving us with 'features' that are highly artificial looking in comparison to a subtly shaped cut and fill in a localised area. When moving large quantities of dirt, the concept of building landforms—ridges, hills, valleys and so forth—that fit in with the natural terrain should be the first priority, with the golf-course features then incorporated into those landforms.

In summary, efficient dirt-moving involves the following steps:

- understanding the natural processes at work on the site that will affect turf-grass development and health; namely, the soil qualities, texture, classification and structure, plus the hydrology of the site;
- studying the terrain to know all its intricacies—recognising and respecting the qualities, and leaving them intact;
- when possible, working with the terrain and natural processes by cutting and filling in a localised area to reduce impact on soil structure and to simplify and reduce construction and transportation of materials; and
- if moving larger quantities of dirt, building landforms and then incorporating golf-course features into them.

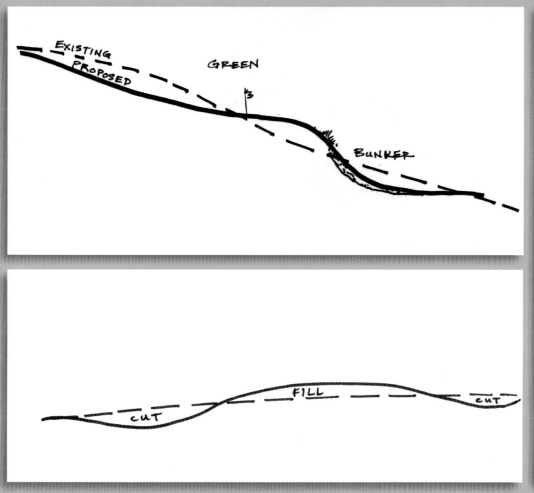

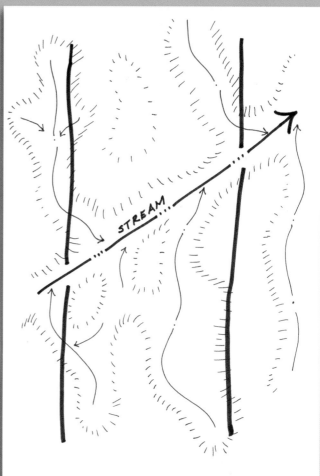

Dispelling the myth of Donald Ross's greens

W. Dunlop White III

Hang around the game of golf long enough and you will invariably hear someone—a commentator, journalist, even a knowledgeable fan—refer to the green complexes designed by Donald Ross as being 'crowned', which is a fancy way of saying his greens are shaped like inverted punch bowls.

The so-called experts describe Ross's greens this way in order to offer golf fans a more vivid mental picture of the difficulty of stopping a shot safely on a convex putting surface rife with what are commonly considered Ross's symbolic fall-away edges.

It's an understandable enough notion given that Pinehurst Number Two, which Ross designed, lived on and nurtured until his death in 1948, has become infamous for

offering up some of the most dramatic, dome-shaped greens in all of golf.

Yet, unfortunately, as exciting and adventuresome as these descriptions sound, they are nothing short of fallacy. Frankly, there's enough misinformation out there about Donald Ross green types to spoil restoration efforts throughout the country. In fact, today's turtleback greens at Number Two do not resemble their original identity, nor are they even in the ballpark of what the Scottish-born architect ever intended.

In the beginning

Early historical photographs reveal that Number Two originally manifested large sand greens, which were perfectly square

and relatively flat, compared to their inflated counterparts today. By 1915, these sand greens evolved with rounder dimensions yet still lacked any significant internal contours because of the possibility of erosion and washouts. Sand greens also integrated with their surrounds 'at grade' making bump-and-run shots and 'Texas wedges' (putts from off the green) a rather simple task from any angle.

In 1935, Ross developed grass greens on all eighteen holes in preparation for the 1936 PGA Championship. Grass enabled Ross to craft greens and their approaches with much more contour without fear of erosion.

Vintage photos of the United North and South Open in 1936 reveal that Ross articu-

OPPOSITE **Pinehurst Country Club (Number Two), North Carolina, USA:** Taken on the fourth hole during the 1936 United North and South Open, this image reveals a low-profile green with outer spines and edges that turn in toward the interior of the putting surface. (Photograph courtesy of the Tufts Archives.)

lated the outer edges of Number Two's greens up-and-down around the perimeter in an irregular fashion. Spines and mounds would, typically, rise out of swales—and then seamlessly roll back into hollows—around the circumference of the entire green.

According to Peter Tufts, the late great-grandson of Pinehurst founder, James W. Tufts, Ross paid as much attention to the green surrounds as he did to the greens themselves. 'Ross wanted to emphasise chipping in a stronger manner around the green', said Tufts.[19]

In the *Pinehurst Outlook*, the local newspaper at the time, Ross described the green surrounds as having been 'cunningly devised in

dips and undulations with bunkers and apparent natural divergence in contour' so one would never have the same shot twice. Ross thought that these humps and hollows presented the golfer 'with an infinite variety of nasty short shots that no other form of hazard could provide'.[20]

In addition to undulations, Ross thought that higher grass cuts would also promote the art of chipping, instead of putting, from around greens. 'Ross stopped the fairway mowing at the edge of the green', said Tufts, who was also Ross's godson. 'If you missed a green, it might roll a little ways off the green surface until the higher grass cuts would stop it, but it would never roll twenty or thirty feet away', said Tufts[21] [like it does today]. Ross never intended for his green surrounds to be closely cropped, nor did he envisage putting to be an option from these locations.

The surrounding humps and bumps also helped visually define the green surface from the approach by breaking up the horizon line on such a flat expanse of property. These landforms, however, varied in location around the border of every green.

Sometimes putting surfaces 'flipped-up' toward the zenith of mounds at the green corners, while other times they 'flashed-up' the peak of spines flanking a side or back-centre location. The 'tie-ins' raised the outer edges of his greens at the high points, thus leaning the putting surfaces back toward the centre of the green, instead of tipping them down as we see today.

Also, hundreds of original green sketches indicate that Ross preferred the portion of his greens bordering bunkers to be 'stiffened'—a term Ross commonly used in his notes to specify a slightly raised edge of approximately one to one-and-a-half feet at the top of the bunker face. The rationale, of course, was to deflect surface drainage away from the sand. Once again, the outer edge of the putting surface adjacent to bunkers originally tilted toward the centre of the green, instead of spilling down into these same bunkers as they do today.

In contrast, the lower cross-sections of his putting surfaces—between these articulating landforms—would gradually float out through a dip or hollow and tie in with the

surrounds 'at grade', but seldom rolled over to the extent we see today.

Number Two's green evolution

Between 1936 and 1970, Ross's greens grew over a foot (in height) through countless applications of topdressing. It was difficult to notice this transgression from one season to the next, but over a span of thirty years Pinehurst's greens gradually mushroomed skyward on every application of topdressing.

Throughout the summer months, maintenance crews would routinely spread a thin layer of sand across their grainy Bermuda grass greens. The sand particles would effectively work their way down between the leafy grass blades to offer a smoother, more consistent putting surface for their resort clientele.

Each fall, Pinehurst would overseed their greens with ryegrass in preparation for their 'busy season' each winter. According to Ron Whitten, golf architecture and design editor for *Golf Digest*, records indicate that superintendent, Frank Maples, topsoiled each green with a quarter of an inch of sand every month during the cool season between 1947 and 1949. Essentially, this meant that more than an inch of sand was applied to the green surfaces each year—just during this three-year timeframe. There's no telling how much more build-up accumulated over the next two decades as the practice continued.

Whitten also notes that aerification—the process of pulling green plugs and refilling them with sand—would have helped counteract this build-up, but Pinehurst didn't begin aerifying until the late 1960s.[22]

Like many other Golden Age venues, Pinehurst, interestingly, would only topdress to the green's edge and never out into the slopes around them. While these green surfaces rose more than a foot, the surrounding contours retained their original profile. Consequently, each green evolved with a sharp drop-off at the collar that no longer tied in with their surrounding landforms. Small saddles or low-area 'birdbaths' then formed between the evolved inner lift and Ross's distinctive scalloped edges.

After Diamondhead purchased Pinehurst from the Tufts family in 1969, the greens would change forever. In an attempt to integrate the evolved green forms with their surrounds, Diamondhead sliced off the topsoil ledges with a bulldozer and shaved away Ross's authentic articulations. In doing so, they carved away more than perimeter green surfaces. Peter Tufts laments, 'they flattened out Ross's beautiful architecture around the greens'.

In 1987, Jack Nicklaus's design team renovated Number Two's greens using USGA specifications, by coring out directly 'on top' of the existing profile. They also converted the greens from Bermuda to Penncross bent and carefully reproduced the contours with a digital terrain remodelling system. No effort was made to lower their evolved elevations to account for years of top-dressing build-up.

Brad Kocher, who came to Pinehurst with the Club Corp acquisition in 1984, acknowledges that the greens have 'inched-up' somewhat over the years, as was evident from the varying layers of soil, sand and organic matter that he witnessed in the subgrade wall. Kocher, who currently serves as Director of Golf Maintenance, isn't convinced that

ABOVE Pinehurst: An archival shot of Number Two's eleventh green, showing how it gradually 'floated' out and tied-in with the surrounds (at grade), while the bunker edges were slightly raised or 'stiffened' to divert water from the sand. (Photograph courtesy of the Tufts Archives.)

BELOW Pinehurst: The eleventh green again, this time captured in 2008. Notice how the middle of the green looks bloated and starts tipping over into the bunkers (and the approach) from well within the interior of the putting surface. (Photograph courtesy of Craig Disher.)

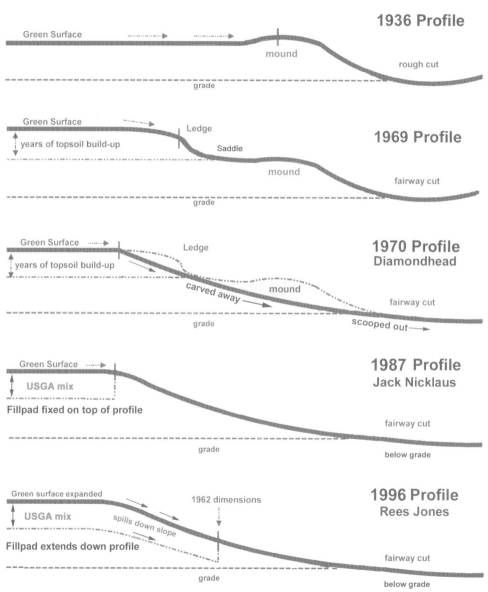

Green Evolution Graph of Pinehurst No. 2
(1936 ~ 1997)

1936 Profile

Green Surface
mound
rough cut
grade

1969 Profile

Green Surface
years of topsoil build-up
Ledge
Saddle
mound
fairway cut
grade

1970 Profile
Diamondhead

Green Surface
years of topsoil build-up
Ledge
carved away
mound
fairway cut
grade
scooped out

1987 Profile
Jack Nicklaus

Green Surface
USGA mix
Fillpad fixed on top of profile
fairway cut
grade
below grade

1996 Profile
Rees Jones

Green surface expanded
USGA mix
1962 dimensions
spills down slope
Fillpad extends down profile
fairway cut
grade
below grade

Number Two's greens have risen too drastically though. He offers the following explanation:

When you scoop out all around the surrounds [as Diamondhead did], the height of the green appears accentuated because of the depth of the depressions around it. But if you look at the topography from a remote perspective—to see the fairway level and how it dips before it comes in—then you'll realise the green levels are not that high in comparison.[23]

In 1996, Rees Jones supervised the next green reconstruction in preparation for the 1999 US Open. During construction, a 1962 map was discovered at the Tufts Archives—the Donald Ross repository in the Village of Pinehurst—which indicated that Number Two's greens were once substantially larger than their 1996 renditions.

In turn, Jones had his construction crew core out and expand the greens mix out to those 1962 dimensions (approximately 60 x 100 feet on every hole). This greatly enlarged the new G2 bentgrass greens, spilling them over the same side-slopes that were carved away by Diamonhead. Yet, once again, there was no attempt to soften the green elevations.

Alas, only the 'slope legends' can put this green metamorphosis into proper light. A case in point: the putting surface on the fifth hole currently occupies 5,897 square feet. Remarkably, only 1,976 square feet (thirty-four per cent) of the green surface slopes less than three per cent and, therefore, can be considered for pin positions given modern green speeds. This, most would agree, is a rather small target-area for a 485-yard par-4.

Even more amazing: fifty-one per cent of the putting surface on the fifth hole slopes in excess of four per cent. A golf ball cannot come to rest in a stationary position on a four per cent plus incline. Somewhat ironic, these are the roll-away slopes around the perimeter that comprise more than half the green surface today.

However extraordinary and special Pinehurst's greens are—some would even say 'magical'—they don't reflect the craftsmanship of master architect Donald Ross.

OPPOSITE **Pinehurst: Depicted from a cross-section perspective, this Illustration charts the evolution of the greens at Ross's Number Two. Due to maintenance practices and architectural adjustments, the profiles of the greens have changed over the years—especially, with how they tie-in with their surrounds. (Drawing by W. Dunlop White III.)**

Landmark Canadian golf courses

Jeff Mingay, with Ian Andrew

Canadian golfers are very fortunate: our country is replete with a remarkable collection of classic pre-Second World War era golf-courses.

Throughout the so-called Golden Age of Golf Design—roughly the years between World Wars—legendary non-Canadian golf-course designers Willie Park Jr, Donald Ross, Walter Travis, Alister Mackenzie and Herbert Strong, and home-based talents Vernon Macan and Stanley Thompson left their marks over tremendously varied and dynamic landscapes, coast to coast.

A number of these courses are true classics, including Park's Mount Bruno near Montreal; Ross's Essex in Windsor, Ontario, Mackenzie's nine-hole course at Winnipeg's St Charles; Strong's Manoir Richelieu in Quebec; Macan's Royal Colwood in Victoria, British Columbia; and, of course, an extraordinary number of Thompson designs, including Jasper, St George's and Capilano.

But which, if any, of Canada's Golden Age designs are truly landmark courses? By definition, a landmark is a building, or other place, that is of outstanding historical, aesthetic or cultural importance.

Thompson's outstanding Highlands Links, on the remote north-east coast Cape Breton, Nova Scotia, is certainly a candidate. Constructed at the onset of the Second World War, Cape Breton Highlands Links is definitely one of the world's great golf courses. The layout's historical and cultural significance, allied to its aesthetic importance, is indisputable. But, at least in part due to its remote location, Cape Breton Highlands Links did not have a significant influence on golf-course architecture in Canada until decades after all of its eighteen holes were opened for play in 1941.

Examining the history of golf-course architecture in Canada, within the context of this essay, two golf courses, Toronto and Banff Springs, blatantly stand out as being most influential on the development of golf-course design and construction in our country. These particular golf courses elevated golf-course architecture to new heights, not only in Canada, but throughout the world as well. They are unquestioned landmarks.

OPPOSITE **Banff Springs Golf Course, Banff, Alberta, Canada:** The 178-yard second hole, 'Rundle'—originally the sixth hole, when the course opened for play in 1927—was named for the rugged mountain looming in the distance. Stanley Thompson's original sequence of holes was changed in 1989, when a new nine-hole course and clubhouse were constructed at Banff Springs. Today, the course begins at Thompson's par-4 fifth hole. (Photograph by David Scaletti.)

Harry Colt's Toronto Golf Club

The most significant event in the history of golf-course architecture in our country occurred in spring 1911, when legendary British golf-course designer Harry Colt visited Canada to lay out a new course for Toronto Golf Club. The property was conducive: a rolling, sandy tract along the banks of the Etobicoke River, east of the city.

To this point in time, Canada was without a course that could truly stand comparison to the world's best. Colt was about to change this unfortunate circumstance. In the process, he also set a new standard for golf-course design and construction in our country, in much the same manner that Charles Blair Macdonald's landmark design at the National Golf Links of America, on the eastern tip of Long Island, New York, did for golf-course architecture in the United States only a few years earlier.

Shortly after Colt's new Toronto course was ready for play, in fall 1912, British golf writer Henry Leach reported that 'Colt's finished work, as I've seen it, must rank as one of his masterpieces'.[24]

Not surprisingly, the brilliance of Colt's Toronto course stems from a clever routing that takes advantage of the best natural attributes of a nearly ideal property for golf. The Toronto course features an outstanding collection of varied, interesting and distinctive holes. Particularly noteworthy are its par-3 holes, especially the fourth hole—a clever and difficult, modified version of North Berwick's famous Redan hole in Scotland.

Colt, typically, concentrated on placing one-shot holes in the most dramatic settings throughout a property, then utilised longer holes to connect those natural par-3s. He was also one of the first golf-course architects to apply a studious, intellectual approach to design. Unlike so many turn-of-the-twentieth-century layouts, Colt's golf-course designs—beginning with Swinley Forest and Stoke Poges in the heathlands outside London, England—were not purely penal.

Inspired by the classic links of the British Isles, most notably St Andrews Old, Colt's golf-course designs are strategic in concept. The original design of individual holes at Toronto featured bunkers that set up angles and guarded preferred positions from which to attack thoughtfully designed greens. At the same time, a majority of his golf holes provided enough lateral 'forgiveness' for less-skilled golfers to enjoy a round.

Colt aimed to enhance the inherently physical test of golf by presenting cerebral problems for all golfers to solve as well. He succeeded in this endeavour at Toronto, and most definitely had a major influence on a young Toronto Golf Club caddie—none other than Stanley Thompson—who grew up to become Canada's most admired and reverential figure in golf-course architecture.

Geoffrey Cornish, an accomplished golf-course designer and historian who worked for Thompson during the late 1930s and 1940s, recalls his former boss openly professing great admiration for Colt. Another former associate, Robert Moote, confirms that when routing a golf course, Thompson also chose sites for the par-3s first. He, too, then routed the rest of the course around these important, natural holes.

Thompson, who was also exposed to Colt's work at Hamilton Golf and Country

Toronto Golf Club, Port Credit, Ontario, Canada: The par-4 tenth hole at Toronto features an elevated tee-shot that entices golfers to try for the green, 331 yards away. However, the selection of a driver brings thick forest at right and a deep fairway bunker, left, into play. The real defense of this short hole continues to be its steep, back-to-front green, set high atop a crown which repels all but the most accurate and delicate approach shots. (Photograph by David Scaletti.)

OPPOSITE Banff Springs: The 424-yard par-4 eleventh, 'Magpie', is one of the most challenging holes at Banff Springs. Golfers must avoid a large cluster of bunkers at left off the tee, as well as a dominant spruce tree on the opposite side of the fairway, to set-up a preferred angle of approach to the green. While Stanley Thompson typically provides option to play the ball along the ground, onto the putting surface, Banff Springs' eleventh green is fronted by a deep, broad swale that dictates an aerial approach. (Photograph by David Scaletti.)

Club in Ontario, Canada, created some of the most memorable par-3 holes in the world, including, for example, the famous Devil's Cauldron at Banff Springs amid Alberta's stunningly beautiful Rocky Mountains. Thompson's one-shot holes are frequently located in the most picturesque settings. They're consistently excellent holes as well, which etch themselves deep in a golfer's memory.

As exhibited at Banff Springs Golf Course, which was ready for play in 1927, Thompson's work shared other similarities to Colt's golf-course architecture.

Stanley Thompson's Banff Springs Golf Course

Thompson's golf-course architecture is also deeply rooted in the so-called strategic school of design. Like Colt, he aimed to challenge all golfers both mentally and physically and, at the same time, provide an enjoyable round for golfers of varying abilities.

Thompson's courses don't provide golfers with a golden, clear-cut guide along the 'straight and narrow' path—for instance,

between flanking hazards. They're more like 'obstacle' courses, where every player must think about their route, then tack their way from tees to naturally sited greens through a maze of sand hazards, seemingly (but not actually) placed randomly over the inherent landscape.

No other course exemplifies Thompson's Colt-influenced style of strategic design more than Banff Springs. With this design, alone, Thompson elevated his golf-course architecture to new heights and, in turn, positively influenced future golf-course design and construction in Canada, and throughout the world.

Stunning scenery aside, Banff Springs was not an ideal site upon which to construct a golf course during the mid-1920s. Thompson's phenomenal and nearly unparalleled powers of visualisation within the golf-architecture industry resulted in a major construction effort at Banff Springs. A workforce of more than nearly 200 men was required to remove blasted rock, reshape the land and cap fairways with imported river sand to create a workable golf course.

Thompson's landmark design at Banff Springs proved, for the first time in history, that world-class golf-course architecture was possible in the most extreme settings. The successful creation of Banff Springs permitted golf-course architects and developers to begin to consider designing and building golf courses at difficult properties elsewhere throughout the world.

By the mid-1920s, when Thompson was commissioned by the Canadian Pacific Railway to design a new eighteen-hole course at the company's beautiful and massive Banff Springs Hotel, he had acquired nearly a decade of experience at designing and building golf courses. Thompson had recently finished another exceptional 'mountain course' at Jasper, Alberta, which Alister Mackenzie once suggested was a major step in the development of golf-course architecture worldwide. Thompson's understandings of scale and, more importantly, the all-encompassing elements of golf-course construction, were major assets at wild, rocky Banff Springs. And so was his gained confidence, and inherent strength of personality.

Upon completion, Banff Springs was reported to be the most expensive golf course ever constructed. Apparently, Thompson and company ran out of money halfway through the course's construction. This, of course, could have been Thompson's own report. He was an excellent self-promoter, and a showman of sorts. Either way, the total tab for construction of Banff Springs was reportedly CDN$1 million (nearly CDN$13 million today).

It is said that Thompson never let a budget stand in his way of creating the greatest golf course possible. He was of the mind that his wealthy clients, including Canadian Pacific Railway, wouldn't care about the extent of construction costs once his golf-course designs were completed and heralded, inevitably, as some of Canada's—and perhaps the even world's—greatest. Banff Springs certainly was.

Thompson exhibited a learned, artistic flair and genius at Banff Springs that wasn't evident to this point in his career. The bunkers at Banff Springs, which originally numbered nearly 200, were particularly clever in design and ruggedly attractive, especially in comparison to Thompson's sand hazards at Jasper, which were relatively rudimentary in form. In fact, shortly after Banff Springs was completed, Canadian National Railway—which developed the Jasper course—insisted that Thompson return to 'jazz-up' the bunkers there, so as to compare with the aesthetic superiority of Banff Springs' sand hazards. He did.

Thompson's achievement at Banff Springs elevated him into the upper-echelon of golf-course designers worldwide. The golf course was widely recognised in 1939, when the *National Golf Review*—a short-lived publication created from the ashes of *The American Golfer* and *Golf Illustrated*—assembled a panel of golfing experts, including Bobby Jones, Walter Hagen, Gene Sarazen, Bernard Darwin and Grantland Rice, plus golf-course architects, Tom Simpson, Charles Alison and Robert Trent Jones, to rank the world's best golf courses. Banff Springs featured impressively, at number eight on this list, ahead of, for example, such venerable golf-course designs as Royal Melbourne and Augusta National. Jasper ranked thirty-sixth.

Remarkably, eighty-years since it was first ready for play, Banff Springs Golf Course continues to exemplify the monumental possibilities in golf-course architecture through bold, artistic vision, flamboyance and intelligent design influenced by tradition and enduring principles.

The brilliance of this landmark golf-course at Banff Springs can be traced back to Toronto Golf Club, where Harry Colt set an important new standard for golf-course design and construction in Canada. In the process, this great English golf-course architect influenced and inspired the fertile and creative mind of a young caddie called Stanley Thompson.

OPPOSITE **Toronto Golf Club: Routed over a narrow spine of land that falls away into thick trees and bushes at both sides, the 222-yard par-3 seventeenth hole has ruined many good rounds at Toronto Golf Club. A deep, grass-face 'coffin' bunker short-left of the putting surface tends to save errant shots from reaching trees, but recovery play from this hazard barely offers a reprieve. Indeed, the 'most difficult shot in golf' is presented: a long blast from sand, from at least five-feet below the level of the fairway and green. (Photograph by David Scaletti.)**

Port Fairy Golf Club, Australia

Situated 290 kilometres west of Melbourne, the township of Port Fairy is located at the mouth of the Moyne River, which provides a beautiful harbour, complete with yachts and fishing boats.

With its many historic buildings (over fifty are classified by the National Trust), antique outlets and its range of quaint cottages and bed and breakfast accommodation, the town is a magnet for those who like a healthy dose of culture, amid a relaxed coastal setting.

Port Fairy's population is barely 3,000, and its residents enjoy an enviable pace of life. Each March, however, madness descends with the annual staging of the Port Fairy Folk Festival—the largest of its type in Australia.

While the region's whaling and sealing past is acknowledged, the marine harvest has shifted to smaller species; namely, crayfish and fish. And with fine restaurants and access to excellent land produce, Port Fairy, today, is a gastronome's delight.

Port Fairy's outward links to Ireland, supported by a cultivated Irish atmosphere, is readily apparent to visitors. The connection is interesting: with the Southern Right Whales in the early 1840s teetering upon near-extinction, the fishing village was rejuvenated by two Irish land developers, James Atkinson and William Rutledge. In the process, they introduced a name change: Belfast. This, more or less, coincided with the dreadful Irish potato famine, which led to the emigration of many skilled potato growers to Port Fairy, Koroit and nearby settlements. The Irish dye was set!

When looking at Perry Cho's soothing photography, another link to Ireland is easily established: the distinctively 'Irish' look and feel of Port Fairy Golf Club's layout. While never purporting to be a championship course, it serves, on the contrary, as the antithesis to big-scale commercial golf.

A round over the multi-levelled layout provides insight to what links golf in Ireland must have been like before the international golf traffic came—in other words, before legendary writer Herbert Warren Wind 'blew the whistle' about Ballybunion—of what golf in a sublime coastal setting is all about; of what can be achieved on a 'shoe-string' budget, given the right terrain and club direction. It's indicative, too, of a golf course that hasn't suffered the effects of over-design.

Port Fairy's design and maintenance is simplistic and uncomplicated: it's straightaway and unremarkable. In some contexts that description could be viewed as a slight. But in its intended context … it's the highest praise.

Photography by Perry Cho

ABOVE **Port Fairy Golf Club, Victoria, Australia: Although the club enjoys a solid membership base, visitors are welcome to tackle the 5,887-metre layout. Impressively, green fees are still less than the price of a run-of-the-mill steak! (Photograph by Perry Cho.)**

OPPOSITE **Port Fairy: The 'links aspect' of the 408-metre par-4 fourteenth hole—generally thought to be Port Fairy's signature hole—was greatly enhanced following the wholesale removal of trees that occupied the right-hand side of the fairway. The prevailing breeze blows golf balls away from the right-side dunal vegetation and out of bounds. Mills Reef can be seen to the right, as part of the hole's commanding ocean backdrop. (Photograph by Perry Cho.)**

Port Fairy: The 349-metre sixteenth hole sweeps leftward and climbs to an elevated greensite—which, when added to the wind, greatly influences approach shots. As the photograph shows; the sand-based rumpled fairway has all the ingredients to excite any true lover of the links game. (Photograph by Perry Cho.)

OPPOSITE Port Fairy: A downhill par-3, the 122-metre eighth hole has been enhanced in recent years with the addition of a new 'fast' green and deep, greenside bunkers. All that aside, the hole's simple elegance and beguiling background makes you want to play! (Photograph by Perry Cho.)

ABOVE AND INSET Port Fairy: Two images of the uphill, 448-metre par-5 fifth hole; the smaller, inset image was taken from behind the green. (Photograph by Perry Cho.)

OPPOSITE ABOVE Port Fairy: Some years ago, Michael Clayton moved the tee of the 178-metre par-3 fifteenth hole considerably to the right, attaining more of a wild, dunal location. Accolades quickly followed. (Photograph by Perry Cho.)

OPPOSITE BELOW Port Fairy: Looking back to the fifteenth hole and the awesome Southern Ocean coastline, from beyond the green. (Photograph by Perry Cho.)

Club de Golf del Uruguay
David Wood

Oh what fun it must have been to be Dr Alister Mackenzie in the 1920s! Having gained fame for his revolutionary course designs, he had assembled a mighty resume in his chosen profession. Offers for his time and services poured in from all over the globe. The golfing world was truly his oyster.

From England to points beyond—Scotland, Ireland, the new world of North America, New Zealand and Australia—Mackenzie left a trail of golfing gems in his brilliantly creative wake that he designed from scratch, revised or co-designed. Other times, he merely advised. Mackenzie was the Michelangelo of his trade; and on his palette was some of the most conducive golfing turf the world had to offer.

In those roaring twenties, Lahinch, Royal Melbourne, Pasatiempo, Royal Adelaide, Titirangi and New South Wales were all glittering examples in the joyous galaxy of his works. Mackenzie's masterpiece, Cypress Point—golf's Sistine Chapel on the Monterey Peninsula in California—had just been completed in 1928. In the case of Royal Melbourne, the layout (now known as the West Course) didn't materialise on its new site until five years after his 1926 visit.

In 1930, with the depression in the United States gathering steam, Mackenzie was asked to travel to the economic boom land of Argentina to bring golf to The Jockey Club in San Isidro—the most chic suburb of flourishing Buenos Aires. He travelled to Argentina via steamer through the Panama Canal, and designed what were to become the Red and Blue courses of The Jockey Club; all while he basked in the high-life of Buenos Aires society. He was the toast of the town.

Two hours by ferry across the tremendously wide Rio de al Plata from Buenos Aires, Montevideo had long suffered in the shadow of fashionable Argentina. Not wanting to be outdone, the Club de Golf del Uruguay sent their vice-president, Jose Pedro Urioste, to visit Mackenzie in Buenos Aires and ask if he would visit their course to see if he might be interested in turning the existing nine-hole layout into the full complement.

Mackenzie agreed and immediately was taken with the property. He was known to

OPPOSITE **Club de Golf del Uruguay: Designed in 1930 by Alister Mackenzie, the South American course is one of his lesser-known gifts to golf. (Sketch by Barry King.)**

have stated that the Club de Golf del Uruguay sat upon one of the finest pieces of golfing land he had ever come across.

With downtown Montevideo grandly in view, the Club de Golf sits on a headland standing sentinel over a picturesque beach on the long gradual harbour of the Rio de al Plata. Because the bluff slopes toward the river, it affords grand water views from numerous points. Mackenzie felt he had the chance to build something special. He was paid $1,000 for the job, a king's ransom at the time, and completed the design in 1930. His original plan hangs at a place of honour inside the charming low-key clubhouse.

At 6,653 yards and a par of seventy-three, you immediately know you're on a Mackenzie course, courtesy of the sloping greens and camouflage bunkering. The layout is both aesthetically pleasing to the eye and punishing to the foolhardy golfer without a plan of attack. Sadly, the club has changed aspects of his original plan. Mackenzie's primary design featured wildly undulating putting surfaces with as much as six feet of relief on several of the greens. Having been so taken

with the giant sweeping mounds on the putting greens of St Andrews, Mackenzie often looked to put a similar stamp on his courses.

The course that Mackenzie designed featured common Bermuda grass, but when sand-based bentgrass was installed in the 1990s many of the severe contours were, in essence, shaved down. Mackenzie wouldn't have been overly pleased with this development. His career-long battles with Green Committees had begun at the first course he had a hand in changing—his original home club of Alwoodley in England. These 'turf wars' were to become the bane of his existence.

The Club de Golf has many of the 'Essential Features' of an ideal golf course that Mackenzie put forth in *Golf Architecture* (1920). Mackenzie felt that, whenever possible, the different nines should be arranged in two unique loops allowing golfers to tee-off on either the first or the tenth when the club was busy. This practice has become commonplace in golf and shows how Mackenzie was ahead of time. A case in point: the 320-yard, par-4 opener and the difficult 389-yard, par-4

tenth are both in close proximity to the clubhouse. Like St Andrews, Mackenzie felt there should be little walking between greens and tees. With narrow groves of trees usually separating the putting surfaces and the hitting-area for the next hole, Mackenzie again succeeded nicely with respect to his ideal for course design.

Mackenzie believed there should be a 'large proportion of good two-shot holes, two or three drive-and-pitch holes, and at least four one-shot holes'.[25] Mackenzie's use of 'two-shot holes' refers to par-4s and par-5s— he didn't use the word 'par' in his early writing. The Club de Golf has a host of stellar two-shot holes. After the first hole—where par is not beyond your grasp if you successfully avoid the narrow bunker that flanks the slightly raised green—golfers face a string of four consecutive holes that will most likely determine whether a decent score will eventuate on any given day.

The stout 447-yard second hole requires two well-struck shots to a small green that slants smartly from right to left. Hitting the putting surface is paramount on your approach because missing the green requires a deft third shot with the added difficulty of negotiating the slope with your pitch. Because of his love of slope and undulations on his greens, Mackenzie's short-game examination tests your nerve.

The third and fourth holes are both par-4s and play downhill toward the Rio de la Plata. Getting your tee-shot *in play* is mandatory if hopeful of having any chance of holding your second shots on these small, elusive greens. Mackenzie's signature of natural, deceptive bunkering is evident and offers protection from the golfer taking dead aim at the portion of the green that would offer the easiest chance of two-putting. Again, missing either green requires the touch of a cat-burglar on your pitch to get 'up-and-down'.

The fifth hole, being the first of the four excellent par-5s, plays to 495 yards and doglegs slightly right to a well-bunkered, arduous green. This hole plays from the lowest point on the property back toward the clubhouse. After just five holes, you sense that every part of your game has been scrutinised, and Mackenzie has exposed your mor-tal coil. If your scorecard has ballooned, at least you can enjoy the walk with the breeze off the water cooling your golfing mind.

Mackenzie may well have been among the first of the designers to factor in the physical beauty of the land as one the major components in an ideal golf course. The greens and bunkering at Club de Golf del Uruguay have the feel that they were hiding undiscovered for centuries and just needed someone to come in and remove the dustcover sheets and open the windows. Mackenzie was the master of the natural.

The excellent 366-yard, par-4 thirteenth hole runs parallel to the Rio de la Plata and is a fine example of Mackenzie's genius. A deep greenside bunker protects the left side of the elevated green that slopes heavily from back to front. To take the bunker out of play, your second shot has to err to the back of the green, while putting back down the hill to the protected pin requires skilful touch.

A celebrated short par-4s is the 337-yard, par-4 sixteenth hole, playing slightly uphill and offering two routes for the golfer to take. The closer the drive hugs the left side of the fairway, the better chance you have to take the bunkers out of play that protect the small, severely sloped green. One must be brave, in a golfing sense, to attempt such a tee-shot strategy for the *heroic* route brings the out-of-bounds fence abutting the far end of the property well into the realm of possibility. The safe route of driving is to the right portion of the fairway; however, that brings all the hazards lurking near the green into play for a second shot that plays longer than the yardage suggests. The sixteenth is the epitome of a hole that requires a well-thought-out plan as well as execution.

One doesn't naturally think of golf and Uruguay in the same sentence, let alone a world-class course designed by the renowned Dr Alister Mackenzie. I played the course three days in a row during my journey round the golfing globe for my book, *Around the World in Eighty Rounds* (2008). What a discovery to find a gem of a course in an unlikely locale. I could happily play the Club de Golf del Uruguay every day for the rest of my golfing life.

The timeless elegance of the Fenway Golf Club, USA

Phil Young

You open the door and step out of the professional's shop and take some steps (about fifteen), and in those few moments find yourself journeying back through time some eighty years to when Gatsby partied and elegant people played a game on golf courses few could begin to imagine. All these years later, Gatsby is gone but Fenway remains an even grander and greater challenge than first imagined by its creator, A. W. Tillinghast.

Tilly spent a lot of time in Westchester County, New York. It is here where the wealth of Mamaroneck is neighbour to that of Scarsdale, where Winged Foot and Quaker Ridge roll majestically through the gentle hills, that his artistry found canvass on a piece of land between these two world-renowned

golf clubs. It is here that one of his grandest masterpieces has lain quietly hidden from the majority of the golfing world. Elegance in a person might be defined as exquisite beauty carried well ... and elegant is the word that best defines the Fenway Golf Club.

In 1920, a group of Jewish businessmen purchased the mansion and forty-acre estate of publishing magnate Eugene Reynal. His elaborate home would serve as both clubhouse and centre for what would be a terrific golf course. They purchased additional acreage and hired Devereaux Emmet, a golf-course architect who was well known in the metropolitan New York area, to design their course, which opened in early 1922.

Unfortunately for them, the dual courses

at Baltusrol also opened for play that year, as did Fresh Meadow on Long Island and the Suburban Golf Club. Construction was also well underway on other courses that would open the following year just down the road—the Scarsdale Golf Club and both courses at Winged Foot.

The Fenimore Golf Club (as Fenway was originally named) had literally just opened its doors when a number of members—who were both a bit jealous and embarrassed—decided that they needed to accept their loss and start over from scratch. They realised that there was a single common denominator to all of these other wonderful designs and so they approached A. W. Tillinghast, the man who had created them all.

OPPOSITE **Fenway Golf Club, New York, USA:** The 'business' end of A. W. Tillinghast's staggering fifteenth hole—a driveable par-4, where its green complex entrance is barely fifteen feet across where most narrow. At just 2,500 square feet, accuracy when approaching this green is paramount. (Sketch by Barry King.)

Ho, Sunnehanna, Brook Hollow and the Newport Country Clubs, to name just a few, leap from the mind of the master. The Fenimore Golf Club rivalled them all. And the club still does.

The members purchased additional acres of land, and so presented Tilly with 240 of them as a canvass to create a masterpiece for them, too. Today, all who love the game of golf are beholden to those brave men for doing so.

Still, by the time that Winged Foot would host the US Amateur in 1940, twenty-two national championships would have been held on Tillinghast-designed courses, and not one of them would be contested at Fenway!

That egregious oversight—caused by its proximity to so many other Tillinghast creations that have had that privilege—has been both to the detriment of the USGA and the USPGA. Moreover, it ensured that Fenway became among the least-known treasures of the golfing world.

Standing on the first tee ... it all looks so simple and straightforward. A par-4 that is

even drivable for some; yet the closer you get to the putting surface, the more diabolical the green complex reveals itself to be. It takes a player just two holes to appreciate a phrase they may have never given much credence to during a round before: angle of play. Fenway epitomises the importance of this aspect of golf-course architecture.

All eighteen greens at Fenway share a common structure; namely, they typify the very essence of the Tillinghast design style. We can appreciate Tilly's work because of a most sensitive restoration done at the hands of Gil Hanse, who was brought in by the club's Green Chairman in the late 1990s to reverse the deterioration of the course caused by time and economic hardships.

The club, now financially stable once again, encouraged Gil to 'give them back their Tilly'. Mission accomplished. Old records and aerial photographs allowed him to properly define and restore green surfaces and bunkers to their original sizes and shapes. He also recovered some twenty-two bunkers that had been filled in through the years; in the process, he even restored one of

In addition to those courses, this period (1922–1925) would also see the Philadelphia Cricket, Baltimore's Five Farms, Southward

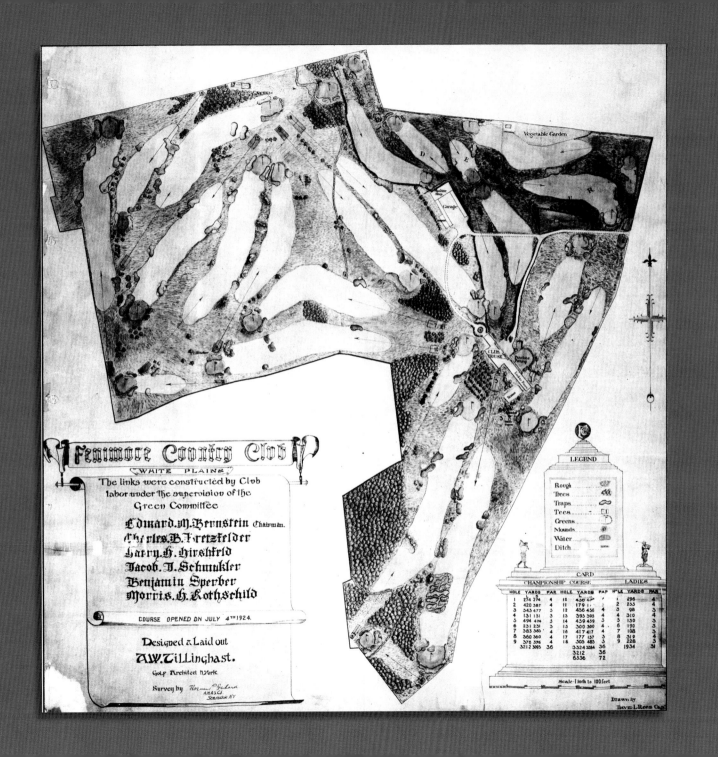

Fenimore Country Club

WHITE PLAINS

The links were constructed by Club
labor under the supervision of the
Green Committee

Edward. M. Bernstein Chairman.
Charles. B. Kretzfelder
Harry. H. Hirshfeld
Jacob. J. Schunkler
Benjamin Sperber
Morris. H. Rothschild

COURSE OPENED ON JULY 4TH 1924.

Designed & Laid out
A.W. Tillinghast.
Golf Architect N.York.

Survey by Norman Eckard
A.M.A.S.C.E
Scarsdale N.Y

LEGEND

Rough
Trees
Traps
Tees
Greens
Mounds
Water
Ditch

CARD

	CHAMPIONSHIP COURSE						LADIES	
HOLE	YARDS	PAR	HOLE	YARDS	PAR	HOLE	YARDS	PAR
1	274 274	4	10	436 437	4	1	296	4
2	420 387	4	11	179 11	3	2	233	3
3	543 477	5	12	456 456	4	3	98	3
4	131 131	3	13	393 393	4	4	310	4
5	494 474	5	14	459 439	5	5	130	3
6	231 231	3	15	300 300	4	6	190	3
7	383 383	4	16	417 417	4	7	108	3
8	360 360	4	17	177 157	3	8	319	3
9	376 376	4	18	305 485	5	9	228	3
	3212 3093	36		3324 3284	36		1934	31
				3212	36			
				6536	72			

Scale 1 inch to 100 feet

Drawn by
David L Rees Capt

Tilly's major design features—the Sahara bunker complex on the third hole.

The length of Fenway was expanded: lengthening holes while making certain that they were so without ever impinging on the shot angles that Tilly had devised with such great care. The work was done so well that it is nearly impossible for someone to separate Gil's work from Tilly's original handiwork. Tilly once wrote:

> The character of the putting greens and their approaches mark the quality of a course to a far greater extent than anything else. No matter how excellent may be the distances; how cunningly placed the hazards, or how carefully considered has been the distribution of shots, if the greens themselves do not stand forth impressively the course itself can never be notable.

I'm not alone in suggesting that Fenway's green complexes and putting surfaces might actually be his finest anywhere. They are easily among Tilly's most bold and dramatic, ranging in size from huge expanses, such as the 10,000-plus square foot eighteenth green, to the tiny and terrifying fifteenth—not even a quarter of the eighteenth's size, yet presenting a front-to-back rise of nearly six feet. These two examples may be among the most challenging and enjoyable holes that a golfer will ever encounter.

The fifteenth hole is an essay in itself: a slightly uphill and drivable par-4 of just over 300 yards. Being a dogleg that eases gently to the left, a well-struck drive may find itself rolling along and up onto the green. One must hope, though, that it is exceptionally accurate, for the green's entrance (unsighted from the tee), is just a tongue of grass barely fifteen feet across. And then it begins its roller-coaster ride of a rise up six or more feet, to an upper portion guarded equally well. The sides of the putting surface are protected by two cavernous and deep bunkers that 'swallow' anything even slightly off-centre. This is where any golfer, regardless of ability, wants least to be.

An aspect of the design that sets Fenway apart from most other courses in the United States is how it still accentuates and encourages the use of a 'ground game' as a viable option of play. Take, for example, the second hole. Today it has been stretched to 455 yards in length, so most players will find themselves with a long-iron or metal-club approach into this green. Cleverly, Tilly fashioned the green's entrance to encourage a properly positioned tee-shot, which, in turn, allows golfers to take advantage of the ground contours, enabling a low-running shot to find the putting surface. In this manner, by paying attention to cerebral design (and play), golfers can avoid the troubles associated with trying to 'carry' the large bunkers.

Tilly believed that a golf course could only be considered great if its par-3s were. At Fenway, the four are diverse, different and singularly dramatic. They range from the deceptively short 145-yard fourth hole, featuring one of the most undulating greens imagineable, to the brutally long 245-yard sixth hole. Yet with the pressure of a close match in doubt, the downhill seventeenth hole—played over a pond to a green that defies you to place a ball on its putting surface—will strike fear into even the bravest of souls.

Fenway has two driveable par-4s, which perfectly balances four others that measure over 430 yards and play far longer than that. It is a course that validates Tilly's design philosophy that holes are 'only as long as they play'[2] and his sentiment that a well-designed one need not play long to be challenging even to the best of players.

The land that Fenway traverses rises and falls with gentle dynamics that help to illustrate Tilly's genius. In spite of the most obvious elevation changes—the course is very open for all to see, as tree growth has been both controlled and contained—there is only one two-shot hole where both tee and approach shots play downhill. Yet the holes that climb the hillocks are inclined to be more across, rather than taxingly uphill. This makes it a wonderful course to walk as well, considerably increasing the pleasure of play.

Over the years Fenway has hosted a number of local tournaments. Take it as read that scoring par on it has become recognised as a badge of honour and something really worth bragging over. Yet even for the average player Fenway is a delightful challenge—one that brings a smile and words of praise from every person who walks off the eighteenth green. And when doing so, you can imagine they can't help but stop and smile and wonder when they will again enjoy the privilege of taking on Tilly's forgotten masterpiece—to once again walk back across the corridors of time to when the game was a truly elegant pastime.

Ballyneal, USA

Doug Sobieski

Travelling through the high plains of eastern Colorado, rural roads connect dozens of small farming and ranching communities—many of which evolved as the result of railroad expansion a century ago. A few miles before reaching the Nebraska border, Holyoke, boasting a population of 2,400 and at an elevation of 3,736 feet, is not dissimilar to many of these towns. Most have a stoplight or two, a grain elevator, a convenience store, an ice-cream stand and, maybe, even a bowling alley. However, as you continue south down miles of dirt roads, an exceptional landform known to locals as the 'Chop Hills' appears in the distance. Hidden within those contours exists Ballyneal, which makes Holyoke distinctly different.

Covering less than five square miles (approximately 3,000 acres), the Chop Hills bare no resemblance to the elegant undulations found throughout most of the Great Plains. Sharp changes in elevation render them unusable for crops or livestock, in complete contrast to the gently rolling land reaching for miles in every direction.

Holyoke native Jim O'Neal would venture to this geological anomaly while in high school to daydream of the golf holes that could exist. He had grown to appreciate the nuances of links golf while watching the Open Championship on television during the heyday of Tom Watson and Seve Ballesteros, recognising that this nearby land could provide the same thrill of playing through rolling, windswept dunes.

Some twenty years later, Jim's brother, Rupert, was considering several options to expand the private hunting club he operated locally. Among his many ideas was a golf course. Fortunately, Jim's dream of playing the game in the aforementioned hills had incubated for two decades. He familiarised Rupert with the accolades that recently built courses in the region had received. Jim also elaborated on his vision for firm, fast-playing conditions, and for fescue turf, too. The golfing model would not include carts. It was to be walking only, unpretentious and laced with strategic design. Rather than simply adding a diversion for hunters, the O'Neals conceived a plan with much greater aspirations.

Jim Urbina, Senior Associate for Tom Doak's Renaissance Golf Design, visited the Ballyneal site in November 2001 to evaluate the opportunity. In spite of being a lifelong Colorado resident, Urbina was unaware that dunes existed in his home state that rivalled

OPPOSITE **Ballyneal, Colorado, USA: An image of the 481-yard seventeenth hole, showcasing the rugged and beautiful desert flora. Over fifty varieties of flowering plants flourish throughout the property, and since it's not possible to re-vegetate the native landscape, great care was taken during construction to ensure that equipment did not scar it. (Photograph by Susan G. Drinker © 2008.)**

OPPOSITE **Ballyneal: Posing a common tee-shot dilemma at Ballyneal; a golfer has an eighty-yard wide fairway at his/her disposal when playing the 375-yard twelfth hole. When accounting for the windy conditions, it can be required! The optimal access route, however, may be as little as fifteen yards wide. (Photograph by Dick Durrance II © 2008.)**

those found at the greatest links around the world. The following spring Doak made his initial visit and recognised character in the land that would enable Ballyneal to be included in any discussion of great golf in the United States, and beyond. During the next eighteen months, Doak surveyed the 1,000 acres of available land with virtually no constraints. Great potential lay in waiting, in every direction, making the routing of the course a challenge and never straightforward. Eventually, the third routing concept, with its roughly two counterclockwise loops, was deemed the best solution.

Isolating and cultivating the Ballyneal 'look' was a constant consideration from the outset. It was critical to make the edges of the golf course 'believable' by blurring the transitions from fairway, to rough, to native landscape. The end result needed to make it appear that there was little in the way of human involvement in the creation. To avoid any accidental evidence that the course was built rather than merely 'discovered', the first order was to establish traffic lanes for any vehicles or machinery to move around the site. Should heavy equipment, for instance,

take a wrong turn through the native desert vegetation it would leave an unsightly scar that would be evident for years. It's not possible to revegetate in order to hide such a mistake, as there are over fifty varieties of flowering plants at Ballyneal. Once these access roads were determined, Bruce Hepner, Doak's lead associate for the project, mowed the entire course-corridor to a height of six inches in a single weekend. Given the steepness of the slopes and the high centre of gravity of the tractor, this proved to be a more dangerous task than expected. Hepner claims he was nearly killed a half-dozen times before they even began shaping!

According to Hepner, 'The first time we walked the routing there were 100 "blind" shots'. He was constantly traversing every fairway on foot to visualise sight lines and to orchestrate what has become known as 'The Big Meltdown'. This became the term for the softening of abrupt contours into their surrounds in order to minimise the 'blind' element, improve playability and to ensure that the property retained a natural look. The fairways, however, remain as wrinkled as one is likely to find in the United States—and it's

still possible for the overly cautious player to face a 'blind' shot on nearly every hole.

Although built entirely on a sand base with no rocks or trees to hinder construction, there was still a problem caused by a beautiful flowering plant. An evergreen shrub called yucca—evolved to survive in harsh, dry environments—was found in vast quantities throughout the entire site. Unlike most undesirable flora, each individual plant had to be extracted by an excavator to a depth of six feet to prevent it from returning. With thousands of individual plants, this process took many months and continued throughout construction, as the plants would re-emerge in fairways and greens. Eventually, the yucca flower became the logo for Ballyneal. Not surprisingly, it also became an 'inside' joke to those involved with construction!

According to Doak, 'Working in sand is like desktop publishing. You can move and revise things very quickly, and nobody can see the edits'. Once a concept is conceived, the designers can literally shape something and reverse it within minutes with little effort. This allowed the team to exchange creative ideas in the field until achieving that 'Eureka'

ABOVE Ballyneal: In contrast to the convex nature of the eleventh green; a shot clearing the fronting dune on the 237-yard fifteenth hole will funnel onto the green from all sides. (Photograph by Dick Durrance II © 2008.)

LEFT Ballyneal: The 200-yard par-3 eleventh hole is perched atop a plateau, where, not uncommonly, the terrain sends balls cascading over fifteen yards from the putting surface. (Photograph by Susan G. Drinker © 2008.)

moment where they felt they got it exactly right. The green of Ballyneal's driveable seventh hole—an irresistible, short par-4—has become a favourite of nearly everyone who has played the course, and it's a prime example of this process.

Doak had been contemplating ideas for the seventh-hole green complex for nearly a year. It was originally to be located high on a ridge, but with the addition of a back tee on the eighth hole, a decision was made to relocate it down to the left into what was essentially a long, narrow half-pipe between two dunes. Once the determination was made to take the grassing line up and over a mound on the left—so the rough into native transition could attain the desired 'look'—Doak immediately seized the chance to build something truly memorable. It eventually took only three hours (from conception to completion) for one of the most imaginative greens in golf to emerge: an E-shaped green, having three distinct sections with intervening bunkers and countless ways to manoeuvre your ball to reach any hole-location.

One consequence of working in sand in a windy environment is that 'final' shaping can disappear overnight, so it was important to safeguard against this scenario. On completion of each hole, irrigation was quickly established so hydroseeding could commence with a fine fescue/Colonial bentgrass/bluegrass mixture. Acting like hairspray, it held everything in place. The fine fescue is becoming the preferred turf, and Superintendent Dave Hensley is training the grass so that his long-range plan won't necessitate having to irrigate during the summer months.

The team knew that they were part of something special, but they made a conscious effort to avoid such talk, hoping that the course could stand on its own merits. Ballyneal was basically built in just twenty-one weeks with nothing but a one-page construction plan, a 'human grading plan' without detailed blueprints, an irrigation crew of locals and an abundance of design talent. This gifted group included the entire Renaissance roster as well as individuals normally associated with other design firms (Pete Dye's and Coore & Crenshaw's), and architect Kye Goalby, too. The result is a collaborative effort that Doak likens to his first job working for Pete Dye at Long Cove on Hilton Head

Island. According to Tom, 'Ballyneal was just a dozen guys having a great time'.

In addition to the publicity the club has brought to Holyoke, Ballyneal is now the largest non-agricultural employer in town. Although it's a private club, the citizens have a sense of ownership and the O'Neals ensure that the club gives back to the community. Over sixty local kids are employed, with caddie scholarships awarded annually. Residents can enjoy the club, via social memberships, with a nominal initiation fee and dues of a couple hundred dollars per year. Seventy-five per cent of that money is directed back to the community through local charities and scholarships.

Although Holyoke may not make an immediate impact on those passing through, the O'Neals can rest assured that Ballyneal will continue to differentiate their hometown from any other in the United States.

OPPOSITE **Ballyneal: Abrupt elevation changes found in the 'Chop Hills' are reflected in Doak's sharply contoured greens, where players often have options to manoeuver their ball toward the hole from multiple directions. Ballyneal's par-4 twelfth hole is 375 yards. (Photograph by Dick Durrance II © 2008.)**

ABOVE Ballyneal: Measuring 7,147 yards with a par of seventy-one, the course features several 'half' par holes, including the sixteenth hole—a 546-yard par-5 that can play with endless variety, depending upon wind conditions and from where a group elects to tee-off. Of note: there are no designated tee-markers at Ballyneal. (Photograph by Dick Durrance II © 2008.)

RIGHT Ballyneal: An overly cautious player can be left with a 'blind' second shot on nearly every hole at Ballyneal. To illustrate the point: a player who steers clear of the bunker complex to the right of the 509-yard par-4 tenth hole will be penalised by that shot 'feeding' into a bowl that offers a view of only the Colorado sky. (Photograph by Dick Durrance II © 2008.)

Ballyneal: Working hard to blur the transition from golf course to native vegetation, the design team was committed, according to Doak, 'to making it appear believable'. The look and feel of Ballyneal is readily apparent from the seventh tee. (Photograph by Dick Durrance II © 2008.)

OPPOSITE ABOVE LEFT Ballyneal: The tee-shot on the 573 yard fourth hole provides a majestic panorama of the 'Chop Hills'. The club's policy of 'walking-only' ensures that there are no cart paths to spoil the view, or damage vegetation. (Photograph by Dick Durrance II © 2008.)

OPPOSITE ABOVE RIGHT Ballyneal: An E-shaped green on the driveable 352-yard seventh hole provides endless opportunity for players to indulge in creative, 'child-like' short-game problem-solving; such is the pitch of the terrain. And yet ... the green complex was conceived and shaped by Doak, and his team, in just three hours. (Photograph by Dick Durrance II © 2008.)

OPPOSITE BELOW LEFT Ballyneal: Firm, fescue turf conditions throughout the layout encourage a player to keep their ball close to the ground on most holes, such as when approaching the ninth hole—a 362-yard par-4 culminating in a green that sits in a bowl. (Photograph by Dick Durrance II © 2008.)

OPPOSITE BELOW RIGHT Ballyneal: The 145-yard third hole reveals the sandy nature of the site, which allowed the design team to refine contours with minimal effort. Without detailed blueprints, the Renaissance team used what they refer to as: 'a human grading plan'. (Photograph by Dick Durrance II © 2008.)

ABOVE Ballyneal: An image of the 481-yard par-4 seventeenth hole, showing how the teeing ground areas blend seamlessly with the surrounding contours and native landscape. Many holes can be played from widely varying angles, as dictated by the chosen teeing ground. (Photograph by Susan G. Drinker © 2008.)

OPPOSITE Ballyneal: Sharp contours throughout the layout needed to be 'melted down' to minimise the 'blind' shotmaking element. Despite this intervention, the fairways are still among the most undulating in the United States. An image of the 362-yard fourteenth hole. (Photograph by Dick Durrance II © 2008.)

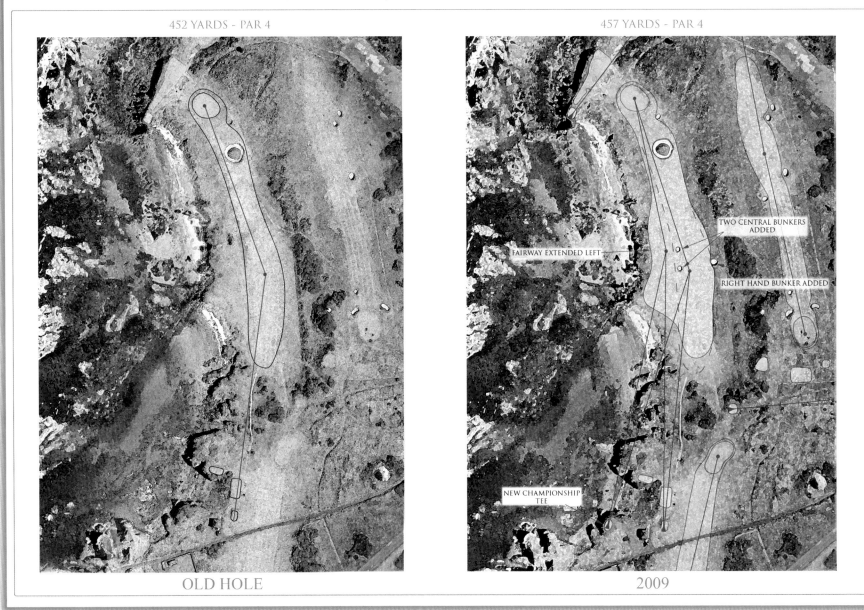

452 YARDS - PAR 4

457 YARDS - PAR 4

FAIRWAY EXTENDED LEFT

TWO CENTRAL BUNKERS
ADDED

RIGHT HAND BUNKER ADDED

NEW CHAMPIONSHIP
TEE

OLD HOLE

2009

Preparation for the Open Championship: Turnberry, UK

Martin Ebert

The Opens played at Turnberry in 1977, 1986 and 1994 were all classics in their own right. The 1977 'Duel in the Sun' was, perhaps, the finest example of two players at the peak of their games going head-to-head and exhibiting the highest level of their skills. Tom Watson could not be denied by the experience and dominant presence of Jack Nicklaus.

Greg Norman triumphed in such style in 1986, playing what could well be the best round in the history of the Open to record a sixty-three in such inclement conditions.

Nick Price's victory in 1994 will forever be remembered for the green-length eagle putt on the seventeenth, which catapulted him to victory at the pinnacle of his career. His victory was achieved with four rounds in the sixties and a winning total of 268 that was just one shot above Greg Norman's record low aggregate at Royal St George's the previous year.

It was a concern that low scoring would be taken to a new level that partly prompted a comprehensive review of the Ailsa Course at Turnberry. There was a feeling that, given benign weather conditions, the course with the most spectacular setting of all Open venues could be seriously brought to its knees by the world's finest exponents of the game. This led Turnberry and the Royal & Ancient to commission a study of the course by Donald Steel & Company, although the final report and co-ordination of the construction work was carried out under the auspices of Mackenzie & Ebert Ltd. Donald Steel and I visited the course in October 2003 to make a full review. Donald had known the course for many years, and had a heartfelt affection for the course and its iconic hotel. I had been involved at Turnberry previously, working upon the creation of the Kintyre Course, using additional coastal land to rework the old Arran Course.

All aspects of the course were studied during the review process. Statistics from previous Opens were considered, including an assessment of the different clubs played by the three Open champions. Although conditions were different for the three events, this revealed a trend for shorter clubs being required to reach greens, as could be expected

OPPOSITE **An Illustration showing the dramatic new alignment of tee-shot and fairway for the tenth hole on the Ailsa—Turnberry's course used in the Open Championship. (Illustration by Mackenzie & Ebert Ltd.)**

given the advances in technology throughout the years. The fear was that the greater advances of ball and club technology since 1994 would render the course highly vulnerable to the power players of the contemporary era. While great care needs to be taken when lengthening any course or individual holes, it was clear that all opportunities for increasing the yardage would need to be considered to preserve the challenge of the Ailsa.

Making more of the natural features of the course was another aspect of the review process. For instance, a sharp-sided crater to the left of the seventh hole was not making as much impact on the hole as it could have done so; this was cut further into the approach to take it closer to the centre line of the hole.

Quite often these exercises are a case of evaluating the ideas and proposals of others and, in the case of Turnberry, George Brown—the Course Manager who had been in his position since the 1986 Open—provided a wealth of experience and ideas. One of the projects that he had always dreamed about was placing a new Championship tenth tee on a rocky outcrop right on the shore line. On plan, the tenth hole looked spectacular playing along the coast line; but, in reality, the shore played little part in the golfer's negotiation of the hole. How that has changed with the new tee perched on the rock! This will be one of the most exhilarating tee-shots in championship golf with a 200-yard carry over the bay. Our expertise was used to ensure that the challenge presented by this new line of tee-shot was fair in all conditions, and also to keep the hole 'sensible' from the main tees on the original playing line. The final proposal included extending the fairway as close to the shore line as possible and the addition of three bunkers, two of which are located in the centre of the fairway and designed to pose a fundamental strategic question from the new championship tee. The most daring tee-shot line is to take on the narrow gap between beach and bunkers. A good drive in still conditions will leave no more than a wedge. A more cautious strategy, but one that will leave an approach of around 150 yards to the green, requires the bunkers to be negotiated. The third option, a safe tee-shot to the right and short of the bunkers, leaves a shot in the region of 200 yards. Ideally, an array of shot-making choices, via sound design, should be offered to participants; we see this time and again with the most thought-provoking golf courses.

Another suggestion offered by George Brown and his team of greenkeepers related to the par-5 seventeenth hole: take the tee back some sixty yards. The old hole was playing far shorter than its 497 yards as a result of the downslope, which could be reached by the longer hitters from the tee. Eduardo Romero reached the green in the 2006 Seniors Open with a drive and a sand-iron on one occasion! The original report had suggested moving the green further on, but there were problems with this suggestion in relation to its proximity with the eighteenth-hole tee-shot; at any rate, such a move would not have addressed the issue of tee-shots landing on the downslope. However, the new idea of moving the tee back had a serious consequence for the sixteenth hole: the new seventeenth tee would lie on the edge of the old sixteenth fairway, requiring a rerouting of that fairway. There was room to dogleg the

AILSA COURSE, TURNBERRY - 16TH HOLE

409 YARDS - PAR 4

455 YARDS - PAR 4

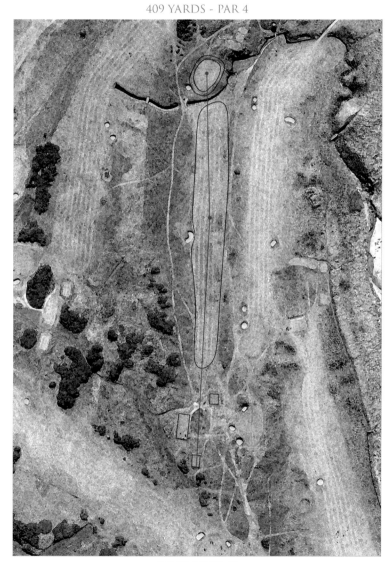

DUNE

CRATER

OLD FAIRWAY LINE

ENTIRE FAIRWAY MOVED TO THE LEFT

DUNE

CRATER AND DUNES CREATED FOR NEW FAIRWAY TO DOGLEG AROUND

EXISTING BUNKER RETAINED

TEES RECONFIGURED AND EXTENDED BACK

OLD HOLE

2009

497 YARDS - PAR 5

558 YARDS - PAR 5

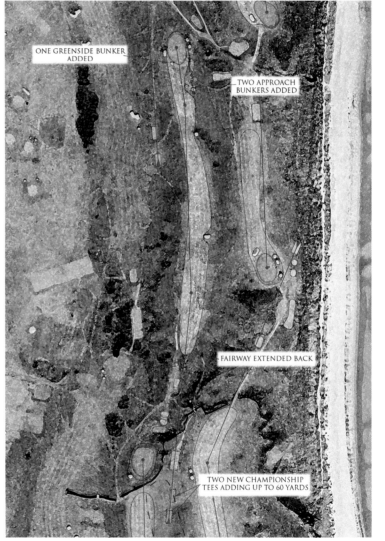

ONE GREENSIDE BUNKER ADDED

TWO APPROACH BUNKERS ADDED

FAIRWAY EXTENDED BACK

TWO NEW CHAMPIONSHIP TEES ADDING UP TO 60 YARDS

OLD HOLE

2009

hole left to right, making room for the seventeenth tee; but the key was to make such a change of angle of the hole look natural. The concept that we recommended was to excavate a deep crater at the corner of the dogleg, and to use the material from the excavation to form dunes before and after the crater.

There are a number of examples of such craters around the course, blown into shape by the wind. These were used as inspiration for the shaping. When the first day's excavation had been completed, there was concern from some quarters—on account of the deep pit created in the centre of the fairway—that we had lost our minds. Pleasingly, faith was retained and we were given latitude to ensure the entire right side of the hole blends in really well with the shapes around it.

One of the ways in which this seamless result was achieved was to lift the rough turf, containing marram grass and heather, from the rough to the left of the old hole and lay it on the new shapes. This process gave the area of rough instant maturity. The turf from the original fairway was lifted and replaced upon the new fairway. The hole has also been lengthened with a new tee; the change of angle means that the tighter the tee-shot is played to the strong features down the right side of the hole, the easier the approach to the green. A safer drive to the left leaves a much tougher line in with the Wee Burn playing a more dangerous role to the right of the green. Previously, the burn was more of a feature to be carried than a lateral hazard.

This was an ambitious project but the finished result has been very well received by the Turnberry members and visiting golfers. The seventeenth hole was also given two approach bunkers (to the right) and a greenside bunker (to the left), which will tighten the margin for error for the longer second shots played to the green from well-hit drives.

The tenth-hole change and the project involving the sixteenth and seventeenth holes were the most extensive of the improvement program. Indeed, most holes have received some adjustment. New fairway bunkers have been added at the first, third, fifth, eighth, twelfth, thirteenth, fourteenth and eighteenth holes. The thirteenth and fourteenth holes have been further bolstered by the construction of some ridges and hollows. These features will demand far more thought from the tee if an aggressive strategy is to be adopted. New back tees have been constructed at six holes: the third; fifth (utilising an old tee); seventh (existing tee extended to the rear); eighth; twelfth; and eighteenth. This extends the course from 6,957 yards for the 1994 Open to 7,211 yards for the 2009 Open.

The R&A was fully involved with every step of the project and was reportedly pleased with how the revised course played during the 2007 Amateur—in spite of one qualifying round played in such a strong wind that the 200-yard carry to the seventeenth fairway was out of reach unless the tee-shots were struck perfectly from the middle of the club.

It will be fascinating to see how the best players in the world take on the challenges of the Ailsa Course in the 2009 Open.

OPPOSITE Turnberry's par-5 seventeenth hole is now a more complete three-shot hole—even for the better players—due to the tee extension and new bunkering. (Illustration by Mackenzie & Ebert Ltd.)

Heather-clad De Ullerberg, The Netherlands

De Ullerberg makes no pretence to being a highly polished course. It is, however, probably the only course in the world where the fairway playing surface is pure heather.

In the early 1920s, a wealthy Dutch industrialist named Dr F. G. Waller bought Ullerberg, a 600-acre heath-land estate near Ermelo situated in the middle of the Netherlands. This area, called the Veluwe, is unlike most of the country.

Instead, it's rather hilly and very sandy. The reason is simple: this was where the retreating glaciers—from the last Ice Age that covered half of Europe—deposited their sandy sediments, thereby creating an intricate landscape of sandy undulations.

Because he was a businessman, Dr Waller decided to plant trees on his estate to pay for the upkeep of his estate. As avid golfer, too, he thought it the ideal property to construct a private golf course.

He called in the help of Jhr G. M. Del Court van Krimpen, one of Holland's best golfers and the president of Royal Hague. Since his home course was designed by J. F. Abercromby, it seems likely that Del Court van Krimpen developed his design principles from this source, and used them in a number of other designs in the Netherlands, notably Rosendaelsche and Hattem.

A nine-hole course at Ullerberg was laid out in 1923, utilising the southern part of the estate. Since there was no irrigation available, the decision was made to build the fairways out of heather, and only cover the tees and green with naturally present fescue grasses. The heather fairways are cut a number of times during the year and, surprisingly, they are accommodating to the game of golf. To keep the wild boar off the greens, a system of electric wires has been constructed around the greens.

Although the length of Ullerberg falls well short of today's course standards, it still plays as a long one does. As you can imagine, this is due to the heather fairways, which don't yield much roll to the golf ball. Moreover, the firmness of the greens makes the layout challenging, as lengthy approaches struggle to 'hold' the surfaces. Good scoring, therefore, inevitably comes down to clever positioning from the tee, and finesse in the approach game.

The course follows an interesting routing, meandering through the heather fields of the estate, almost forming a letter E. Adding to a golfer's playing enjoyment, the hole-types are diverse: two par-3s; two driveable par-4s; a number of longer, dogleg par-4s; and a tricky par-5.

Very little has changed at De Ullerberg in the last eighty years, something the Waller family, who still own and manage the estate, is quietly rather proud of. There is no golf club, nor are there starting times, but the family allows true lovers of the game to come and play on prior appointment.

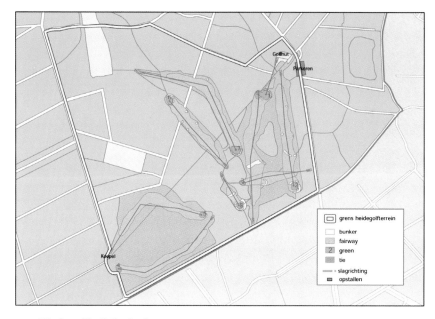

ABOVE **Ullerberg, The Netherlands: The layout of the nine-hole course follows the open spaces of the heathland areas of the estate. In several places the holes cross each other—an aspect of play that doesn't cause any problems, given the low volume of play. (Graphic by Frank Pont.)**

OPPOSITE **Ullerberg: The 106-metre eighth hole has a classic greensite, enclosed by Scottish Pine and ringed by bunkers and grassy hollows. (Photograph by Frank Pont.)**

Ullerberg: An important tee-shot decision is required at the 275-metre sixth hole; namely, whether to place the tee-shot to the left or right of the pine tree, which is located in the middle of the fairway. Going left is wider and easier, but it leaves the harder shot to the green. (Photograph by Frank Pont.)

OPPOSITE TOP
Ullerberg: The fairway of the 320-metre second hole, of which the green is visible in the distance behind the birch. Ullerberg's 125-metre opening hole green can be seen, at right. (Photograph by Frank Pont.)

OPPOSITE BELOW LEFT
Ullerberg: Detail of the first green, showing the electric wires that are necessary to keep the wild boars off the greens. (Photograph by Frank Pont.)

OPPOSITE BELOW RIGHT
Ullerberg: A view to the green from the right side of the sixth fairway. (Photograph by Frank Pont.)

ABOVE **Ullerberg: The approach-shot view toward the green of the 387-metre ninth hole, with the old golfing hut in the background. (Photograph by Frank Pont.)**

OPPOSITE **Ullerberg: The intimidating ninth-hole tee-shot affords players the choice to attack the gaping, fairway-wide bunker, or to safely lay-up before this natural windblown hazard. (Photograph by Frank Pont.)**

Awaking Sleeping Beauty: Restoring Royal Hague's greens

Frank Pont

Royal Hague, built in 1938, was the last of the ten golf courses that Harry Colt's firm designed in the Netherlands. By that time, due to his advancing age, Colt wasn't travelling anymore. In this instance, the on-site design work was undertaken by his close associate, Charles Alison.

Royal Hague is strikingly different from the other remaining Colt courses in the Netherlands. A major part of this difference is the distinctive, dunal landscape in which the course is situated. But Alison's share of the difference is markedly expressed in other areas. Not only is the bunkering larger, deeper and bolder than on the other Colt courses—a mere nineteen bunkers were used on the course, including one bunker on the thirteenth fairway—another clear difference is Alison's routing and the green locations, which are significantly more adventurous. One could even say the green complexes are extreme, in comparison to what Colt had designed in his Dutch work to this point. For these reasons, and others, Royal Hague to this day remains an important gift to golf.

What is still quintessential Colt & Co at Royal Hague are the devilishly difficult, deceptively flat-looking greens, the beautiful shaping of humps and hollows around the greens and, of course, the infinite variety and superb strategy of the holes.

Because the dunes surrounding Royal Hague were relatively barren at the time of its construction—the course was nicknamed 'the Pine Valley of Europe'—the decision was made to transport fertile, clayish soil on to the areas of the greens, tees and fairways. This worked fine in the first decades and allowed for golf to be played in this otherwise barren dunal landscape. It later, however, became problematic: in winter the fairways are softer than desirable for a links-type course. Tellingly, the old clay layer had sunk so deep after seventy years of topdressing on the greens that it had become an impenetrable layer that could not be broken down anymore with normal maintenance equipment. The golf club, therefore, followed the advice of a number of well-known agronomists to rebuild all eighteen greens. I was delighted to assist the worthy cause when Royal Hague commissioned me to provide the architectural and Colt/Alison expertise on this project.

OPPOSITE **Royal Hague Golf & Country Club, The Netherlands: On a clear day, the skyline of The Hague becomes visible in the distance when looking back over the third green. Directed over a broad ravine, the tee-shot on this 350-metre par-4 is among the most exciting on the layout, while the elevated green has a treacherous front that 'swallows' approach shots that come up short. The front also takes care of over-enthusiastic putts back to the flag. (Photograph by Frank Pont.)**

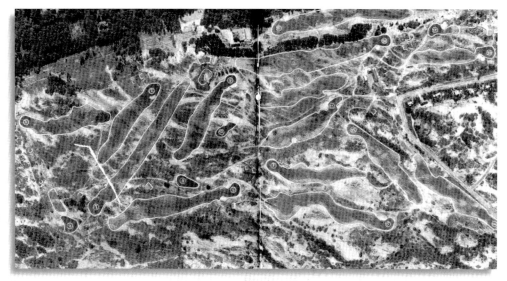

Royal Hague: This aerial of Royal Hague was taken just after WW2, and it shows the routing of the course through the barren dunes. Close study indicates that very little has changed to the basic layout of the holes over the years. (First published in *Golf* magazine.)

BELOW Royal Hague: A 1938 picture taken during the 'grow-in' phase of the course, showing the sandy wilderness surrounding the 230-metre par-3 fourth hole. Note the penal waste area in front of the green, forcing the weaker players to play a safe lay-up shot. (First published in *Golf* magazine.)

De korte 4e hole van 230 meter der Wassenaarsche baan, waarover wij hiernevens een en ander vertellen.

My goals at Royal Hague were two-fold: firstly, to restore the thirteen greens that were still original as accurately as possible; secondly, to create putting surfaces for the five greens that had been changed or moved over the years, so they'd look and play like original Alison greens to knowledgeable visitors. To this end, all the greens were painstakingly detailed measured in 3D, thereby allowing us to rebuild them in exactly the same form.

Two further elements were instrumental in recreating Alison's style at Royal Hague. Firstly, to mirror his large, sand-faced greenside bunkers we studied old aerial pictures of the course to determine their exact locations and contouring. Although the bunkers are rather large and 'in your face', we decided to stick with this peculiar historic style rather than opt for more organic-looking bunkers. Secondly, historical analysis of the grassy hollows (with short grass) that he carefully positioned around his greens was instructive. These had become overgrown and filled-in over the years; we made a concerted effort to bring these important 'hazards' back into play.

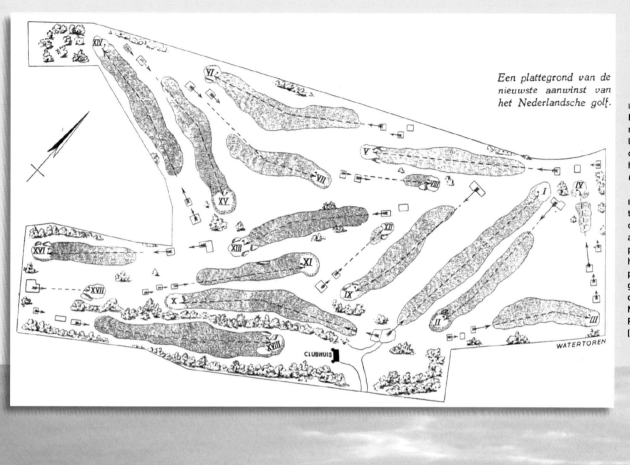

Een plattegrond van de nieuwste aanwinst van het Nederlandsche golf.

LEFT Royal Hague: This rendering of Royal Hague's course routing shows its compact nature—a feature the casual visitor isn't likely to notice during their round, due to the clever way Alison weaved the sequence of holes through the dunes. (First published in *Golf* magazine.)

BELOW Royal Hague: The singular green of the sixth hole bares its 'teeth', on account of a deep, grassy hollow on the right, and an 'even' bunker on the left. The 430-metre par-4 hole, in most cases, forces players to hit long-irons or metal/woods into the prevailing wind to this rather unreceptive green. The hole also holds the distinction of being undeniably the hardest hole in the Netherlands. It also happens to be Kyle Phillips's favourite golf hole, worldwide. (Photograph by Frank Pont.)

Royal Hague: A view of the devilish, short-mown grassy hollows behind the 355-metre par-4 second hole's new green. They are prime examples of the type of 'hazard' that Colt and Alison were keen to utilise; namely, being difficult enough for good players and 'forgiving' for less-talented golfers. (Photograph by Frank Pont.)

Royal Hague: The green of the 328-metre par-4 ninth hole lies high atop a dune ridge, guarded by a deceptively difficult bunker. The unpredictable wind is always a vital factor in choosing one's club for the approach. (Photograph by Frank Pont.)

Royal Hague: The green of the 202-metre par-3 fourth hole, as seen from the back tees, still provides players with a breathtaking view of the dunes and, occasionally, passing ships on the North Sea. It doesn't, however, diminish the threat posed by the three bunkers, or the OOB along the right-hand side of the hole. (Photograph by Frank Pont.)

In restoring the original greens we took great care to recreate the exact playing surfaces; we also repaired some areas that had clearly changed over the years. One example was an enclosed depression in the thirteenth green that clearly was the result of consolidation of the soil over the previous decennia.

Restoring the original greens was rewarding; the highlight of our project, however, was designing and building the new ones. The following text describes some of the thoughts and issues that went into that process.

The first of the newly constructed greens was on the second hole. The previous green had been very small: all upward-sloping, and it had a 'band-like' dune behind it that appeared artificial. The hole is a medium-length par-4 where, due to a massive valley in front of the green, the shot into the green is either approached 'blindly' with a short-iron, or to a visible target with a medium-length iron. The goal was to give the player hitting into the green with the longer shot more room to land on the green, while making the longer hitter's 'blind' wedge shot into the green an even harder proposition. Another goal was to remove as much visual backdrop to the green as possible, so that better players would have a hard time judging the distance to the green.

The new green we built was almost fifty per cent larger. The front of the green remained the old surface, while a new back section was added—flat for the first portion, sloping away from the player, thereafter. Grassy hollows were installed behind the green.

Another new green was installed at the seventh hole, where the main problem again was that the green was too small. The solution here was to lower the green surface by about a metre, which created just enough extra space on the right side to make the total green surface large enough. A welcome, extra dimension of expanding the green to the right has become apparent: it makes the tee-shot even more strategic, for any drive that is not sufficiently leftward on the fairway, leaves a daunting 'blind' shot to the green.

Royal Hague's thirteenth green provided quite a different challenge. The supplanted green was grossly out of character with its two-tiered structure and double-flanking bunkering left and right of the green—clear indications that it wasn't an original green. Because the hole is a difficult par-4 that is usually played into the wind, we were keen to provide players with more space to land a long-iron on the green, and to improve the odds of golf balls staying on the surface. This was achieved by moving the green rearward, making it significantly longer in the process. The new green is defended by a bunker on the front, right side and flanked on the left by a little 'nasty' hump at the entrance to the green. The entire left-hand side and back of the green is defended by three, huge grassy hollows that gather most of the less-accurate shots of the players. Putting on this long, upward-sloping green is far from easy, since it plays 'tricks' with your eyes—from both the front and the rear of the green, it seems the green slopes to the left. Obviously, this is a physical impossibility.

The sixteenth hole is a short par-4, which, from the men's tee, is driveable for the big-hitters. The green had a large pine tree right next to the green, which many members liked, but it wasn't present when the course was built. It certainly didn't fit Alison's design philosophy. The most negative aspect of it

was being a perennial maintenance nightmare for the greenkeepers. We decided the tree had to go, and that it would be replaced by a new bunker, which also would increase the number of greenside bunkers to three. To further amplify the interest of the hole, the valley situated before the green was widened. In this manner, shots into the green that were short, including drives, would roll all the way down to the right of the fairway. From this area, recovery shots can be delicate, tricky or downright murderous depending on one's short game skill.

The final par-3 of the course, the seventeenth hole, represents the last of Royal Hague's new greens. The hole suffered through having its previous green poorly vis-ible from the tee; it didn't assimilate in the existing landscape, and the green only yielded a few interesting pin positions. In designing the new green, along with its surrounding landforms, we wanted to achieve a number of outcomes: the front part of the green should be sloping upward to enhance visibility from the tee; the back-left part of the green should be lower than the top plateau to create a hard-to-hit target; it should be more harmonious with the surrounding landscape. Lastly, we wanted to incorporate three bunkers, each with various degrees of difficulty and flashed-sand faces, to make the defence of the hole more varied. Additional strengthening of the hole was achieved after we constructed a number of low, grassy hollows behind, and to the right of, the green. And last, but not of least importance, we allowed for a less-risky 'bail-out' area for the benefit of older members in the front, left of the green. Now, a relatively easy chip onto the green is possible.

The fortitude that Royal Hague displayed in having all its greens restored has paid off handsomely. Not only are the putting surfaces back to their original high standards and presenting firm and fast greens, but there is real excitement around the club knowing that it now possesses one of the most exciting inward nine holes one could ever hope to play. The 'sleeping beauty' that Alison created has truly woken up; may she live a long and happy life.

Royal Hague: Another long par-3, the 209-metre eighth hole requires a precise tee-shot to keep the ball on the green. The upside of a 'missed' green is the infinite variety of exciting recovery shots one is presented with in trying to scramble a par. (Photograph by Frank Pont.)

OPPOSITE ABOVE
Royal Hague: The new row of bunkers, allied to the enlarged valley in front of the green of the 261-metre par-4 sixteenth hole, makes any effort to drive the green both exciting and potentially dangerous to your score. A great match play hole; it comes at exactly the right moment in the round at Royal Hague. (Photograph by Frank Pont.)

OPPOSITE BELOW
Royal Hague: The last of the par-3s, the 143-metre seventeenth is another hole that offers the player with numerous tee-shot options. The hole's defense is its three bunkers, and the front and back-sloping areas of the green, subjecting players to pin positions that vary from 'easy' to 'impossible'. Always, however, the astute player can find a way to avoid trouble, be it at the loss of a stroke. (Photograph by Frank Pont.)

Royal Hague: The green of the 403-metre par-4 eleventh hole has a deep, 'bathtub'-style hollow in its front entrance that eludes approach shots that are slightly inaccurate—a design element that was a favourite of Colt & Co. Behind the green, grassy hollows were reinstated during the works. (Photograph by Frank Pont.)

BELOW LEFT
Royal Hague: Even though the par-3 twelfth hole has the largest green of the course, and it only measures 158 metres, an always-shifting side wind makes this one of the hardest greens to hit in regulation. Several deep, grassy hollows make the resulting up-and-down shots both interesting and tricky. (Photograph by Frank Pont.)

BELOW RIGHT
Royal Hague: The new thirteenth green now sees the 397-metre par-4 as being almost as challenging as the sixth hole. Not only is the green well-defended by grassy hollows and a bunker, it's bolstered by a hump at its entrance, which serves to push slightly inaccurate shots both left and right. (Photograph by Frank Pont.)

OPPOSITE
Royal Hague: The severely undulating tenth fairway and the hole's contrasting green, as seen from the right-hand side of the fairway. From this photo's general vicinity, long-hitters usually attempt to reach the green of this 439-metre par-5. (Photograph by Frank Pont.)

Tetherow Golf Club, USA

Casey J. Krahenbuhl

Tetherow Golf Club is the newest addition to the DMK Golf Design portfolio. The club, originally known as Cascade Highlands, recently opened as a private club for homeowners and hotel guests only. The hotel is currently under development, thus the club is allowing selective outside play. Martin Chuck, Tetherow's director of golf, has created an atmosphere around the clubhouse that is inviting for members, visitors and all manner of golf aficionados. Tetherow has changed the golf landscape in central Oregon and is generating the kind of buzz that will put it on everyone's must play list. DMK Golf Design has worked diligently to create a singular and timeless golf experience.

The master plan was done by David Kidd and Paul Kimber from DMK golf design in conjunction with the landscape architect and master planner, Hart Howerton. The overall goal was to minimise the impact of the residential lots on the golf experience. Lots are large and set back from the golf. The golf corridors are wide, at a minimum 400 feet wide and often much wider. There are several large swaths of golf land that encompass most of the golf holes, with a few other holes linking these main 'core golf areas'. The driving range was placed directly in front of the clubhouse for ease of access and overall flow. The first tee is a mere 100 feet from the clubhouse door, and the front nine plays out-and-back returning to the clubhouse area. The tenth hole is a short hike from the ninth green and passes behind the eighteenth green to give a preview of the finishing shot.

The blueprint for Tetherow was to bring the aura of the Scottish Highlands to the Cascade Mountains of central Oregon. The challenge was how to achieve that atmosphere. Several key concepts were identified. Firstly, the playing surfaces had to be hard and fast. The 'ground' game would help a player post a lower score, while the lob-wedge would more often than not be the risky option. Secondly, the rugged landscape of lava flows and volcanic activity would need to be mimicked on the golf course. The shaping would need to be aggressive and intimidating. The course should look much harder than it would play. Thirdly, the golf course should flow seamlessly around the property with no noticeable difference from fairway to green. The defined lines from rough to fairway, and fairway to green, should all be blurred. Lastly, the vegetation and natural landscape should dominate the course, giving a frame to each and every

OPPOSITE **Tetherow Golf Club, Oregon, USA: An image of the eleventh green (protected by 'spill-offs' on all sides), looking up the fairway to the turning point. The Oregon high desert is portrayed by the volcanic rock outcroppings, Manzanita, Bitterbrush, Fescue tufts and an occasional pine tree. (Photograph by Wood Sabold.)**

Tetherow: Gazing backward from the par-4 sixth green, a view of the fairway split by a fescue-ridge and dotted with diabolical bunkers. The fescue turf on the greens allowed for aggressive shapes and contours that challenge the golfer. (Photograph by Wood Sabold.)

OPPOSITE Tetherow: Landing area on the fourth hole, also showing how the green is defended by a large bunker on the right side. The golf hole feels like it is being taken over by the native vegetation. Thousands of hours were spent transplanting native plant species throughout the course. (Photograph by Wood Sabold.)

hole and creating a feeling of being unpolished and severe.

One of the most attractive features of the natural site was the high desert vegetation. The site was burned by a forest fire in the early 1990s and has since been overrun by Manzanita, bitterbrush, rabbit brush and fescue tufts. The variation of colour and texture is incredible and made for an excellent palette for the type of experience expected at Tetherow. The golf course needed to feel like it was slowly being taken over by the surrounding plant life. In order to achieve this feel, the course was cleared with the greatest of care in order to reduce the amount of replanting. In spite of the care taken, the developer's labour force spent thousands of hours transplanting the high desert plants back into the cleared areas of the project, especially around hazards. A few large ponderosa pines still stand on the course, and they were used as strategic hazards in the middle of several fairways and just off the edges of the greens.

Tetherow: An enormous fairway greets the golfer on the first tee—the potential for trouble comes on the second shot, when negotiating a 'skinny' green and a long, deep greenside bunker. The green, tan-tinged fescue turf fits seamlessly into the surroundings. (Photograph by Wood Sabold.)

OPPOSITE Tetherow: Defined by the 'spill-offs'... the eighth hole provides a scenic view late in the day. (Photograph by Wood Sabold.)

Before Tetherow, central Oregon was considered Bluegrass Country. Except for a couple of high-end private courses, which have bent grass fairways, every golf course in central Oregon plays on bluegrass fairways and bentgrass greens. The older courses have, for the most part, been inundated with poa in addition to the bentgrass. For that reason, there was a lot of resistance to planting fescues wall-to-wall, as no other project had used fescue before in central Oregon. The team at Tetherow, however, with much convincing by the architect, finally agreed on the grassing plan. The fescue blend was sweetened with a minute amount of Colonial bentgrass to aid in filling thin areas. The fescue blend requires much less water and fertiliser than bluegrass and bentgrass, and plays much faster and harder than standard grass types. Planting the same blends of grass throughout the mowed areas really creates a sense of seamlessness from tee to green. The collar to green transitions become much more subtle, and the greens complexes become entire putting complexes.

To further enhance the ideal of seamlessness, the root zone sand—normally only spread on the greens—was spread throughout the entire greens complex and well out onto the apron. This creates a hard, fast surface out in front of and around the green. It was a hefty cost to the developer to extend the sand areas on the green, but in the end it proved to be a great addition to the playability around the green.

When shaping fairways and roughs, it is very difficult to create anything exotic or groundbreaking. The concept at Tetherow was to leave spill-offs in strategic locations throughout the course. A spill-off, also known as a hillock, hummock or inverted bunker, is a steep hill or hump in the fairway with native vegetation atop. These spill-offs are 'hazards' that defend the most aggressive lines on many of the holes. The fairways have a feel of ruggedness obtained by aggressive shaping and the use of native vegetation on these shapes.

The use of fescue grass helped shape the ideas of the contouring on the greens. With the green speed expected to be around an eight or nine on the stimpmeter, the greens would be benign if left flat or subtle. The hunch was that the greens needed to be real 'roller-coaster' rides. The envelope was pushed inside the putting areas. Plenty of flatter areas were carved in, while large mounds and contours were left to separate the pinnable spots. We were careful to extend these contours outside the green to ensure a seamless feel.

Several different types of bunker sand were tested from separate suppliers around the Northwest to discern the qualities of each. They were shipped to the site and placed in various bunkers. The important factors to be observed were colour, texture, drainage and playability. After hundreds of bunker shots, sand from the coast of Oregon was chosen. Unlike the well-manufactured bunker sands that are crushed, washed and screened to create the perfect particle size, Tetherow's sand was dug straight off the beach and shipped to the site. It was valued for its tan colour and natural feel. The lightness of the sand allowed it to blow around the edges of the bunker and helped blur the edges of the hazards. The bunker floors actually get the ripple effect from the wind often seen on sand-dunes or on the beach.

What about the design/construction of Tetherow's tee complexes: square, round or kidney? In the past, these have been the three distinct shapes of tee boxes. The entire notion of 'tee boxes' is inherently confining and hinders the creative juices flowing in a shaper's or designer's heart. At Tetherow, the tees were shaped as tee complexes with interesting slopes and shapes outside and inside the hitting-areas. The tees were given the same painstaking attention to detail as the greens and bunkers. Tees don't need to be flat or perfectly sloped. There was not even a dictated number of teeing areas. The guidelines were that there needed to be varying locations of teeing areas for differing levels of golf skills and that there needed to be ample square footage of area in order to allow the slow-growing fescue to recover. Some holes have as many as nine teeing areas, while others as few as three.

Tetherow's layout will surely draw both compliments and complaints—such is the way of golf. Either way, all golfers will have strong opinions regarding its playability and appearance of the club. And that is just as the team intended. Tetherow is, by design, unlike anything in Central Oregon and, maybe, anywhere in the world.

Ganton Golf Club, UK

Ian Douglas

The Ganton Golf Club was founded in 1891, on what was, for centuries, poor pasture situated on the edge of the English village of Ganton near Scarborough, North Yorkshire. The original layout of the course remains virtually intact to this day. Some movement of tees and greens has achieved the necessity for added length.

In 1890, the founding members asked Tom Chisholm of St Andrews to design them an eighteen-hole course. He was assisted in this task by the appointed professional/greenkeeper, Robert C. Bird. In 1894, Tom Dunn, who was one of the most prolific golf-course designers, made many changes to the initial layout. Further improvements were made on the advice of the Ganton professionals, Harry Vardon and Ted Ray.

In 1907, the Committee invited Harry S. Colt to give his views on possible improvements. His recommendations were duly approved by the membership and the changes that were adopted created the features, which bear a close resemblance to the present layout. Colt paid two more visits to Ganton; the last in 1930 was significant and resulted in changes to the fourth, thirteenth and seventeenth holes. Minor adjustments, mainly to the bunkers, were made when Alister Mackenzie visited Ganton in 1912 and 1920, and after Tom Simpson visited the course in 1934 to undertake minor changes to the eighth and twelfth holes. In 1949 and 1952, C. K. Cotton was invited to offer advice; he was responsible for the conversion of the twelfth hole from a short par-3 to a dogleg par-4. This work took place after the staging of the 1949 Ryder Cup.

Ganton was very fortunate in its early history to have the services of Harry Vardon, followed by Ted Ray as professional/greenkeeper. Both were born and raised on the Channel Island of Jersey; however, they were markedly different in character. The quiet and methodical Vardon—whose six wins in the Open Championship may never be equalled—contrasted with the extroverted, more erratic, big-hitting Ray. Like Vardon, Ray also won both the US and the Open Championships.

Harry Vardon was a member of the triumvirate that dominated golf before and after the turn of the twentieth century. Vardon, John Henry Taylor and James Braid

PRACTICE GROUND &
DRIVING RANGE

SAND PIT

PLANTATION

GANTON
G G

THE PRESENT COURSE
2006

N

accumulated sixteen Open Championships and, in 1900, Vardon brought home to Ganton the US Open Trophy won at Wheaton, Chicago. It was during his period at Ganton (or Scarborough Golf Club as it was known for the first sixteen years of its existence) that both his and the club's reputation were forged.

Ganton is situated twelve miles inland from the sea, and has many of the characteristics of a links. Before the last Ice Age, the land was submerged as part of an inlet from the North Sea. To this day, seashells come to light when the green staff are at work on the bunkers, which number one hundred and fourteen. The quality of the turf on the fairways, as well as the humps and hollows, ensures that Ganton is highly reminiscent of seaside golf. Yet another feature adds to the golfers' difficulty: the abundance of gorse and broom that gathers up any errant golf balls.

The railway system was an important factor in the positioning of UK golf clubs, and Ganton is no exception. In 1891, the North Eastern Railway had a halt (small station) only 300 yards from the proposed new clubhouse. This afforded golfers an easy journey from Scarborough—a thriving Spa resort— as well as from the more populated areas of West Riding, Yorkshire and north-east England.

Helped by a sympathetic landlord named Sir Charles Legard (Ganton's first president) and the enthusiastic founding members, golf took hold and has flourished ever since.

The three most important Matchplay Cup events in the United Kingdom have all been held at Ganton: the Ryder Cup (1949); the Curtis Cup (2000); the Walker Cup (2003). It now seems likely, on account of the changes to the style and administration of

Ganton: An aerial of the present course, from the South-west corner of the property. (Photograph courtesy of Tom Ward)

round of the final of the English Amateur Championship in 1977, Sir Michael Bonallack OBE returned a score of sixty-one against a par of seventy-one.

One of the most interesting features of Ganton concerns the changes in direction of the holes. This aspect plays an important part in the enjoyment of the round, as wind is a constant companion—on only two occasions do holes follow the same direction. The long, par-5 ninth hole is followed by the short, par-3 tenth—in an east-north easterly direction. The short, par-4 fourteenth hole and the lengthy fifteenth are configured in an east-south easterly direction.

Ganton is basically a flat course, but there are many undulations and subtle slopes that come into play, particularly during dry weather. One of the most important features of the course is the bunkering. A high percentage of these are deep, so the first consideration for the golfer must be 'getting out', especially with respect to the fairway bunkers: take the punishment and accept the dropping of a shot! Philip Baldock, the head greenkeeper, and his staff, constantly alter

professional golf, that the few clubs that have hosted all of theses events—The Honourable Company of Edinburgh Golfers (Muirfield), The Royal Birkdale Golf Club and Ganton Golf Club—will remain as a select threesome.

The club has hosted three Amateur Championships (1964, 1977 and 1991), and it's still the only non-seaside golf club to have done so. One round over the layout shines like a beacon: while playing in the morning

the shape of bunkers, filling where necessary and excavating new sites positioned to meet the demands of the contemporary golfer and today's equipment.

It is beholden on any golf club committee to ensure that their course is kept abreast of developments. Ganton has been fortunate in this respect and uses the most up-to-date course maintenance products. The club also places a very high premium on appropriate staff training.

The following holes at Ganton stand out during a round:

Second hole (448-yard par-4). Demanding a well-executed drive over the bunker on the left; this is followed by a shot with a mid-iron to a green that slopes sharply from front to back, with a hollow immediately behind it.

Fourth hole (412-yard par-4). A drive directed toward the left-hand side of the fairway produces the best line for the second shot, which is across a hollow to the plateau green designed by Harry Colt.

ABOVE LEFT Ganton: The victorious US Ryder Cup team at Ganton in 1949. Ben Hogan, the non-playing US Captain, is shown proudly holding the trophy. (Photograph courtesy of Ganton Golf Club.)

ABOVE RIGHT Ganton: Wilf Dalby and Nick maintaining the 'Pandy' left of the eighteenth fairway in 1937. (Photograph courtesy of Ganton Golf Club.)

BELOW LEFT Ganton Hall, circa 1910, was home of the club's Founding President, Sir Charles Legard. It is now owned by the Wrigley family. (Photograph courtesy of Ganton Golf Club.)

BELOW CENTRE Ganton: Harry Vardon, the great six-time Open Championship winner, was professional at Ganton from 1896 to 1903. (Photograph courtesy of Ganton Golf Club.)

BELOW RIGHT Ganton: A gregarious type, Ted Ray won the Open Championship and the US Open. Even so, he was just as often singled-out for his big frame, penchant for pipe-smoking and his prodigious length off the tee. Ray was the professional at Ganton from 1903 to 1912, and is pictured standing with Harry Vardon at the club entrance. (Photograph courtesy of Ganton Golf Club.)

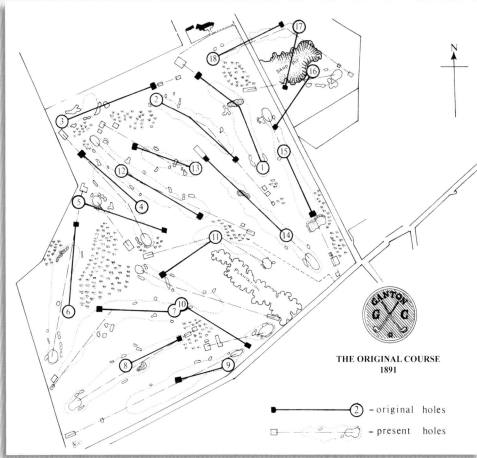

THE ORIGINAL COURSE
1891

2 — original holes

— present holes

If the drive is missed to the right, it will find rough, leaving a ditch to be carried. A large bunker to the right—intruding on the angle of approach—will also need to be negotiated. An over-hit shot, meanwhile, is threatened by gorse behind the green.

Sixth hole (474-yard par-4). The direction of the hole is against the prevailing wind: but two good shots, especially today, will reach the green. A drive over the obliquely lying right-hand bunker provides an opportunity to achieve this objective. The fairway narrows on approach to the forward-sloping green, with bunkers on either side.

Seventh hole (441-yard par-4). A dogleg from left to right, with a nest of bunkers filling the angle, these bunkers can be accounted for with a solid drive, leaving a short- to mid-iron second shot. The safer route is down the left-hand side of the fairway, leaving a longer shot to a tricky, two-tier green sloping downwards from right to left and guarded by bunkers on both sides.

OPPOSITE **Ganton: A view from the tee at the par-5 thirteenth hole. (Photograph courtesy of Ganton Golf Club.)**

Tenth hole (171-yard par-3). The second par-3 at Ganton is surrounded by six bunkers, requiring an accurate shot to the centre of a saucer-shaped green.

Eleventh hole (428-yard par-4). The left-hand side of the fairway is guarded by a pot bunker, while the bunker on the right-hand side appears to have a fateful attraction for golfers. The cross-bunkers short of the green—not easily visible from the tee or the fairway—must be avoided, as should the steep-sided bunkers strategically flanking both sides of the green.

Ganton is renowned for its tough finish and the last four holes are included in the description. Indeed, many feel the run home ranks among the sternest test of golf in the United Kingdom.

Fifteenth hole (465-yard par-4). This hole requires both length and accuracy. The drive is followed by a long-iron (or metal-headed club) that needs to find the correct part of the complex green

characterised by a number of subtle slopes and borrows.

Sixteenth hole (450-yard par-4). The drive over the massive cross-bunker can fall away from the fairway if it lands off-centre. A long drive—past the single tree on the left—is rewarded by finishing on relatively level ground. The lengthy approach is played to a flat, well-bunkered green.

Seventeenth hole (251-yard par-3). With the prevailing wind behind, a fairway-metal or long-iron will reach this challenging par-3. The fairway slopes up to the elevated green guarded by 'gathering' bunkers to each side.

Eighteenth hole (438-yard par-4). The right-hand side of the fairway is the ideal line for the drive; this strategy avoids the golfer's second shot being blocked out by a copse of pines. An undulating home green waits—the longest on the course—and it slopes from front to back and left to right toward two steep-faced bunkers.

Ganton Golf Club, with its proud traditions, has always been pleased to share its facility with visitors. The current members offer a warm welcome to any golfer who wishes to play their famous championship course.

Ganton: The tenth-hole view. (Photograph courtesy of Ganton Golf Club.)

OPPOSITE ABOVE LEFT
Ganton: The tenth green. (Photograph courtesy of Ganton Golf Club.)

OPPOSITE ABOVE RIGHT
Ganton: The eighteenth fairway. (Photograph courtesy of Ganton Golf Club.)

OPPOSITE BELOW LEFT
Ganton: The sixteenth green. (Photograph courtesy of Ganton Golf Club.)

OPPOSITE BELOW RIGHT
Ganton: A view of the seventeenth hole, from the tee. (Photograph courtesy of Ganton Golf Club.)

Ganton: A view of the second green, showing the deep bunker in place to catch approach shots. (Photograph courtesy of Ganton Golf Club.)

The Royal and Ancient Golf Club (Old Course), St Andrews, Scotland

One great result.

visit www.toro.com

TORO® **Count on it.**

Donald Ross revisited

Gerry Stratford

In the millennium of titanium, graphite and plastics when many golf courses are being lengthened and redesigned to require heroic carries, why would The Peninsula Golf & Country Club seek to emulate and preserve a design philosophy that is eighty years old? To answer this question is to examine basic issues about the game itself, and consider the answers proposed by the ambassador from Dornoch, Donald Ross.

Ross worked at Peninsula (then called the Beresford Club) for twenty-one days in 1923 and, in spite of ill-conceived modifications made by various Green Chairmen, the course retained hints of his signature for eighty years.

When members of the club determined to develop a Masterplan in 2003, club histo-rian Michael Jamieson suggested that they contact the Donald Ross Society (DRS), and it was this group that made the club's leadership aware of recent trends in course restorations. Nevertheless, the first question that Jamieson and his committee needed to answer was: if Donald Ross, himself, was still alive, would he be the architect of choice to address modifications at Peninsula? When this question was put to the respected agronomist John Zoller, he answered emphatically, 'Unless you intend to maintain the golf course with firm and fast fairways and reasonable green speeds, a Ross restoration is meaningless'.

Thus it was that architectural questions came to coincide with discussion about agronomy. Peninsula was built on heavy clay soil that required excessive irrigation in the summer months and became a virtual quag-mire from November through February. A similar problem had plagued several holes at nearby Spyglass Hill and the superintend-ent there had recently completed a major retrofit that had proved remarkably effective in solving water-retention issues. The tech-nique, referred to as 'sand-capping', entailed the removal of five inches of topsoil, trench-ing even lower for irrigation pipes and drain tile, and the addition of an eight-inch-thick layer of sand as a growing medium. The new holes at Spyglass drained beautifully and, even more to the point, they played 'firm and fast'.

Anticipating the playing characteristics that the sand-capping would provide, the

OPPOSITE **The Peninsula Golf & Country Club, California, USA: The seventeenth hole is a drivable par-4, but its green is protected by strong bunkering and a graceful willow. The prudent tee-shot is a lay-up to the left side of the fairway, which opens up this view of the hole. (Photograph courtesy of Gerry Stratford.)**

Peninsula: The combination of 'deceptive' fairway contours and adjacent bunkers enables the short, par-4 sixth hole to be highly challenging. (Photograph courtesy of Gerry Stratford.)

decision to restore the Ross design philosophy soon followed. In Ron Forse, who has offices in far off Pennsylvania, the club found a golf-course architect with a profound respect for Donald Ross. Once again, the club brought an easterner out to the West Coast.

On an introductory site visit, Ron was walking up the fourteenth fairway with Michael Jamieson. As they approached the elevated green, Ron stopped and said, 'Wow ... this hole reminds me of the uphill par-4 at Wannamoisett Country Club in Rhode Island. But there, Ross had raised mounds on both sides of the entrance to the green indicating the target boundaries for the "blind" shot. This hole is missing one of those mounds'. Jamieson was amazed, for he remembered that the original design had indeed incorporated two mounds—Robert Trent Jones had the left-hand mound removed in 1953.

When a parkland course is faced with the need to respond to evolving technology, maintenance practices and the playing styles of the modern game, it is faced with a severe constraint—limited space. However, an interesting fact about many of the golf courses of the Golden Age is that length was never the basis of their challenge. Ross, in particular, delighted in the shorter holes. Moreover, the options that he presents off of the tee are always about accuracy and choice of position for the ensuing play; not about brute force.

Donald Ross was a greenkeeper before he was an architect; when he built greens he was always sure to provide effective surface drainage, and this emphasis, combined with his penchant for offering optional routes of play, explains some of his recognisable green features.

On modern courses, and even some constructed by other architects during the classic era, players can often shape their shots so as to start the ball toward the centre of a green and then have it curve toward a flag located near the edge. This conservative shot-making strategy avoids problems if the ball is hit a bit short, or if the applied fade or draw is less than anticipated. But Ross greens often have descending slopes near the edges, making the same strategy ill-advised. If a player wants to get the ball close to such a cupping area, the shot needs to be brought in from the outside of the green toward the upslope. Such a shot, if miss-hit, will not find the green at all. On Ross greens, different cupping areas require distinctly different approach shots with options for either safe run-ups that may leave long, difficult putts or bolder shots that risk roll into collection areas or greenside bunkers. And, because angle and shape of approach depend upon hole location, so too will the ideal position of the tee-shot in the fairway

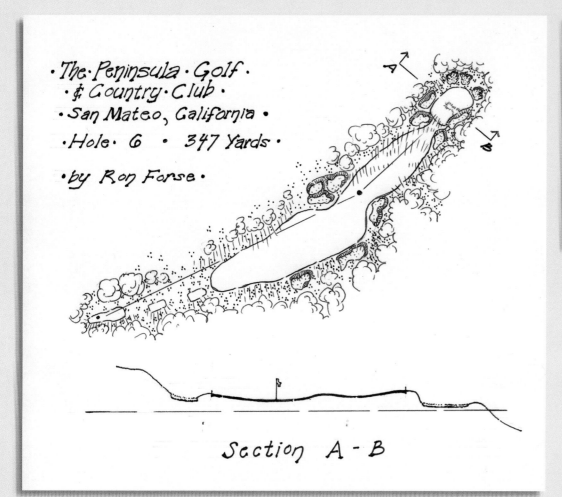

The Peninsula Golf
& Country Club
San Mateo, California
Hole 6 • 347 Yards
by Ron Forse

Section A - B

ABOVE Peninsula: The photograph shows the sixth green from the left rough on a line, perpendicular to section A-B, as depicted in Forse's rendering. (Photograph courtesy of Gerry Stratford.)

LEFT Peninsula: In this classic rendering, architect Ron Forse reveals the sixth hole's formidable defenses. (Rendering by Ron Forse.)

Peninsula: The elevated sixth green, with its severe false front, as viewed from the dogleg 125 yards out. (Photograph courtesy of Gerry Stratford.)

change, depending upon where the hole is cut on any given day.

R. T. Jones Sr, who modified Peninsula in the 1950s, had eliminated a delightful par-3 to make way for a new entrance to the clubhouse. When Forse examined the original Ross plans he was captivated. Visible from the main dining room was a non-descript par-3 green, much modified by various Green Committees over the years. Ron Forse suggested that we rebuild it with the contours of the 'lost' green. Forse also restored original features on several other large, round greens that Jones had built—once again referring to original plans that showed distinct contours and dramatic bunkering.

Before the restoration, Peninsula's sixth hole was an awkward dogleg left, to an elevated green. A huge eucalypt dominated the inside corner and the fairway sloped toward neighbouring houses on the right, exaggerating the tee-shot errors of golfers. Sale of some of the club's property during a financially troubled time in the 1950s had eliminated portions of two holes, and Jones had shoe-horned this hole into a corner with the green very close to the boundary fence.

The original suggestion by Forse was that we move the green away from the fence and create a challenging, uphill par-3. This could be achieved by moving the tee forward and eliminating the dogleg. He suggested that the preceding hole could be lengthened into a par-5 (actually, part of the original Ross layout), which would improve that hole as well. Many members objected to this suggestion, essentially, because it would deliberately orchestrate two par-3s in a row. Arguments pointing out the consecutive par-3s at Mackenzie's Cypress Point were to no avail, and Forse was sent back to the drawing board.

It sometimes turns out to be a blessing when a designer is asked to rethink a solution for arbitrary reasons. Instead of implementing the first idea that presents itself, additional time spent can result in an even better, albeit more allusive, solution.

Forse shortened the hole by moving the green away from the property line, he asked Wadsworth Construction to use their heavy equipment to level the fairway and we con-vinced the membership to allow the removal of the eucalyptus tree. An undulating, challenging, false-fronted green, and the construction of thirteen bunkers, make this totally new hole one of the best short par-4s in Northern California. And it never would have materialised if the membership hadn't rejected the first proposal.

The restoration of Donald Ross architecture at the Peninsula Golf & Country Club has turned an architecturally unsophisticated membership into impassioned advocates of classical golf-course architecture. It has drawn Ross aficionados from all over the country, and it has proved that courses do not have to be long to be challenging.

Design considerations on flat sites

Tyler Kearns

Every golf-course architect has a vision for the ideal terrain upon which to practise their craft. They eagerly anticipate each trip to scope out a potential new project in the hope it will prove to be that 'once-in-a-lifetime' site—their very own Cypress Point, Sand Hills or Barnbougle Dunes. But more often than not, the proposed golf course has been resigned to less-than-ideal topography, or worse yet, a site devoid of relief. How can we turn 200 acres into a compelling, enjoyable and visually appealing golf experience with only a few feet of elevation change? Where do we start when nature has provided little in the way of guidance?

Unlike those idyllic environments where the native landforms beg to be exploited and suggest natural golf strategies to the architect, a dead-flat site does not yield these blessings. On the positive side, it poses few limitations on the routing of the golf holes, which can be as long and wide as strategically necessary and more easily sequenced and oriented as desired. A flat site barring an unlimited budget might make it impossible to create a world-class venue, but it need not spell folly. With a modest yet reasonable budget, a golf-course architect can shape a level site into a well-patronised golf facility by focusing efforts on the areas where players want to hit the ball, and avoiding that which is superfluous.

With only so much money available for earthmoving, it seems prudent to allocate those funds to contouring the portions of the property from which golfers want to play—the fairways and the greens. Golfers never tire of clever and occasionally wild green contours, and it is those rumpled fairways of the ancient links that have beguiled golfers for centuries by offering a variety of stances and lies, not to mention fortunate and less-than-fortunate bounces that help make the game so special. 'Undulation is the soul of golf',[26] wrote John Low, so what a waste it is to see such effort put into lining flat, nondescript fairways with containment mounding, all in an attempt to disguise the true nature of the landscape. A four-foot mound biting into the front of the green will interact with golfers in a much more pro-

OPPOSITE **Elevating key design features such as greens, tees, bunkers and fairways promotes positive surface drainage, while transforming a flat landscape into interesting golf country. (Photograph by Tyler Kearns.)**

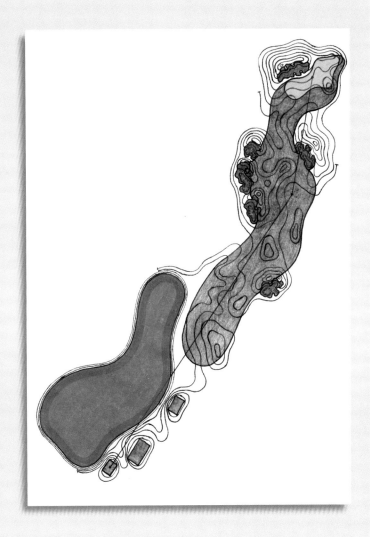

found manner than both rows of containment mounds.

Drainage, the most important aspect of golf-course architecture, is accentuated on flat sites, where the entire drainage network needs to be designed. This provides the opportunity to create those interesting contours. Excavating lakes provides the bulk of the material required to elevate greens, tees, bunkers and fairways, providing the macro-undulations that enable surface drainage and enforce strategy. The lakes are fed by a series of swales, ditches and creeks, providing the fill to form the more engaging micro-contours of the golf course. By merely flipping the dirt from a gentle one-and-a-half foot deep swale in the immediate vicinity, we create a three-foot roll that can affect how golfers attack the hole. Purists may cringe at the thought of artificial lakes dotting a golf course; however, they serve the necessary purpose of storing water for the irrigation system and, ultimately, it is the golf architect's choice whether the lakes will play an integral role in the strategy of the golf course.

Dealing with limited topography is all about moving water away from the closely mown areas of the golf course, reinforcing the need to spend the time building up and shaping those surfaces, helping the turf stay drier and healthier, and keeping the register open after inclement weather. The alternative approach—playing between rows of containment mounding—often leads to a reliance on catch basins and large diameter sub-surface drain lines. Moreover, it's a costly remedy, and proves ineffectual in colder climates during the spring when lines remain frozen for weeks after snow melt. And another thing: containment mounding has an adverse affect on turf grass!

It can be easy to get carried away, but level sites require long, gentle slopes to more seamlessly blend the hand of the architect with that of the native environment and random, irregular contours with those found in nature. The golf-course architect must be restrained when constructing golf features on such terrain, as lay-of-the-land courses are more conducive to the characteristics of flat sites, in addition to being more

Elevating key design features such as greens, tees, bunkers and fairways promotes positive surface drainage, while transforming a flat landscape into interesting golf country. (Photograph by Tyler Kearns.)

OPPOSITE The pond has been kept out-of-play; however, its visual appeal has been exploited, and the fill generated through its excavation has been used to create the landforms for good golf on the closely-mown portions of the hole. (Sketch by Tyler Kearns.)

budget 'friendly' and natural in appearance. We want the green complexes, tees and fairway bunkers to flow effortlessly back into the earth, not erupt from the ground like a volcano.

Rarely featured in golf calendars and magazine covers, golf courses on flat sites generally lack the visual 'punch' that many golfers have come to expect. Because of this, architects dealing with such sites must be extra-vigilant in appropriating existing elements that are beneficial to the course such as specimen trees, natural water bodies and off-site views. Exploiting what Mother Nature has accomplished in thousands of years can greatly enhance the feel of the course, instilling a much-needed vintage character that shifts attention away from the flatness of the site. Furthermore, fescue rough can be employed liberally throughout the out-of-play portions of the site. Under current environmental standards and economic times, it simply makes sense to devote some property to a virtually maintenance-free regimen. Additionally, it also

helps to break-up the horizon on flat landscapes, obscuring the relative lack of relief, and yields exceptional hues and textures that add greatly to the visual character of the completed golf course.

Flat sites are the 'blank' canvases that allow the imagination of the golf-course architect to run wild; and that's a tantalising prospect for any creative mind. When tackling a project of this type, the following edict cannot be over-stressed: focus energy on those surfaces that golfers desire to play from—fairways and greens, and keep them dry! The drainage network creates the contour, which, in turn, instils the strategy and ensures both a challenging and enjoyable experience.

OPPOSITE **With an eye on the budget, fill from an adjacent pond was employed judiciously at the green complex and landing area, while leaving the less-frequented area in between relatively flat. (Photograph by Tyler Kearns.)**

Peterborough Golf Course, Australia

The seaside haven of Peterborough, with a population less than 500, rests at the mouth of the Curdies Inlet, and is located on Victoria's notorious Shipwreck Coast. The Port Campbell National Park, stretching from Princetown to Peterborough, is where several of Australia's most recognisable and photographed natural wonders reside, such as Loch Ard Gorge, the Blowhole, Mutton Bird Island, the Grotto and London Bridge—of the latter, a section famously collapsed in 1990 and stranded tourists. National headlines followed. The most famous of all local landmarks is none other than the Twelve Apostles—huge limestone 'stacks' that rise up from the ocean— thirteen kilometres from Peterborough.

Such rugged, dramatic landform (soft limestone) has been carved by the relentless pounding of the seas and southerly storms. And it's not altogether different to what supports the ocean-hugging boundary of the nine-hole Peterborough Golf Course.

Laid out upon a compact, cliff-top swathe, commanding coastal views from all points of the course are endless. Most eerily, perhaps, at the par-3 sixth, where golfers hit across a gouged-out section of coastline.

Authorities keep a constant watch for coastal erosion across the entire Shipwreck Coast. At Peterborough, it reared its ugly head some years ago when the cliff-top third tee suffered a mauling from the elements.

Bereft of adornments, Peterborough's windswept layout makes do without bunkers or par-5s. It's virtually treeless; has out-of-bounds fences behind a few greens; some punchbowl greens; and less 'forgiving' fairways than elsewhere. With lengthy and test- ing par-3s, small greens and without any 'gimme' par-5s to rescue your scorecard, golfers rarely 'take apart' Peterborough Golf Course—especially if the wind is up.

The fairway lies, if taken in the right spirit, will bring a smile to any purist's face: they're hardly lush. To be presented in that manner would be completely out of char- acter in such an invigorating, salty golfing environment. If anything, the fairway lies are at the other end of the spectrum: lean and occasionally 'spiteful'.

Anyone who pits their golfing skill against Peterborough's layout is in for a treat, as there's nothing else like it in Australia.

Photography by Perry Cho

Peterborough Golf Course, Victoria, Australia: From the first tee, a stirring ocean and country vista instantly makes its mark—golfers can easily be excused for thinking they're playing a famous British links. Captured looking back down the second fairway and green, this combination (first tee to second green) is used on 'Cross Country Day', when the design is thrown away. Without fail, a fun day is had by all. (Photograph by Perry Cho).

FOLLOWING PAGES (LEFT)
Peterborough: The 205-metre par-3 ninth hole is listed as the Stroke Index No. One hole. Like most golf courses, the key to playing Peterborough is being accurate and knowing where to err in the advent of a 'missed' shot. For instance, you're 'safe' if you go through the ninth green—unless you go a long way through—it's the powerful miss to the left that will end up OOB in the club's car park, or in somebody's front yard. Heavy bush, to the right, carries its own wicked penalty. (Photograph by Perry Cho).

FOLLOWING PAGES (RIGHT)
Peterborough: A view of the daunting prospect from the Women's sixth tee. In spite of being just 103 metres in length; if you waver at all, your ball will end up on the beach. From the Men's tee, some forty metres behind, at least the beach is hidden! (Photograph by Perry Cho).

ABOVE LEFT **Peterborough: A good drive on the 246-metre par-4 fifth hole will hit the green down below. To the left is water; to the right, the territory over the road is out of bounds. Clearly, the golfer needs to be ultra-straight when playing the fifth. (Photograph by Perry Cho).**

ABOVE RIGHT **Peterborough: An image of the none-too-forgiving bush on the right of the ninth hole, where local 'urchins' hover in the bushes. If you have the misfortune to stray in this vicinity, you may be able to buy your ball back. (Photograph by Perry Cho).**

BELOW **Peterborough: A view from the tee of the 287-metre par-4 first hole. Doglegging gently from right to left, modern equipment technology has given golfers the confidence to 'straighten-out' the tee-shot—the swamp is usually cleared without raising too much of sweat. The second shot is a short-iron to the type of green that doesn't always 'hold'. (Photograph by Perry Cho).**

OPPOSITE **Peterborough: The second hole is a 235-metre par-4, with rough on the left, and the ocean if you drive too far left. For good measure, many poorly struck tee-shots succumb to the swamp on the right. The saucer-shaped green is the greenkeeper's delight; he often derives great joy in placing the pin on the 'slippery' slope. (Photograph by Perry Cho).**

The New Deal and the democratisation of golf

Kevin Kenny

Pulitzer Prize winner Carl Degler believed that the Great Depression of the 1930s rivalled the Civil War for its cataclysmic impact on US society and came close to 'overturning the basic institutions of American life'.[27] While the opportunities for food and employment were among the casualties to which Degler referred, leisure activities, such as golf, also suffered. However, while the Depression impacted on many aspects of the game, it will be argued here that the 1930s also saw golf attract new converts to the game. That this happened was in no small way due to the New Deal policies of Franklin Delano Roosevelt (FDR).

When writing about the Depression era, America's pre-eminent golf historian, Herbert Warren Wind, suggested that, 'beginning in 1937, professional golf grad-uated into big business'.[28] However, if the professional game made progress, it is clear that other areas of golf suffered, such as membership numbers, which fell by up to sixty-five per cent.[29] This was not surprising considering the drop in disposable income compared to the prosperous 1920s when golf boomed and when many golfers belonged to more than one club.

In addition to the impact on club membership, golf architects suffered greatly with fewer new courses being built and with many existing courses closing. Sure, the Alister Mackenzie-designed Augusta National opened in 1932, but the picture appeared bleak. Even the prolific and successful Scots-born golf-course architect Donald Ross, whose resume included Pinehurst Number Two and Oakland Hills—and whose company once had 3,000 employees—saw his business dramatically reduced.

However, the golf-course design business was to receive a boost from an unlikely source: FDR's New Deal. After his first election victory in 1932 (he would win three more), Roosevelt was charged with the responsibility of restoring prosperity and hope to Americans. The New Deal was a milestone in US history as the Federal Government abandoned laissez faire policies and actively took control of the economy. With unemployment running at almost twenty-five per cent—it was just three per cent, nationally, in 1929—the main aim of the New Deal was to get Americans back to work. One of the many initiatives introduced, and among the most successful, was the Works Progress Administration (WPA) of 1935. This scheme was headed by Harry Hopkins, who argued that 'hunger is not debatable' and whose brief was to 'provide millions of jobs quickly'.[30] Hopkins and his team achieved their aims, often by recruiting

OPPOSITE **Asheboro Municipal Golf Course, North Carolina, USA:** Formally opened in May 1937, Asheboro was at that time the only course between Greensboro, and perhaps the most famous of all Donald Ross courses, Pinehurst. Asheboro remains a nine-hole course and has kept the classic Ross features of some bowl-shaped greens. It has stayed true to its roots, with green fees priced at just fourteen to twenty-four dollars, inclusive of a cart. (Photograph courtesy of Asheboro.)

unskilled labour. By the time the WPA ceased operations during the Second World War, it had left a lasting legacy of bridges, roads and schools.

That leisure was also part of this initiative was no great shock, given that Roosevelt was a sports fan who believed that games benefited Americans, 'physically, mentally and morally'.[31] In this regard, an ambitious program was devised that would provide employment and, simultaneously, offer sporting facilities. Many swimming pools were built and the WPA also started a circus—at one time, it gave work to a young acrobat called Burt Lancaster.

Part of this program also included the construction of hundreds of new golf courses. Despite the fact that this initiative came under the heading of Public Works, some courses were private, such as Prairie Dunes, which later held both the Curtis Cup and the US Women's Amateur Champion-ship. Southern Hills was another, which hosted both the PGA and US Open Championships. Perry Maxwell, who designed many courses on the WPA program, was responsible for both of these courses.

However, most of the WPA-constructed golf courses were municipal; either by design or by chance, it fitted neatly into Roosevelt's aim of creating a more egalitarian society. While golf had begun to cross class boundaries ever since ex-caddie Francis Ouimet's seminal US Open victory of 1913, the 'Country Club' image remained very much part of US golf. In this climate, well-designed courses where you could turn up and play would make golf more accessible and more affordable for the average American.

A prominent example of the municipal program was The Mark Twain Course at Elmira (NY) designed by Donald Ross. Located near the author's birth place, the course opened in May 1937 with an exhibition four-ball that included Walter Hagen. As with other WPA projects, Elmira did not just house a golf course; the project also comprised a pavilion, shower room and a pro-shop complete with living quarters. It was also a feature of many WPA clubs that both men's *and* women's changing rooms were built. Ross also designed municipal courses at Asheboro, North Carolina, as well as the George Wright course in the working class district of Hyde Park, Boston.

A. W. Tillinghast, of Baltusrol and Winged Foot fame, also became involved in the WPA program when his regular design work dried up. His most notable project was at Bethpage, New York, in the mid-1930s. While there is debate as to whether he or course superintendent, Joe Burbeck, had more influence in the creation of the 2002 US Open venue, Bethpage Black, there is no doubt that Tillinghast was heavily involved in this ambitious WPA venture which saw five courses built.

Texas also profited from the WPA program with the opening of Houston's Memorial Park in 1936. The noted golf-course architect John Bredemus, who also co-designed Ben Hogan's Colonial with Perry Maxwell, was responsible for the project, which saw 500 men employed. The course officially opened in June 1936, with green fees set at thirty-five cents on weekdays and fifty cents at weekends. In general, the cost of golf at WPA courses ranged from twenty-five cents for nine holes, to thirty-five/fifty cents for the full round. Determining exact levels of disposable income during this time is difficult, but with the monthly rates of pay for WPA workers ranging from forty dollars (unskilled) to seventy-five dollars (skilled), it seems safe to suggest that a weekly round of golf was an affordable pastime for many.

Overall, the scale of the WPA golf initiative can best be gauged by the following statistic: in 1936 alone, 247 projects were ongoing in forty states—from Florida to Montana, from New Jersey to Oregon. These comprised new layouts and the updating of existing courses. The government's golfing expenditure during this landmark year was five-and-a-half-million dollars.[32]

With all of these new and affordable courses being built, it was important that tuition in golf was available to the new golfers. It is worth recalling, therefore, that many of the WPA projects included professional shops where teaching was on offer. At the Donald Ross-designed Asheboro, for example, Henry Mills was appointed professional in 1937. Perhaps, more importantly, local government initiatives were also designed to kindle interest in golf. For example, Cincinnati's Public Recreation Commission, along with the *Cincinnati Daily Post*, sponsored golf lessons in schools, community centres and industrial plants. These lessons ranged from a lecture on the history of the game, to putting, and according to *Golfdom* magazine, such programs were instrumental in seeing 11,500 players registered on the city's two municipal courses in 1936 compared to a figure of 4,000 in 1934.[33]

Apart from the impact the WPA had on creating golf courses and in stimulating interest in the game, there were also spin-offs for the equipment industry. Clearly, more people playing the game meant more demand for clubs and balls. One of the first to see the possibilities was A. G. Spalding & Bros when, in May 1936, it sent Horton Smith, Jimmy Thomson and Lawson Little on an exhibition tour. According to company Vice-President Milton Reach, it was aimed at the 'democratisation of golf'. Bob Jones, Spalding's signature player, backed this effort, which took place almost exclusively at public courses, claiming 'the potential development of public course jobs for pros qualified to expertly operate a public utility, legitimate promise of millions of dollars increase in pro income during the next decade'.[34] Jones spoke from a position of some feeling here, as he consulted personally with Harry Hopkins on the WPA golf program. Indeed, in his view, affordable golf was one sure way to popularise the game.[35] While there is little doubt that this initiative was a smart piece of marketing aimed at promoting Spalding goods, the use of the word 'democratisation' fitted perfectly with the mood of the time.

The success of these marketing strategies aimed at new converts to the game must be viewed against the economic background of the 1930s and the considerable drop in disposable incomes. However, there is little doubt that the growth in the number of municipal courses, and the resultant demand for clubs and balls, helped equipment companies survive the Great Depression.

In April 1940, journalist Bob Considine promoted Roosevelt for The Vardon Trophy for his services to golf and suggested that the President had helped create a new average US player, 'John Doe, successor to John Dough'.[36] These claims may seem extravagant and, of course, Roosevelt was not eligible for the Vardon award—which went to the golf professional with the lowest scoring average for the year. In any event, Roosevelt received his own stamp of approval from the golfing community when a WPA-funded municipal course in Philadelphia was named in his honour.[37] However, it is fitting that the man who delivered a New Deal for Americans was also the architect of a project that brought about a new deal for US golfers.

Bending the 'rules' to cut construction costs

Edwin Roald

How much does it cost to build a golf course? This is the million dollar question—or is it? Every golf-course architect has been asked this often enough to establish some kind of an auto-reply—a patent answer that comes in handy in social gatherings or in the meeting room.

Clients differ in their knowledge of the game and their background. Those who have little or no idea of the intricacies of this fascinating game want to have an understanding or to be assured that they are getting a first-class product. They perhaps feel uneasy about the very thing that makes golf so unique: the fact that no two golf courses are alike, or should not be alike. The process would, in many ways, be easier for them if a golf course

had predetermined dimensions such as an Olympic swimming pool, in which case very specific details need to be fulfilled.

Also, clients want to know how their golf course can achieve a so-called 'international standard'. This term is not dissimilar from the common, yet tedious label: 'championship golf course'. This, they ask, while labouring under the impression that golf courses are likely to have some kind of a star rating like hotels and restaurants, and that certain standards are to be followed in their construction. They are often baffled to hear my reply, because there are absolutely no standards. Nothing is written in stone, or is it?

If there is a standard, I believe most will agree that a golf course is required to have

eighteen holes so it may gain acknowledgement among keen and 'knowing' golfers. Still, it is important to stress that countless golf courses throughout the world with fewer holes, mostly nine-hole courses, remain immensely popular.

There is a key positive point that is becoming increasingly helpful. Golf courses that are less expensive to build are gaining more recognition among the world's best. In this regard, Sand Hills in Nebraska has been a huge contributor.

Case study: Geysir Golf Club

In the summer of 2003, I was contacted by a small family that to this day runs a guesthouse across the narrow winding country road from

OPPOSITE **Geysir Golf Club, Haukadalur, Iceland:** A nine-hole layout, Geysir's Out-and-Back routing turns inwards after the par-3 fifth—a hole played diagonally across the Almenningur river. (Photograph by Einar Tryggvason.)

The Great Geysir, the world-renowned geothermal spring in Haukadalur, South Iceland. They wanted to build a nine-hole golf course on their twenty-hectare property.

The size and shape of the property provided little flexibility in routing the golf course. Opting for an 'out' and 'in' layout—a la The Old Course, St Andrews—was necessary. The existing vegetation, consisting of small-scale moss mounds and bumpy terrain covered with heather, wildflowers and shrubs, gave the property a great deal of character. The dominance of moss was a challenge, since it is prone to 'swallow' golf balls straying off-track and beyond the limits of the fairways and adjacent semi-rough.

Since we were focused on keeping construction and running costs to a minimum, we had to flirt with the fine line between playability and difficulty. A nine-hole par-3 course was discussed, but this option was less appealing to the owners. After identifying attractive green sites that could be linked together with the guest house at the start and finish of the round, we proceeded to clear the existing vegetation in the playing corridors,

giving nature the benefit of doubt wherever it arose.

We were hopeful that with each round played, the moss content in the native rough would gradually decrease, or that it would compact and firm up under the feet of golfers. This would increase the player's chance of finding his/her golf ball. Now, in the third playing season after opening, this seems to be coming to fruition. The severity of penalty resulting from an inaccurate shot is gradually decreasing, allowing us to keep grassed areas to a minimum. The existing vegetation needs little maintenance as long as fertiliser does not filter into it. The result is a golf course that can be mown by one person in a single day using a ride-on mower.

Our logic was that it was better to remove too little existing vegetation than too much. This way we could enjoy the benefit of seeing how the course played, and then widen the fairways if necessary. Doing it the other way around would be much more expensive.

The biggest cost factor in the construction of Geysir Golf Club was in the earthworks needed to prepare the tees, of which there are

three sets per hole, and greens. When the design relies almost entirely on existing topography, irrigation, drainage and the acquisition of the right materials for the construction of tees and greens usually rank among the highest cost items.

Making irrigation hard enough

In Northern Europe, fescues are among the most suitable golf turf grass species. Their dominance in the sward over other species is best encouraged by keeping fertility and irrigation at modest levels. An automatic irrigation system, therefore, is not vital for turf health. If anything, it increases the risk of overwatering; although it is accepted that it will help germination and the 'grow-in' phase tremendously.

At Geysir, no automatic sprinklers were installed. We only established pipe infrastructure that could deliver water to a hose point near each green; in most cases we relied on the use of a mobile petrol-powered pump to deliver water directly from the rivers to a nearby green. This is only used in extreme situations. Still, during the dry summer of 2008, it was never used. One can say that making irrigation 'too much bother'—under low to moderate foot traffic—is the way to successfully grow fescues.

When designing a drainage system for Icelandic golf courses on reasonably porous soils, the emphasis should be on getting rid of rain and melting ice and snow during winter, rather than rain during the summer, since it simply does not come in the same volumes as further south in the world. Inlets or catch basins are, therefore, the logical solution.

However, any pipe infrastructure connecting these inlets and channelling water to a desirable exit or storage point is expensive. At Geysir, we found that there was a layer of fine gravel and coarse sand at a depth of two to six metres depth below the surface. Instead of installing pipes, we drilled approximately twenty-five holes extending into this layer, insulating them with PVC-pipe and backfilling with gravel. This is a technique that we are repeating on at least one project in Eastern Europe, where winters are not unlike what global warming seems to be bringing to Iceland in the off-season.

Geysir: Brother to The Great Geysir, Strokkur gets ready to erupt and throw massive volumes of boiling water high into the air—an occurrence that is guaranteed to happen while playing the last two holes at Geysir. (Photograph by Einar Tryggvason.)

Geysir: Acceptance of a few blind shots opened-up new possibilities when routing of the course. For many players, the tee-shot on the eighth hole is the highlight of the round—a not surprising fact, given the crashing sound of the Almenningur river and spectacular Mt Bjarnarfell in the background. (Photograph by Frimann B. Baldursson.)

Geysir: Although cost effective, construction of the course still required substantial earthmoving, such as importing soil to place on top of the rocky terrain occupied by the second green as well as third tees and fairway. (Photograph by Einar Tryggvason.)

Home-made greens

The most important attribute of any golf course is the quality of its greens. Therefore, the main focus at Geysir was on the construction of the greens. It was clear that building greens strictly to the USGA specification would dwarf other cost items in the project. None of the materials we ended up using conformed to USGA specifications. On the adjacent property we found sand that had good enough particle size distribution and other key attributes for effective grass growth, given the anticipated traffic volume.

At Geysir, there is no herringbone drainage pattern in the compacted soil base underneath. The construction profile of the greens is 700 millimetres deep. This is a depth we determined necessary to get below the 'frost-line', namely, the depth to which frost is likely to reach in the ground during winter. Throughout Iceland, winter heaving—the uneven lifting of the surface due to frost—is common. The gravel, which we found on-site, was poured into the green cavity to a thickness of 400 millimetres. Then, to prevent the finer particles in the root zone from filtering into the gravel, an intermediate layer was used. This we took from left-over material from nearby roadworks.

The greens were then established by seeding. Most importantly, this method of greens construction has given the client a medium to grow in and manage greens to a high standard. The Geysir greens have received special mention and praise from a large portion of those who have played the course.

Acceptance of the occasional 'blind' shot

The topography and terrain of the property seemed to lend itself to the holes having the following par sequence: five; five; four; four;

three; four; three; four; five—a par of thirty-seven and, therefore, seventy-four over eighteen holes. Attempting to reach a more conventional layout would most likely have resulted in extensive earthworks and longer walks from green to tee. A decision was also made to accept the two 'blind' tee-shots that the routing included; the more significant of the two, being the drive on the eighth hole. Interestingly, feedback suggests that this tee-shot has become the highlight of the round for many players. In the more detailed design, we made sure all grassed areas could be cut with a ride-on mower. Also, we decided to grass all walkways. If they got worn out, we would introduce a suitable substitute. This is a positive problem occurring from increased traffic. The total number of sand bunkers on the course is less than an average of one-per-hole: seven!

At Geysir, we weren't reinventing the wheel, and nobody involved there will claim to have done so. We had many things going our way on this project; what we did on-site would be virtually impossible in many climates. Still, the bottom line is that we built a nine-hole golf course that continues to increase in popularity—and we did it for amounts lower than the price of an average home. We did it by keeping our eyes, ears and minds open.

Fescue to the rescue

Among all the factors that contributed to the cost savings in the construction of Geysir Golf Club, the climate, perhaps, is the dominant one. The ability to grow and successfully manage fescues was a key element in our quest to keep the expenditure manageable. In northern latitudes, more experts are arriving at the conclusion that fine fescues are the future. This choice of species and cultivars is part of their recommended approach; namely, to rely mostly on cultural practices in an effort to control weeds and disease, instead of the application of chemicals.

This prompts one to wonder if northern latitudes—including the coastlines of the North Atlantic and other maritime climates in similar latitudes—have potential to become the golfer's 'paradise' of the twenty-first century. Could it become one of few places on Earth where the stand-alone golf course will be economically viable? Applying the approach outlined in this essay, where applicable—and assuming the greater creative freedom and more flexible land use involved in the design of such a facility—it is not unreasonable to conclude that this region will have increased chances to attract a lot more players in the future, both domestic players and visitors from abroad.

Links lessons vital to the future of US golf

Tim Liddy

Although many Americans profess a huge love for links golf—the traditional game the Scots gave to the world more than half a millennium ago—the simple truth is that very few of us actually understand what it is, how to fully appreciate it, or have any idea of just how important it is to the game of golf around the world. This has become very clear to me in recent years while working in Scotland with increased exposure to the 'real' game and understanding its relevance to golf on the wider front.

For most Americans, experience of links golf is a much-looked-forward-to trip to Scotland or Ireland that involves an organised (but usually manic) chase around a few of the icons of links golf—a trip digitally recorded for posterity or for 'bragging rights' for the boys and girls back home. Inevitably, it will have been hugely enjoyable but the truth is that, at best, it's largely a superficial experience. A few rounds on great links courses will set the golfing juices flowing but they cannot begin to unlock an understanding of what this form of the game is really all about.

There isn't enough time to truly appreciate that links golf is one of Nature's great gifts: seaside dunes tumbling down to the shoreline; the colouring of brown fescue; dark green gorse and purple heather against the rumpled green (and often brown) fairways. And what a singular experience is the firm turf under foot: immediately broadcasting a well-executed iron shot through the fingertips, the hands and arms, and directly into the soul. Centuries-old links golf has much to teach us about golf in the United States, and elsewhere, but I am afraid we are not listening.

What I had not realised until I became immersed in the best of Scottish golf, was just how vital the lessons of links golf and links golf-course architecture are to the future of golf in the United States, and elsewhere. Links, with their sandy soil, firm turf and natural features can teach us as much today as when they originated over 500 years ago. Scottish-based golf writer, Malcolm Campbell, so elegantly captures this in *The Scottish Golf Book*. He states:

> With few exceptions, golf in Scotland has remained true to the traditional principles of the game handed down over the generations. There are, thankfully, few

examples of the tricked-up wares of self-styled architects—mostly, it has to be said, American—who arrogantly proclaim their creations as 'Scottish-style' championship links, when, in fact, they are as often as not nothing more than vaguely planned dumpings of dirt that turn honest countryside into fields of upturned egg-boxes to boost the sales of real estate.

From the virtues of sustainability in their maintenance practices, playability for all levels of golfers and providing affordable golf, the United States, I am sorry to say, is lagging far behind. Al Gore has tried to open our eyes to the future perils for our planet and the limited resources at our disposal. Golf in the United States has not answered the call. We still routinely irrigate over a million gallons daily on many of our golf courses. Our repeated failure is to judge the maintenance of these courses—on something akin to a 'scale of green'—inappropriately against the most artificial golf course *ever built*, Augusta National. Perhaps it's more accurate to suggest: *ever maintained*. We have reached the point, in my view, where many searching

questions now have to be asked. Among them: is this high maintenance, artificial form of the game sustainable? Is US golf now too expensive as a result? Are we making it harder for future generations to enjoy this great game?

There is a horrible irony at play: being 'green' in golf is not the same as being 'green' in other aspects of the environment. In the United States, dormant Bermuda grass is the closest playing condition to links turf than any other grass in the southern United States; yet while we continually profess to want to emulate Scottish or Irish links golf, we consistently overseed dormant Bermuda to achieve soft, green conditions for the winter golfer—an expensive and grotesquely wasteful use of resources.

Sustainability should be the new buzz word for golf in the United States. For lessons in sustainability we need to look to the origins of the game. British links have been sustainable for centuries requiring little or no water, low fertilisation and low maintenance costs. This explains, in a nutshell, why Scotland still enjoys inexpensive golf. And were it the opposite, golf participation would not be the

national pastime it is.

Which begs another question: how much is a round of golf actually worth—$50, $100, $200? If we could follow the example set by links golf courses, our maintenance cost would be hugely reduced; our development of golf courses would be less costly; and our green fees rates would go down significantly! And the benefits to the environment would be considerable.

The agronomic characteristics of links turf—dry, lean and firm—trumpet proper maintenance practices developed over many centuries. There is no *Poa trivialis* on a links golf course—emblematic of too much irrigation and fertilisation. *Poa trivialis*, an annual bluegrass commonly referred to as poa, is prominent in overwatered golf courses in the United States. It invades because superintendents, fearful for their jobs, overwater their golf courses in an attempt to keep their courses 'Augusta'-green and their members living an egotistical and unsustainable dream. It is a regime that allows poa to overtake the drought-tolerant bents originally planted. Once the poa is established the superintendent is stuck with overwatering to keep what is essentially a weed, alive.

With poa endemic on your golf course it is time to look seriously at maintenance practices. It will take time, maybe years, to fully eradicate the infestation, but less water and fertiliser minimises disease growth, allows the bent grasses to return and provides a firm, sturdy turf—ideal for golf and essential for sustainable golf.

Links fairways in Scotland, for the most part, are not green in the summer. They turn, instead, a golden tan colour in dry conditions with only a hint of green; and yet they remain not only alive and healthy but provide a wonderful surface from which to play. Minimal watering of putting surfaces, applied only in the driest conditions, ensures greens remain firm and fast.

Playability for all levels of golfers is an important characteristic of a links. Because of the way golf developed—heightened by the arrival of the Haskell rubber-core golf ball around 1902—golf 'more on the ground' was an integral part of the design strategy of the early links. The ability to play golf 'less through the air' adds greatly to the enjoyment of the game for the average player, while offering more options for the better player. It also encourages an improvement in skill levels.

Yardage means nothing as the variable wind and firm conditions provide a test that is different every day. Five sets of tees are simply not needed; primarily, because yardage differences are not as important without the forced carries and target golf so prevalent in the modern United States-led version of the game.

The Old Course at St Andrews, for example, was brilliantly set up to match the dry conditions of the 2000 Open. Fairways rolled, in some cases, faster than the greens! These conditions defended the golf course against the power-hitters. Tee-shots travelled to the edges of the fairways where serious hazards awaited, while approach shots to firm greens had to be played from the right place in the fairway. Course management was just about the whole story, from a playing perspective.

Tiger Woods, the eventual clear winner, displayed wonderful strategic skills throughout the event, best exemplified by his tee-shot at the twelfth hole (Heathery). Here, a 'moonscape' of bunkers dot the fairway on this short par-4, where finding a safe placement for the drive is critical. Woods, with his tremendous power, opted to defend against the hazards—not by laying up short that would leave a difficult and unpredictable second to a severely contoured green—by launching a driver over the green and beyond all the fairway/approach hazards. This left him a relatively easy chip back from beyond the green, eliminating the need to negotiate the fairway hazards, the pot-bunker and a severe tier at the front of the green. It was the stroke of a master who had absorbed the essence of the game of golf as it is played under links conditions—the original and purest form of the game.

Alister Mackenzie in *The Spirit of St Andrews* outlined the playability of the Old Course with his diagram of the fourteenth hole (Long), illustrating four alternative routes in playing the same hole. The route varies daily depending on a golfer's ability, the hole-location on the green and the prevailing breeze. Strategy is paramount and decisions that will have major impact on success or potentially embarrassing failure have to be made on this hole before any shot is played. Circumstances and, therefore, decisions change quickly. The art of playing links golf is to appreciate the first and be able to respond with the second.

At its best golf is a chess game with different pieces and a different board every day. It requires as much, and perhaps more, skill and strategy than power. In the United States, by contrast, we play only one way. We fly the ball to the green, making golf a one-dimensional game.

Clearly it is not possible to have golf links everywhere; there has to be compromise. However, the guiding principles of the traditional form of the game in terms of sustainability and all-year playability are just as relevant to every golf course, regardless of the climate or latitude.

Minimum water and fertilisation is paramount and many inland golf courses on heavy soils would benefit from understanding and employing this sound agronomic principle. Understanding the importance of top-dressing heavy soils with sand; understanding that poa is the hallmark of too much water and fertiliser; understanding that green is not always the preferred colour on a golf course ... are vital lessons to the future of sustainable golf in the United States.

Many golf courses throughout the world, including the heathland golf courses of England, such as Sunningdale and Swinley Forest as well as Golf de Morfontaine in France and Royal Melbourne and Kingston Heath in Australia, extol these virtues. Putting superb design to one side—that is why they are great golf courses and why they continue to stand the test of time.

To remain relevant, golf in the United States must take on its competition. Golf can offer solitude and natural elegance against the crass, modern society—a private experience instead of mass media. But we need to stop building artificial golf courses with cart paths, range finders (and other nuisance gadgets) and yardage markers. If we drive our golf cart and play to yardages all day, why not just play to targets on a driving range. What is the difference?

To compete in today's society golf needs to offer the antithesis of today's society, not a reflection of it. Golf links provide the natural, sustainable model for a healthy outdoor exercise that, in the words of David R. Forgan, son of the famous St Andrews clubmaker, 'affords the opportunity to play the man and act the gentlemen'. Or, as Malcolm Campbell states: 'It opens up the joys of the great outdoors, the chance to pit one's skill against nature, an opponent and most importantly, one's self'.

It is the principle of working *with nature*, not *against it*, and it's becoming increasingly vital to the future of golf in the United States that we understand the underlying message and act upon it before it is too late.

Figure 1

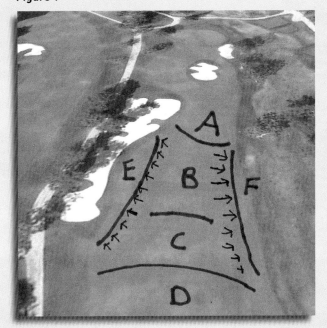

Figure 2

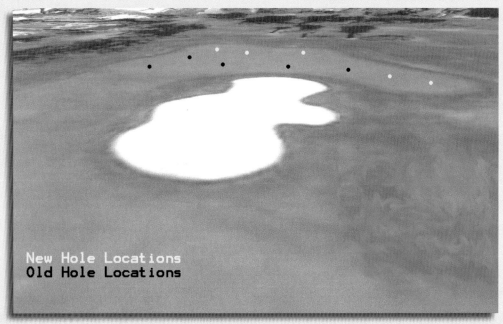

Riviera Country Club, California, USA: Figure 1 depicts how the tee-shot options at the par-4 seventh hole have increased following Tom Fazio's design work; both in numbers, and in complexity. The combination of the new camel-back fairway grading, the restoration of the barranca right of the fairway and a previously existing fairway bunker ('lost' many years ago), now presents six options from the tee—each, of which, possesses varying risks and rewards to consider. (Copyright Google, with illustration by Sam Kestin.)

Riviera: Figure 2 shows the additional opening green hole-locations created by Tom Fazio's design firm. The enlarged pockets of green in the front-right, back-centre and left allow for a gaggle of new hole-locations that dictate different lines of play on lay-up second shots. All of this, of course, is geared toward obtaining an ideal approach angle for the third shot. (Copyright Google, with computer graphics by Sam Kestin.)

The 'new' Riviera Country Club, USA

Sam Kestin

Though he visits the venue annually at the PGA Tour's Northern Trust Open, Steve Elkington will never again get a chance to duplicate what he called 'the round of my life'[38]: a blistering sixty-four in Sunday's final round of the 1995 PGA Championship at Riviera Country Club. That day, Elkington rolled in an eight-yard birdie putt on the final green to win the Wannamaker Trophy in a playoff over Colin Montgomerie. Fourteen years later, the eighteenth hole is just one of fifteen holes at storied Riviera that have undergone changes in the years since his winning putt.

Leaving only the second, fourth and sixteenth holes untouched, the club has narrowed some fairways, reconfigured a number of greens, added new tees, and repositioned and regraded many of the bunkers. In some cases, entire holes have been recreated to old designs that hadn't existed on the grounds for decades. The changes, most of which were planned and executed by Tom Fazio's design firm, have been greeted with mixed feelings. Riviera's Head Professional, Todd Yoshitake, bills the effort, 'a restoration of the intent of George Thomas's original design',[39] while others feel that the changes are out of character with the golf course as it was designed.

The critics' assault on the work at Riviera as 'out-of-character' prompts one to pause and consider exactly how to define the character of Riviera Country Club. For guidance, let's turn to the most basic principle espoused by the course's famed designer, George C. Thomas Jr. Thomas believed, above all else, that 'the strategy of the golf course is the soul of the game'.[40] Analysing the 'new' Riviera, there-fore, we should scrutinise first and foremost the strategic impact of the changes the club has made. To that end, one must take note of the effect of the alterations on the course's various strategic and tactical examinations.

Many of the changes made to Riviera serve to increase the number and importance of the golfers' choices between options. At each changed hole, alterations have increased the penalty of failure, or value of success, for many different playing tactics. Specifically, the changes to the drive at seventh hole pro-vide an excellent illustration of this principle.

In 1995, Elkington played this short, dog-leg-right par-4 with the fairway defended on the left by rough—blocked out behind three eucalyptus trees—and on the right by some rough and a bunker rendered obsolete by technology. The aggressive play then was a

OPPOSITE **Riviera Country Club, California, USA: a snap-shot of two of the key changes made by Tom Fazio to this storied layout.**

270-yard drive bleeding from left to right, between the right rough and the trees on the left. Those who erred were either blocked out by the trees on the left—from where a shot would be manufactured up to the green, and the cross bunker some forty-five yards from the green's front edge would become a factor—or forced to gouge a ball out of the unpredictable rough on the right. Golfers who succeeded in hitting the 'proper' shot were gifted a shorter approach to the green from a better angle. The golfer who declined the option of taking on this challenging tee-shot route could lay back from the trees with a safer club and be spared the burden of shaping the tee-shot at the expense of a having to hit a longer club into the small, contoured green.

Today, the seventh hole has grown in complexity, as depicted in *Figure 1*. The combination of the new camel-back fairway grading, the restoration of the barranca right of the fairway and a previously existing fairway bunker ('lost' in a flood over fifty years ago), now demands the player choose between six different options—each of which possesses varying risks and rewards. The ideal drive at present (to 'A' in the diagram) is still one that drifts to the right, but now it must cover 290–295 yards. The reward is still a shorter

approach and better angle. The new risk, however, is a lost ball in the right-side hazard, or one that is found but draws a horrid lie behind a tree. Others may gamble upon a tee-shot that challenges the left bunker; with this attack, one's ball may nestle too close to one of the many fingers and tongues that Fazio's crew installed—leaving the golfer unable to reach the green.

The golfer who elects not to take on the biggest risk at 'A' can settle for 'B' in the diagram. This fairway position can be attained by various shot-patterns; one must ensure the tee-shot is not overly shaped to the right, as a ball landing at 'F' in the diagram will most likely find the right hazard. A tee-shot curving excessively to the left and landing at 'E' will, most likely, find the perilous left bunker. Highly conservative golfers can play to the 'fatter' parts of the fairway at 'C' and 'D'. On face-value, position 'C' would appear preferable to 'D' (being closer to the hole), yet it presents golfers with a greater possibility of drawing an uneven lie. Two other options: a 250–270 yard fade to 'E', or a similar distance draw to 'F', provide different angles, with 'F' providing a good angle into the green but the lowest chance of a flat lie. Both 'E' and 'F' have the advantage of gambling the least with

the camel-back down the centre of the fairway, but the disadvantage of being so close to the nearby hazards.

An increase in the complexity of Riviera's strategic choices, such as those described on the seventh hole, is also experienced following changes to the tee-shots at the eighth, ninth, fifteenth and seventeenth holes. The new eighth, for instance, is a restoration of Thomas's original double-fairway hole, which presents the player with three options spread across two fairways. The added Championship tee on the ninth hole extends the par-4 by some forty yards, and now presents the three options originally prescribed for the hole. The repositioning of tees and fairway bunkers at the fifteenth and seventeenth holes restore and create choices (and challenges) similar to the ones presented at the ninth hole due to its new tee and existing bunker positions. Previously, fairway bunkers on both the fifteenth and seventeenth holes no longer encroached far enough into the landing-zone to influence the tee-shot strategy for championship-calibre golfers.

Changes at all the par-5s—recontoured and reconfigured green sites at the first, eleventh and seventeenth hole—create variety in the daily tactics employed on these holes. At the first hole, newly created back-left and front-right hole locations require the third shot to be played from the right side of the lay-up area, while the new, back-centre hole location demands the approach to be played from the left side (*Figure 2*). Similarly, new hole locations in the front right and back right of the eleventh green examine the ability of the golfer to properly place the lay-up shot. For instance, the new right-hand pin locations demand a left-sided approach. At the seventeenth hole, the new back-left hole location requires a right-sided approach, while the front-right and back-right hole locations require a left-sided approach. This harmonious interaction of the new hole locations, and the increased relevance of the greenside bunkers, surely would serve to ease Thomas's usual concern that three-shot par-5s often have weak and unimportant lay-up shots.

Additionally, the green complexes at the third, sixth, eighth, ninth, twelfth and thirteenth holes have been enlarged to create additional hole locations. Many of these new complexes have pin positions that require varying trajectories to attain a birdie opportunity; thereby, creating a tactical advantage for the golfer who has the ability to place a variety of shots with varying shapes and trajectories.

In addition to being created for the sake of preserving Thomas's original strategic intent, new tees built at Riviera's fifth, sixth, eighth, ninth, twelfth, thirteenth, fifteenth, seventeenth and eighteenth holes enable the length of the golf course to be commensurate with the contemporary golf ball. These additions strengthen Riviera's total yardage from 6,946 yards—as it was presented during the 1995 USPGA Championship—to 7,279 yards. Many of these new tees restore the club selection decisions faced on approach shots by those who tamed Riviera in the past. In 1950, for instance, Sam Snead came to the eighteenth tee needing a birdie to defeat Ben Hogan in that year's emotionally charged Los Angeles Open—Hogan's comeback tournament following the near-fatal automobile accident he'd experienced in early 1949. Snead hit a solid drive and a well-executed one-iron to finish off the 'Hawk'. By the late 1990s, however, Riviera's home hole had been reduced by technology to a driver and a mid-iron, or less, for championship participants. Today, a new tee stretches the hole to nearly 480 yards and, once again, dictates the green be approached in the same arduous manner demanded of men like Snead and Elkington in the past.

Despite the criticisms of many, the 'soul of the game' that Thomas held so dear is far from absent at the 'new' Riviera. The strategic problems posed to the golfer at Riviera today, can be aligned, as an analogy, to updated versions of the Scholastic Aptitude Test (SAT) or Law School Admissions Test (LSAT) faced by US undergraduates during entrance exams. Those tests, every few years, have been refurbished with new questions, but the ethos of their examinations remains intact. Likewise, at Riviera, some test questions have changed, but Thomas's strategic ethos remains alive and well. Indeed, let's allow the famous architect of Riviera to have the final say:

The spirit of golf is to dare a hazard,
and by negotiating it reap a reward,
while he who fears or declines the issue
of carry, has a longer or harder shot for
his second, or his second or third on
long holes; yet the player who avoids
the unwise effort gains advantage over
one who tries for man than in him lies,
or fails under the test.[41]

Four Mile Ranch Golf Club, USA

Four Mile Ranch Golf Club is a daily-fee golf course located in Canon City, Colorado. The Jim Engh-designed layout opened for public play in July 2008.

The golf course is the centrepiece of a new residential community in Central Colorado. This region, affectionately known as the 'Banana Belt' of Colorado, features 325 days of sunshine a year and has a much milder climate than nearby Denver. Canon City also serves as a gateway to the Rocky Mountains and the famous Royal Gorge, a mile-deep canyon carved by the Arkansas River. Hiking, biking, fishing, skiing and rafting have made Canon City a paradise for outdoor types.

The course flows seamlessly through the spectacular high desert terrain of the front nine and the rugged Pinon Pine mesas of the back nine. Golfers are greeted with views of the Sangre de Christo and Wet Mountains from every hole. With such a breathtaking canvas to work with, Jim Engh felt that traditional bunkers would only distract from the natural beauty. Instead, he went about creating a completely new hazard: the 'hogback'. The 'hogbacks' are small, shale-topped outcroppings and mimic those that appear naturally throughout the site. While intimidating in appearance, golfers will discover that they are more 'bark than bite'.

The par-72 layout plays to 7,053 yards and features five par-3s and five par-5s. Jim Engh's fondness for the seaside links in Ireland is apparent from the first tee-shot at Four Mile Ranch. Perfectly struck drives will disappear into the natural contours of the fairway and the results are only revealed as the golfers get closer to their balls. The topography dictated some 'blind' and partially 'blind' shots; Engh, however, has provided ample room to accommodate most shots. The greens also feature dramatic contouring and so an automatic two-putt is never a given.

Jim Engh has created a golf course that is sure to be talked about for many years to come. Golfers may come, initially, for the course, but they will be equally charmed by the town.

Four Mile Ranch, Colorado, USA: The most conducive second-shot approach angle at the par-4 fifth hole is obtained by driving down the left side of this dramatically sloping fairway. By contrast, driving too far to the right is destined to leave a partially 'blind' second shot to the heavily contoured green. (Photograph by Jim Engh.)

ABOVE LEFT Four Mile Ranch: The opener, an interesting par-4, features a beautiful arroyo which needs to be avoided when approaching its ridgeline green. (Photograph by Jim Engh.)

ABOVE RIGHT Four Mile Ranch: A view of one of three 'Hogbacks' to be negotiated when playing the short, par-4 fourth hole. A deft touch is required around the slightly elevated green. (Photograph by Jim Engh.)

BELOW Four Mile Ranch: At the par-5 fifteenth hole, many golfers will be tempted to go for the green on their second shot-frequently, with only a mid- to long-iron in their hands. The green, however, is completely 'blind' from the fairway; only a second shot with proper trajectory and line will reward those bold enough to give it a go. (Photograph by Jim Engh.)

OPPOSITE Four Mile Ranch: A dramatic thirteenth-hole tee-shot to the wide, tumbling fairway below disguises the difficulty ahead. This par-4's green is protected by a wildly undulating approach and a near twenty-foot fall-off to the right of the putting surface. (Photograph by Jim Engh.)

Four Mile Ranch: The angled green on the par-3 seventeenth hole is tucked into an inviting amphitheatre. The tee-shot is slightly uphill, so determining the correct pin-location will not be easy task. (Photograph by Jim Engh.)

Four Mile Ranch: With a nod to the 'Dell' hole at Lahinch, the green-complex at the par-3 fourteenth hole is 'hidden' in a natural depression. Of note: the green is more than seventy yards wide from left to right, while its sloping surrounds will prove beneficial to most golfers. (Photograph by Jim Engh.)

Growing golf
Ronald Fream

Promoting luxurious golf courses with high costs to play or join is all well and good. This situation will never change. However, if golf is to prosper into the coming decades, more attention must be given to accessibility and affordability.

In many countries, the rate of new golfers entering the game is declining. In some instances, government actions have slowed the creation of new courses. Economic trauma and rising land prices have curtailed new courses in the United States and elsewhere. In India, growing demand is offset by water shortages and land availability. Land cost, competition between housing, agriculture, commercial development and golf, limits the growth of golf. Golf is not a necessity. A worldwide economic slowdown, initiated by the decay of the US housing market, has restricted golf development. After all, in many markets, golf remains a luxury. In too many markets, golf has become so expensive middle-class people are shying away.

If golf is to prosper into the next decade, the industry as a whole must rethink and refocus its priorities. Although long-established as the foundation and basis of golf, country clubs offer only social prestige, exclusivity and a refuge from the less-gifted players found outside its walls. The profitability of these clubs is often not an issue or a concern of members. Selective access is a primary desire.

Private clubs will continue. More and more-expensive clubs will be constructed. Those fortunate enough to earn or inherit ample funds will always prefer to luxuriate in the real and perceived social cocoon of the private golf club exclusivity. Good for them. Social equality does not exist. Some have; some have less; and some have nothing at all.

Money and private clubs do not grow the game. Private clubs often are very exclusionary. One learns and becomes addicted to golf before putting out the fee to join. Once there, more lessons follow to try to reduce one's handicap and inflate the ego. Yes, the children are exposed, but outside and aspiring non-member golfers are not often welcomed.

OPPOSITE **Shore Gate Golf Course, New Jersey, USA:** An aerial of the green-complex at the ninth hole, showing one of the smaller sets of bunkers on this highly popular daily-fee course. (Courtesy of Inkworks, photograph by Chris John.)

To prosper, golf must grow. Those seeking long-term economic benefit from the business of golf must participate in growing the game, expanding usage and bringing formerly disenfranchised players into the pro-shop.

Private clubs with multi-year waiting lists to join bring decline to the game, as their ageing members continue to foster the following illusion: the longer the waiting list; the more prestigious the club. Check the books. At many of these status venues, profitability is rare. So, too, is the much-needed youth golf program.

Two, interrelated avenues to move golf forward exist: public accessibility and affordability. In each case, access must be available to new or aspiring players. In addition, golf must be promoted widely as a tourist/visitor-friendly venue. Access yields more interest and more addicted players. Access will enhance operating profits.

Access will only succeed if affordability co-exists. In the golf boom years of the 1990s, the long-term, cost-to-operate calculations were not always considered. The merit of the new course, alone, was based upon how much was spent—not how well. Spending more money does not assure better playing or a more beautiful course. More money spent raises operating costs, which mandates higher entry or green-fee rates. Higher costs will decrease play in any market.

In some situations, money is no concern. We've seen this with golf development of the past decade in South Korea, or the Tiger Woods virgin effort as a golf architect in Dubai. In these cases, profit is not the motive. If they are not well-connected, access to new, young and senior players at these courses is restrictive or nonexistent.

Into the future, accessible and affordable golf, with long-term profitability as focus, must be the model. Growing the game benefits everyone in the golf industry one way or another. Private clubs will remain and persevere. Open-to-the-public, daily-fee 'pay and play' and resort courses with a welcoming atmosphere, user-friendly service and realistic green-fees, will continue as overpriced country clubs convert to daily fees or disappear. Daily-fee courses created with excessive operating costs are, as a result of losing play due to the high green-fees, in a deal of trouble.

In the hyper-capitalistic economy of the United States, between seventy and seventy-five per cent of all courses operating today are open to the public. These courses, approximately 12,000, are not often municipal or public-agency owned. The exceptions stand out: Torrey Pines and Bethpage Black are 'muni' courses that host the US Open. However, the vast majority are pay-to-play layouts owned by various entities that operate for profit. Something like seventy-five per cent of all golf played in the United States is on publicly accessible courses. This pay and play model is successful in the United Kingdom, too. Pay and play should be the general model.

Creative business men who convert bankrupt private Japanese clubs into daily-fee pay and play courses through insightful management and revised operations bring affordable golf to many now. What may seem a

high greens fee, US$200 or so, is far more affordable than the once higher joining fees.

More evidence emerges as the world economy contracts that high-priced golf is not finding the market demand it once was. The high-priced course, big joining fee or excessive green-fees, are finding fewer takers. The days of 'more is better' in golf only raised prices; it did not raise playing volume. It must be noted, however, that what is an affordable fee in one country may still be considered excessive in another. For many, the current Japanese green-fee scale is still excessive.

To grow golf, and begin producing younger players who will grow old with the game, the accessibility factor is paramount. Getting young people out from in front of a computer or video game will have lasting benefit, perhaps even for national health systems a few decades from now.

With too few daily-fee, pay-to-play courses in Asia, and too many status-driven clubs emerging in Eastern Europe and Russia, access for the up-and-coming wannabes is

Yeti Golf, Fulbari Hotel, Nepal: Across the canyon lies a hand-built golf course—one of the world's most exotic, unique tourist courses—while further beyond is the formidable 8,000-metre Annapurna Massif. (Photograph by Ronald Fream.)

OPPOSITE Pezula: Nature dictated the design solution—the twelfth hole. (Photograph by Juan Espi.)

lacking in many markets. The Russian golf model now is the prestige exclusive club, not daily-fee. In Brazil, its population of about 180 million shares only some eighty-seven golf courses. Demand is limited as clubs are mostly private and joining fees high with few openings available. California with its population of 35 million has some 800 courses.

As the US model demonstrates, the long-term operating profit margin is not with the private club, but resides with the daily-fee

course that is affordable and can also offer a game that attracts travelling and tourist golfers. The problem has been developers who seek quick payoffs, via memberships, and then abandon the course to a barely functioning club management.

Many high-end prestige projects include some form of residential component. A 'name brand' professional golfer-cum-designer attaches his/her signature to the drawing. Great cost is expended. Houses sell, golfers come. But the operating future after all the home sale profits have been consumed remains in question. Will the high investment, high-profile project be self-sustaining into the future?

Hanging a name brand player's image on the signboard at the course or residential community does not guarantee lasting financial success. Playing golf well is no guarantee that the design product attributed to the professional golfer is stylistically original, creative or strategically playable by a twenty handicap golfer. Often, a name brand pro poses, expresses profound admiration, then leaves as soon as possible to visit the next lucrative photograph opportunity. One thing is certain: name brand pro attachment is not beneficial if affordable golf is the goal.

Excessive costs for design, construction and seeking unattainable Augusta National-inspired maintenance drives up long-term costs. Excessive building for the clubhouse eats profits. Fream's law of profitable golf operations is simple: the larger the clubhouse, the smaller the operating profits! Golfers come to play an enjoyable, memo-rable course, not to be overwhelmed by an ostentatious clubhouse.

Creative design solutions are not always the product of the pro player. Original design is the product of artistic and creative talent, not clubhead speed. To be successful, golf must offer something memorable. Too many golf courses are the product of wannabe designers who produce stereotyped, boring copies of some other boring course.

Creative design must be coupled with know-how and experience to build the course for value. By building it right the first time, on budget and on time, it naturally produces what will be an affordable layout to play.

The Tiger Woods Foundation, the USGA First Tee, the Royal & Ancient's Golf Development and even the Bhutan Youth Golf Association help introduce and promote the growth of golf. Not enough entry-level golf access is yet at hand. Bringing the youngsters into the game earlier is an important aspect of the sport's survival.

Excessively priced high-tech club equipment, and costly golf balls, also diminishes the ability to play. There has been no corre-sponding inverse average decrease in players' handicaps as the level of technology and price of golf equipment has risen. Too-high equipment costs; too-high greens fees; and too-few accessible courses are not an omen of health into the future. More expensive equipment has not, and will not, increase employment opportunities in emerging markets.

Tourism is the world's largest single industry. Golfers still number around sixty million—a number that has remained almost flat-lined since the turn of the century. Making golf affordable and accessible makes golf enjoyable and popular.

It is possible to design, build and operate courses that don't require a micro bank loan to buy a green fee. Profitable operations are good for golf. Accessible and affordable facilities will be good for the game.

Golf-course architecture in Wales

Ian Scott-Taylor

When you think and talk about Wales, the imagination takes over: castles; mountains; quaint villages; the Arthurian legend, Merlin; the land of Princes; Rugby, for starters. In fact, there is more to the land of song and Celtic myths; more than the 641 castles and 690 miles of coastline. It's also the undiscovered land of early development in classic British golf-course architecture.

Many of the great British golf-course architects plied their trade in Wales, and even inspired one architect to transport an idea to California. From the Isle of Anglesey in the north to Glamorgan in the south, Wales is full of golf history and golf courses that showcase some of the most spectacular scenery in the world—there are around 200 golf courses to play.

Harry Colt, Tom Simpson, James Braid, the great names are endless a *Who's Who* of famous golf-course architects—culminating in Royal St David's, Aberdovey, Southerndown, Royal Porthcawl and Conway, to name a few courses that sit in the land of song and, not only inspired the architect, but inspire the player and touch the soul of the connoisseur.

With the spray of the sea, or the wind from the mountains, where else can you play golf under an eleventh-century castle, stand on a tee and look down an entire coast line one way, then up the snow-capped Snowdon valley another; play golf where US Masters champion Ian Woosnam and I, as juniors, battled it out for honours (which I lost); tour golf courses where members of the Royal Family played many times; or tackle a golf course that witnessed the Lion of Scotland defeating the Tiger of America and my friend, and Walker Cup captain, Clive Brown's victorious team triumph over the old advisory, America? The golfer can take a car and travel the length and breadth of the principality and not get bored with the next golfing experience, but leave wanting more and breathless with anticipation at the next course.

Where do you start? Well, let's start in the north, where I was raised. Isle of Anglesey—'the Mother of Wales'—is an island that

OPPOSITE **Nefyn Golf Club, Gwynedd, Wales: As part of a twenty-six hole complex, the short par-3 fourteen hole—played from a tee on a stone tower—is not the place to over-club! Golf started at Nefyn as early as 1907, with a course upgrade several years later, followed by the addtion of another nine holes in 1933. (Photograph by David Scaletti.)**

houses four main early designed golf courses among its total of eight. One of my favourites, Holyhead, was built in 1911 by James Braid for the London & North Western Railway. It is short (6,000 yards) by today's standards, but when the wind blows it plays the equivalent of about 7,200 yards.

Holyhead's par-3 fourth hole is just 114 yards and can be a mere 'flick' with a sand-wedge on a calm day—but you always have to be accurate. With bunkers front and left, a plateau green that's about 2,500 square feet, plus out of bounds not more than twelve feet off the back, the hole is far from straightforward. In a strong wind off the Irish Sea, I have hit two drivers and a wedge and still been short of the green. Bull Bay Golf Club is situated on the north of the Island; on the first green, the views of Liverpool Bay and the Skerries Lighthouse are spectacular.

On mainland Wales lies St Deiniol's (James Braid), where standing on the fifteenth tee the golfer can look west down the Llyn Peninsula and east down the coast toward the Great Orme.

Where else can a golfer in the space of a 100-mile circle play golf courses that have been designed by the great architects of the day; where the famous triumvirate of James Braid, J. H. Taylor, and Harry Vardon designed their first and last golf courses; where seaside links, parkland and mountain courses are in abundance, and architectural styles are plentiful and varied; or play courses that show the development of British golf-course architecture from the late 1800s to the present-day US-style course of the 2010 Ryder Cup venue at Celtic Manor in Newport?

The design of British golf courses can be tracked in your trip through Wales, from the early functional designs of tee, fairway and green, to the strategic explosion of the John Low-era, encompassing penal, strategic and the heroic designs that are a staple of today.

In North Wales you have Nefyn and District Golf Club built in 1907 as a nine-holer and extended in 1912. It was here where my grandfather, Dr David Scott-Taylor, brought his guest, Dr Alister Mackenzie, to play one day. The good doctor not only 'lost'

a few pounds for his trouble, but the stretch of holes from the twelfth to the seventeenth inspired Mackenzie to look for land to emulate his Nefyn experience. The fruits of that labour are well known: Cypress Point in California, USA.

In South Wales another member of the famous triumvirate, J. H. Taylor, worked on Ashburnham Golf Club in 1910 and again in 1914. A superb links layout, it tests every club in your bag. This exhibits the penal school of architecture, with later additions made to the design; the bunkering has changed to produce a more strategic layout that still holds the need for a good golfing brain and deft touch around the greens.

Harry Vardon, the last of this illustrious trio, ventured into Wales as early as 1894 at Llandrindod Wells in Mid-Wales. Much of his original course still exists today. This includes his remodelled effort of 1905, and it survives as a great example of pre-strategic golf architecture and, dare I mention, a great pint of beer in the clubhouse! Other courses by Vardon include Aberystwyth (1911) and

Knighton (1908) on the Welsh Marches.

The famous Royal St David's was where the future King of England, Edward the Seventh, was Captain in 1934. It's a fine links design that any budding golf architect should explore, with the golf course following the contours of the land to perfection, and creating one of the finest tests of golf in the United Kingdom under the shadow of Edward the First's mighty Harlech Castle (1190s).

Up the coast a little is Porthmadoc Golf Club; it's here that golfers encounter one of the finest strategic short par-4s in the world. The twelfth hole (a right-to-left dogleg) is played along the shore line of Samson's Bay—you can birdie or double-bogey the hole in the blink of an eye, yet still be left with a smile on your face and a peaceful feeling as you look to the bay with the mountains and the sea breeze in your face. With a modest length of 290 yards, it strikes worry into the player on the tee, even though length is not the premium. A good tee-shot into the fairway is half the battle, as the second shot (a wedge or less) is played to a raised green fraught with danger. A par is a really fine score: take it and breathe again!

As an aficionado and student of golf-course design, Tom Simpson, who co-authored *The Architectural Side of Golf* (1929), embodies all of his theories at Rhos-on-Sea in North Wales and the Glamorganshire and Royal Porthcawl (1937) in South Wales. Simpson also tinkered with the Mid-Glamorgan Golf Club in the same year. Many of his theories outlined in the book are seen to good effect at these clubs.

Another renowned golf-course architect to have designed in Wales is Willie Park Jr. He did so at Brynhill in 1920, along with his remodelling work at the Glamorganshire. The Glamorganshire club is full of history and is a great place to observe Park Jr's architecture in practice. One of the club's famous members was Guy Gibson, the man who commanded the famous Dam Busters raid on Germany during the Second World War. On the night he was awarded the Victoria Cross, he celebrated at the golf club. These two courses are fine examples of Park's work, notably of the penal school. Park Jr, of course, is also famous for being the mentor of Donald J. Ross.

Harry S. Colt is yet another architect to visit Wales, designing Clynne Golf Club (where I played a lot of my college golf), Pyle and Kenfig Golf Club (1922), and St Melons, with famous British golf professional Henry Cotton and Fred Hawtree (1937). Colt was one of the great early architects and his theories on design are again evident on these links designs. Clynne is a course of length and it requires golfers to have a good short game to score well, given its greens. Colt has used the land and local weather conditions to great effect, so visiting this course is a must on your Welsh golfing journey.

A more modern architect than those previously described is Frank Pennink. He remodelled the Caernarvonshire Golf Club (Conway) and designed St Pierre with C. K. Cotton (1962), Cradoc Golf Club (1967) and remodelled Langland Bay (1982). St Pierre is a parkland layout, which hosted the 'Benson and Hedges' event for many years on the European Tour.

While you're in South Wales there are two necessities for golf-course architects. The first is to break from older courses and visit the former home of the founder of the Rolls Royce car company, 'The Rolls of Monmouth'—a fantastic old manor setting for a golf course. Here, one finds heritage and golf all wrapped-up in one. Indulge yourself in the old ways!

The other is Royal Porthcawl—a links akin to a golf architecture museum, as it displays a plethora of architectural styles from famous architects. Porthcawl is also the ideal destination to either start or finish your Welsh adventure. For any golf architect, Wales is a true dictionary of design form—from the very old to the new. And there's always something new that you missed on your last trip.

Endnotes

1. Scott Macpherson, *St Andrews: the Evolution of The Old Course: The Impact on Golf of Time, Tradition & Technology* (Christchurch: Hazard Press, 2007) 29.

2. Bernard Darwin, *Green Memories* (London: Hodder and Stoughton, 1928) 52.

3. Jeff Shelley and Michael Riste, *Championships & Friendships: The First 100 Years of the Pacific Northwest Golf Association* (Seattle: PNGA, 1999) 44.

4. Geoffrey S. Cornish and Ronald E. Whitten, *The Golf Course* (New York: The Rutledge Press, 1988 edition) 216.

5. Royal Colwood Golf Club: www.royalcolwood.org/macan.html (Accessed 1 October 2008).

6. Jeff Shelley and Michael Riste, *Championships & Friendships: The First 100 Years of the Pacific Northwest Golf Association* (Seattle: PNGA, 1999) Shelley and Riste (1999) 43.

7. Arthur Vernon Macan, 'A letter to Green Chair of Overlake Golf Club', 1958.

8. Geoffrey S. Cornish and Ronald E. Whitten, *The Golf Course* (New York: The Rutledge Press, 1988 edition) 216.

9. Royal Queensland Golf Club, Seventh Annual Report and Balance Sheet (extract from Alister Mackenzie's report), 31 January 1927.

10. Ibid

11. Ibid

12. *Golf Magazine*, Sept 2003.

13. Hal Phillips, 'Small Wonder', *Sports Illustrated*, 27 October 1997.

14. Dan Jenkins, 'America's Best 18 Holes', *Golf Digest*, February 2000.

15. Malcolm Gladwell, 'The Ketchup Conundrum', *The New Yorker*, 6 September 2004.

16. Ibid

17. Ibid

18. Walter Hagen, with Margaret Seaton Heck, *The Walter Hagen Story* (London: Heinemann, 1957) 104.

19. Richard Mandell, *Pinehurst: Home of American Golf* (Pinehurst: T. Eliot Press, 2007) 145.

20. Richard Mandell, *Pinehurst: Home of American Golf*, (Manuscript and Notes), 2005.

21. Ron Whitten, 'Donald Ross Wouldn't Recognise these Greens', *Golf Digest*, June 2005.

22. Richard Mandell, *Pinehurst: Home of American Golf* (Manuscript and Notes), 2005.

23. Brad Kocher, 'Slope Map Legends for Pinehurst No. 2', Hobbs, Upchurch and Associates, 1997.

24. Jack Batten, *The Toronto Golf Club, 1876–1976* (Toronto: privately printed by Toronto Golf Club, 1976) 39.

25. Alister Mackenzie, *Golf Architecture* (London: Simpkin, Marshall, Hamilton, Kent & Co., 1920) 23.

26. John L. Low, *Concerning Golf* (London: Hodder & Stoughton, 1903).

27. Carl N. Degler, *Out of Our Past: The Forces That Shaped Modern America* (New York: Harper, 1970) 379.

28. Herbert Warren Wind, *The Story of American Golf: Its Champions and Its Championships* (New York: Farrar, Strauss, 1975) 263 and 272.

29. Ibid, 214.

30. George B. Tindall and David E. Shi, *America: A Narrative History* (New York: W. W. Norton & Company, 1993) 734.

31. Franklin D. Roosevelt, 'The Presidential Papers of Franklin D. Roosevelt' (Item 18), 23 January 1937.

32. *Golfdom*, Oct 1936, 19–20.

33. Ibid, May 1937, 21.

34. *Golfdom*, June 1936, 34.

35. *New York Times*, 8 April 1936.

36. *Golf*, April 1940, 12.

37. The FDR Golf Club, Philadelphia, was opened in the mid-1930 and is still thriving.

38. Larry Dorman, *New York Times*, August 14, 1995.

39. Robert Thomas, *Fore* (Los Angeles: Southern California Golf Association, March/April 2002 issue).

40. George C. Thomas Jr, *Golf Architecture in America, Its Strategy and Construction* (Los Angeles: The Times Mirror Press, 1927) 37.

41. Ibid, 37.

Picture credits

Kimbal Baker: 66; 71 (above); 72 (above); 75 (above); 127 (above); 127 (below); 128; 129; 130; 131 (above); 131 (below)

Frimann B. Baldursson: 295 (below)

Jay Blasi: 98 (set of 12 photographs)

Aidan Bradley: ii; 88; 92–93; 95; 96; 97 (below); 100; 102–103; 104; 108; 109

Tom Breazeale: i; xviii; 2–3; 5; 6 (above); 6 (below); 6–7; 8; 10; 11 (above left); 11 (above right); 11 (below); 12 (above); 12 (below); 13; 14–15

Walt Bukva, Bukva Imaging Group Inc.: 76; 79; 84; 85; 86 (above left); 86 (above right); 86 below; 87

Perry Cho: 194; 195; 196; 197; 198 (above); 198 (below); 199 (above); 199 (below); 282–283; 284; 285; 286; 287 (above left); 287 (above right); 287 (below)

Trevor Colvin: 24; 26 (above left); 26 (above right); 26 (below right); 30 (below)

Courtesy of Asheboro Municipal Golf Course: 288

Courtesy of the Borneo Highlands Resort: xii

Courtesy of Brae Burn Country Club: 142

Courtesy of the California Club of San Francisco: 161; 164 (above left); 164 (above right); 164 (below right); 164 (below left)

Courtesy of Michael Cocking, Michael Clayton Golf Design: 74

Courtesy of Craig Disher: 181 (below); 182 (below)

Courtesy of Foxfield Links: 154 (above)

Courtesy of Ganton Golf Club: 256; 258; 259; 261 (above left); 261 (above right); 261 (below right); 261 (below middle); 261 (below left); 262 (above); 262 (below); 263; 264 (above left); 264 (above right); 264 (below right); 264 (below left); 265; 266

Courtesy of Glenelg Golf Club: x

Courtesy of Golfplan – Fream, Dale & Ramsey: 12 (right)

Courtesy of Hurdzan/Fry Environmental Golf Design: 51 (above); 51 (below); 52; 53 (above); 53 (below); 54 (above); 54 (below)

Courtesy of Inkworks, photograph by Chris John: 312

Courtesy of Jerry Matthews 146

Courtesy of Norwood Hills Country Club: 144

Courtesy of Oak Hill Country Club: 140

Courtesy of Overlake Golf & Country Club: 42; 43 (above right); 43 (below left)

Courtesy of Pierce County, Washington: 91 (middle); 91 (right)

Courtesy of PNGA: 36

Courtesy of Royal Colwood Golf Club: 45;

Courtesy of Royal Queensland Golf Club: 68 (above left); 68 (above right); 68 (below)

Courtesy of RTJII: 91 (left)

Courtesy of Rutland Country Club: 147 (above right)

Courtesy of Scioto Country Club: 50 (above); 50 (below)

Courtesy of Gerry Stratford: 268; 270; 271 (above); 272–273; 275

Courtesy of Taconic Golf Club: 148

Courtesy of the Tillinghast Association: 206; 207

Courtesy of the Tufts Archives: 176; 178; 179; 181 (above); 182 (above)

Courtesy of Tom Ward: 260

Courtesy of Woodhall Spa: 136 (right)

Courtesy of Yarram Golf Club: 27 (above left); 27 (above right); 27 (below); 32

Mike DeVries: 172; 175 (above left); 175 (below); 175 (right)

Susan G. Drinker: 210; 214–215; 222 (above)

Dick Durrance II: xiv; 97 (above left); 97 (above right); 213; 215; 216; 218; 218–219; 220 (above left); 220 (above right); 220 (below right); 220 (below left); 221; 222–223

Jim Engh: 306–307; 308; 309 (above left); 309 (above right); 309 (below); 310; 311

Juan Espi: 316

Shannon E. Fisher: 118; 121 (above); 121 (below); 122 (above); 122 (below); 123 (above); 123 (below right); 123 (below left); 125 (above); 125 (below)

Ron Forse: 271 (left)

Ronald Fream: 317; 319

Golf magazine, The Netherlands (Now defunct): 238 (above); 238 (below); 239 (above)

Euan Grant: 102 (below)

John and Jeannie Henebry: 48; 57

Ross Holden: 102 (above)

Margo MacArthur James: 83 (above left); 83 (above right); 83 (below right); 83 (below left)

Taliferro Jones: 99

Tyler Kearns: 276; 278; 279; 280–281

Sam Kestin: 302 left; 302 (right)

Paul Kimber: 106–107

Barry King: 200; 204

Bob Labbance: 143 (above left); 147 (above left); 147 (below); 149 (left); 149 (right)

Richard Latham: 132; 135; 136 (left); 138 (left); 138 (right); 139

Grant Leversha: 315

Gary Lynagh Photography: 71 (below left); 71 (below right); 72 (below); 73; 75 (below)

Mackenzie & Ebert Ltd.: 224; 227; 228

Kevin Mendik: 143 (above right); 143 (below); 145; 151

Mike Nuzzo: 110; 113; 115; 116

Frank Pont: 230; 231; 232; 233 (above); 233 (below left); 233 (below right); 234; 235; 236; 239 (below); 241 (above left); 241 (above right); 241 (below); 242; 243; 244; 245 (above); 245 (below); 246 (above); 246 (below); 246 (below right)

Tony Ristola: 16; 19; 20; 21

Wood Sabold: 248; 250; 251; 252; 253; 255

David Scaletti: 22; 25; 26 (below left); 28 (above left); 28 (above right); 28 (below); 30 (right); 31; 33; 184; 187; 188; 189; 191; 192; 320; 323; 325

Ian Scott-Taylor: 154 (below)

Joshua C.F. Smith: 158; 162; 163 (above); 163 (below); 168 (above)

Scott Stambaugh: 34; 37 (above); 37 (below); 38 (above left); 38 (above right); 38 (below); 43 (above left); 43 (above middle); 43 (below right); 46

Mike Strantz: 58; 59; 60 (above); 60 (below); 61; 62; 63 (above); 63 (below); 64 (above); 64 (below); 65

Mark Thawley: 165

Einar Tryggvason: 292; 295 (above); 296

George Waters: 160; 167; 168 (below); 169; 170

W. Dunlop White III: 182 (right)

Contributors

Jay Blasi

A resident of Los Gatos, California, and project architect for Robert Trent Jones II, LLC, Jay's representative projects have been Chambers Bay (as project architect), Stanford University Golf Practice Facility and The Patriot. Jay grew up playing golf on the family's backyard green in Madison, Wisconsin. By high school he'd listed his career goal: 'To design a golf course that would play host to the US Open'. Jay majored in landscape architecture at The University of Wisconsin, where he completed two-year long golf projects, including the expansion of UW Ridge. Upon graduation he joined Robert Trent Jones II, LLC in 2001, providing design support to other designers for almost three years. Jay's first opportunity in a leading, creative role was at Chambers Bay.

Bruce Charlton

President and chief design officer of Robert Trent Jones II, LLC, he joined the firm in 1981 following graduation from the University of Arizona with a degree in Landscape Architecture. His more than fifty golf-course designs— which have won countless awards and accolades—include Trans Strait Golf Club and Yalong Bay Golf Club, China; Skjoldenaesholm Golf Center, Denmark; Bro Hof Slott Golf Club, Sweden; Arizona National, Arizona; The Bridges at Rancho Santa Fe, California; Osprey Meadows at Tamarack Resort, Idaho; Southern Highlands, Las Vegas; and Chambers Bay, Washington. Charlton is currently a member of the executive committee of the American Society of Golf Course Architects (ASGCA), and is serving as the organisation's president in 2008/2009. The author of many articles about the golf industry, he enjoys speaking to golf-related audiences. Bruce lives in Los Altos, California, with his wife Maridee and their daughter Casey.

Trevor Colvin

Trevor Colvin plays to a handicap of eight or nine about once every three years; the rest of the time battling to maintain a handicap in the low-twenties. Colvin is a firm believer that golf is a game played in the space between the ears and loves the game for the constant challenge that it presents. His favourite course is 'The Dunes' followed closely by Yarram, both in the Australian state of Victoria. Trevor is a committee member at Yarram and operates a boutique marketing consultancy in South Gippsland having made a sea-change with his wife, Susie, ten years ago. Colvin is also writing a history of Yarram Golf Club's first 100 years.

Mike DeVries

Mike DeVries grew up playing golf with his grandfather and working at the great Alister Mackenzie course, Crystal Downs (Michigan, USA). Those influences led to his working with Tom Doak and Tom Fazio and earning his Master's degree in Landscape Architecture from the University of Michigan. Founder of DeVries Designs, his work includes Kingsley Club, Greywalls at Marquette GC, Mines GC, Pilgrim's Run and Diamond Springs, all in Michigan. He also has long-range restoration projects completed or underway at Meadow Club (California, USA), St Charles CC (Manitoba, Canada), Siwanoy CC (New York, USA) and Sunningdale CC (New York, USA). A new course is under construction near Hanoi, Vietnam, while other projects in the United States and beyond are being developed.

Ian Douglas

Ian McKinnon Douglas was born in 1934, educated at Liverpool College and has enjoyed active involvement in rugby football, cricket and golf. In the case of rugby union, he was a player into his forties, and later refereed for a further ten years. During his National Service with the Black Watch he was stationed in the Far East. Ian's interest in golf continued when he moved to the East Riding, Yorkshire. He was invited to become a member of Ganton Golf Club in 1972, served as its Captain in 1999, and was appointed Club Archivist in 2000. Ian has been married to Judith for fifty years and has three sons, Adam, Graeme and the late-James, along with eight grandchildren.

Martin Ebert

Following Martin's organisation of the Cambridge University's US tour in 1989—a great experience, where he enjoyed playing and studying an array of classic, old courses—a golfing career became his goal. The tour reinforced the appreciation of how golf courses should be eased into the landscape, which was later enhanced while playing many of the great links and inland courses of the United Kingdom. A career in golf-course design began in 1990, leading to fascinating experiences in over twenty countries. Mackenzie & Ebert was formed in 2005, with four of the nine Open Championship venues being advised by the company, along with many new course projects around the world.

Ronald Fream

Ronald Fream has been a golf architect for more than forty-two years. He has been involved in strategic planning, design, construction and turf-grass maintenance in sixty-five countries. Six years of university study concluded when Fream left graduate school to join Robert Trent Jones Inc., in 1966. Golfplan was founded in 1972. Golfplan–Fream, Dale & Ramsey provides comprehensive golf-course architectural services on a worldwide basis. Ronald Fream is a director of the Bhutan Youth Golf Association and is council to the Nepal Golf Federation.

Lester George

A retired Lt Colonel in the US Army Reserve, Lester has been a golf-course architect for twenty years. He has extensive experience in new course design, renovation and restoration. An associate member of the American

Society of Golf Course Architects (ASGCA), Lester was selected by *Golf World* magazine as one of the leading young architects in the country. Lester's most notable golf project to date, Kinloch Golf Club, was awarded several *Golf Digest* honours, including Best New Private Golf Course of 2001, seventh on the list of Best Modern Golf Courses and Number One Golf Course in Virginia. Lester George has also developed a niche in renovating and restoring classic golf courses.

Dr Michael J. Hurdzan

Principal of Hurdzan/Fry Environmental Golf Design, Dr Michael Hurdzan has been honoured many times over the years, including the American Society of Golf Course Architect's (ASGCA) highest honour, the 2007 Donald Ross Award. He has also been presented with the Donald A. Rossi Award by the Golf Course Builders Association of America (GCBAA) for distinguished contributions to his profession. He was *Golf World* magazine's 'Architect of the Year', and *The Board Room* magazine's selection for that same honour, twice. Michael is an internationally recognised authority on golf-course environmental issues. The International Network of Golf awarded Mike and his partner, Dana Fry, industry honours for Achievement in Golf Course Design for their many creative and playable designs. Dr Hurdzan studied turf management at The Ohio State University and earned a Master's degree in Landscape Architecture and a PhD in Environmental Plant Physiology at the University of Vermont. The author of five books, some reviewers have heralded his 400-page book on golf-course architecture as 'the modern "bible" of golf-course design'.

Allan R. Jamieson

Self-employed in the area of real estate finance and development, Allan's thirty-five year affiliation with the California Golf Club has been a focal point of his life, ever since becoming a junior member just a few years after returning from Vietnam. Allan's father, a Scot, introduced him to golf at an early age, and he's been thankful ever since. Allan was married at the club, has won the club championship, enjoyed quality time with his two sons on-site, and has served two terms on the board of directors. Allan has always strongly believed that California's layout belonged in the pantheon of great US courses (as it was in the 1960s), and praises the architectural work of Kyle Phillips for overcoming years of neglect and a lack of vision by key stakeholders.

Charles S. James

Charles is a Senior Managing Director of Fixed Income at PPM America, an investment management advisor based in Chicago, Illinois. A member of the Dunes Club in New Buffalo, Michigan since 2003, he is a self-professed 'average' golfer ... with a handicap of eleven. Charles is a Chartered Financial Analyst, holds a Master's degree in Finance from the University of Chicago, and is the proud owner of an impressive collection of books on golf-course architecture. Youthful summers were spent caddying at Shoreacres in Lake Bluff, Illinois.

Tyler Kearns

A graduate of the Faculty of Architecture at the University of Manitoba, Tyler has worked as a design associate for golf-course architect David Grant since 2001. His interest in golf-course architecture was spurred on at a young age by the shared passion he and his father held for their home course, Donald Ross's Elmhurst Golf & Country Club. It manifests itself today in an extensive golf library and an incessant desire to seek out interesting golf experiences during his travels.

Sam Kestin

Sam Kestin is a twenty-three-year-old New York native, with a major in Political Science and a minor in International Relations. Sam graduated from the University of Southern California in 2009 and is currently living in Los Angeles. In the midst of a busy life, he can either be found at Riviera Country Club, where he maintains a 1.1 USGA index golf handicap; the Seawane Club, where he won the Club

Championship in 2008; or in front of his computer ... indulging his passion for writing. A published author, his work has appeared in local, national and international periodicals—*Emmy Magazine, Southland Golf Magazine* and *Newsweek Japan*, to name a few.

Kevin Kenny

Kevin Kenny is a lecturer with the Open University in Ireland. Among the courses he has taught is 'The Rise of America in the Twentieth Century'. His interest in American history/politics developed in Edinburgh University where, as a mature student, he completed an honours degree in History/Politics. Kevin subsequently completed two post-graduate History degrees while in Scotland; one at Edinburgh, and the other at the University of Aberdeen. He has a longstanding interest in American golf; one of his earliest golfing memories was watching Sam Snead and Arnold Palmer in 1960 win the Canada Cup in Portmarnock, Dublin. This is his first appearance within a golf publication.

Paul Kimber

Paul's love of the outdoors meant a regular nine-to-five job would never suffice. Although a reasonable golfer, his limited ability meant a professional playing career was not an option. His greenkeeping in Sussex allowed free golf, but it wasn't a career that would allow his creativity to flourish. Returning to college, he earned his Master's degree in Landscape Architecture in 1998 at Edinburgh College of Art. With limited opportunities for golf-course design work, Paul freelanced for landscape firms. This allowed spare time to work (gratis) alongside European Golf Design to ensure his resume was primed should an opportunity present. In 2000, Paul became employee number two with DMK Golf Design. Following several international assignments, Paul moved to St Andrews, where he oversaw the design and construction of 'The Castle'. In 2006, Paul was promoted to Director.

Casey Krahenbuhl

Casey graduated from Northern Arizona University, where he started his career by building a local golf course as an irrigation labourer for Wadsworth Golf Construction. After studying his senior year in Mexico, he returned to Arizona to continue building golf courses as a construction superintendent. Ten years later, he met David McLay Kidd and the two quickly gained one another's respect and admiration. Casey reluctantly left Wadsworth and is now a Senior Design Associate for DMK Golf Design. He lives in Bend, Oregon, with his wife Lacy and daughter Ava.

Richard A. Latham

Richard A. Latham has been involved in golf for the past thirty-six years in one capacity or another. He graduated with a degree in Mathematics and worked in the aerospace industry before switching to the golf industry on a full-time basis. He has enjoyed a long and successful amateur playing career and has worked in golf administration for the past eighteen years. He is currently the Director of Operations at Woodhall Spa. The history of golf-course architecture has always been of huge interest to Richard, and he is fascinated by the world's top 100 golf courses and their evolution. He has published *The Definitive Guide to the Hotchkin Course, Woodhall Spa* and *The Evolution of the Links at The Royal County Down Golf Club*. A similar publication studying the development of Muirfield will be published shortly.

Ian Lynagh

The archivist, a past captain and a thirty-five year member of Royal Queensland Golf Club, Ian holds a PhD in Psychology and, for some twenty years, was a consultant sport psychologist to the Australian Institute of Sport. At various periods in the 1980s and 1990s, Ian was the consultant to the PGA's trainee professionals and the QLGU's development squad, introducing them to the mental side of the game. Subsequently, he has worked with many of Queensland's noted golf professionals, both men and women. Ian has travelled widely in relation to athletes, sporting teams and international competition. Other than a stint of a few years in the United States, Ian has resided in Brisbane, Australia—his city of origin.

Jeff Mingay

Jeff Mingay has worked with fellow Canadian golf-course architect Rod Whitman since 2001. As Senior Associate with Rod Whitman Golf Course Design, Mingay participates with every aspect of golf-course design and construction, including feature shaping. Mingay and Whitman have worked on a number of notable designs throughout Canada, including Blackhawk Golf Club in Edmonton, Alberta. Blackhawk currently ranks fifteenth on *SCOREGolf* magazine's list of the top-100 courses in Canada. A keen student of the history of golf and golf-course architecture, Mingay is a noted author as well. His expert essays on golf-course design and construction appear in various publications throughout the world. Renowned golf columnist, Lorne Rubenstein, calls Mingay 'one of the sharpest young men working in and around the field of golf-course design today'.

Mike Nuzzo

Principal of Nuzzo Course Design, Mike recently completed the design of Wolf Point Club on the Gulf Coast of Texas. The design is truly unusual, as was the combination of old-fashioned and modern techniques to build and maintain the course. Using native materials and labour, coupled with digital planning and GPS technology, ensured efficient construction and maintenance programs. His client loves the course, setting out to play it every day; Mike, meanwhile, states, 'It is the most fun course I've played in years'. The author of a blog titled 'An Ideal Golf Course', Mike is quick to point out that it isn't '*The* Ideal Golf Course'.

Tim Liddy

Tim Liddy/Associates, Inc. was formed in 1993. It is a small, select firm providing quality golf-course design services. In the firm's brief history it has won many awards and created golf courses of enduring quality. He has collaborated extensively with Pete Dye for two decades. Among his solo projects are the Trophy Club in Lebanon, Indiana, and a renovation of The Duke's in St Andrews, Scotland. Tim Liddy is a member of the American Society of Golf Course Architects (ASGCA).

Frank Pont

Frank Pont spent most of his working life in civil engineering, strategy consulting and investment banking before deciding to do something 'useful' with his life. He became a golf-course architect. After completing a MSc in Golf Architecture in Scotland, then gaining some experience with David Kidd, he started Infinite Variety Golf Design in Amsterdam in 2004. Since then Frank has established himself as one of the leading restorers of classic golf courses on the continent, specialising on Colt, Simpson and Pennink. He has also completed three new courses and has several exciting projects in the pipeline.

Edwin Roald

Edwin established his golf-course design firm in 2001. Operating internationally, it now has offices in Bulgaria, Philippines and Edwin's home country of Iceland. Edwin believes there is room for lowering construction and operational costs on golf courses, and that this can be achieved, in part, by being more creative and liberal with the canvas provided at the start of each project. With four years of education in marketing and economics, plus in excess of four more years in golf-specific study in Britain, Edwin feels he can help deliver a sound business platform both alongside and through his design.

Ian Scott-Taylor

Ian Scott-Taylor's golf architectural career has spanned twenty years to include involvement with, or leading, over sixty major design projects throughout sixteen countries. A Welshman, he opened his own practice in 1991 in Wales and has worked with David Feherty, Brian Huggett and Ian Woosnam on numerous sites. In 1998, Scott-Taylor relocated to the United States to create a championship British golf course on the Eastern Shore of Maryland—the result, critically acclaimed Hunters Oak Golf Club in Queenstown. Scott-Taylor sees a special need for accurate restoration of classic courses and environmentally sensitive solutions for course improvement and expansion. His goal is to build courses that will become the timeless standard of the game.

Doug Sobieski

While teaching himself to play as a teenager on a nondescript public course in Brighton, Michigan, Doug spent countless hours reading the history of the game and imagining one day playing the most famous courses in the world. After graduating in 1989 from Stetson University in Deland, Florida, he became a PGA Professional while working for Arnold Palmer at the Bay Hill Club in Orlando, Florida. Doug now resides in Dublin, Ohio, with his wife Kerry and daughter Hannah, working in technology leasing. He has fulfilled his lifelong dream of membership in one of the world's greatest courses: Ballyneal in Holyoke, Colorado.

Scott Stambaugh

Scott is currently the Golf Course Superintendent at the A. V. Macan-designed Overlake Golf and Country Club in Medina, Washington, while his career in golf-course management began at the Tacoma Country and Golf Club in Tacoma, Washington. He then relocated to Pebble Beach, California, where he served as the Assistant Golf Course Superintendent at the Monterey Peninsula Country Club. During this period he also supervised the renovation and grow-in of the 1926 Seth Raynor-designed Dunes course, carried out by Rees Jones. Ensuing superintendent roles in the bay area of San Francisco allowed him to live among the vines of the Napa Valley and enjoy his other passion first-hand. A member of the GCSAA, NTA and the GCSANC, Scott lives outside of Seattle, Washington, with his wife Heather and their two daughters.

Gerald W. Stratford

Gerald Stratford is a fourth-generation Californian. Other than brief sojourns for military service and college study, he has continued to call the 'Golden' state his home for sixty-eight years. A Philosophy major and varsity tennis player at UVA, he founded Stratford Design Associates and for several years taught Graphic Design and Architecture to high school students. Since retirement Gerry devotes his time to writing about golf and playing with his eight grandchildren. Gerry is President of the Donald Ross Society, an international organisation dedicated to the restoration and preservation of classic golf courses. He serves on the Olympic Club's Green Committee and on the Steering Committee for the renovation at the PGCC. Gerry is a member of the Northern California Golf Writers Association and regularly publishes articles on the game of Golf, Golf Course Maintenance and Golf Course Architecture. He is the Feature Writer for the Olympic Club Magazine, *The Olympian*.

W. Dunlop White III

A crack amateur golfer and the past president of The Donald Ross Society, Dunlop is a long-time historian of classical golf-course architecture. His treatises on restorations and tree management are covered by most major golf publications. Dunlop also serves on the USGA Architecture Archive Committee, a group committed to the development of a central repository for historic architecture materials at The Arnold Palmer Centre in Far Hills, New Jersey. Dunlop is also active with 'Golf House Carolinas', a similar initiative for The Carolinas Golf Association in Pinehurst, North Carolina. White volunteers as a design panellist for *Golfweek* and *North Carolina Business* and sits on the Board of The Wyndham Championship, a distinguished PGA Tour event long-remembered as The Greater Greensboro Open. Dunlop also acts as a director of the Triad Chapter of The First Tee.

David Wood

David Wood is the author of *Around the World in 80 Rounds* (St Martin's Press, 2008). David writes on golf, travel and humour for numerous periodicals. An in-demand speaker, his keynote presentation for business groups and associations—*Challenge Your Inner Adventurer*—focuses on 'breaking out' of comfort zones and pursuing dreams. David resides in Seattle, Washington.

Philip Young

Philip Young is the Historian for the Tillinghast Association as well as a published author. In addition to numerous articles, short stories and poems, among his books is his biography of the golf-course architect whose work he has studied for many years, *Tillinghast: Creator of Golf Courses*. Phil also owns Golden Age Research, a company that provides research services for golf courses and architects. Phil's passion for golf has been put up with for the more than thirty-three years he has been married to his wife Maria. They have two sons, Joel and Kiel, neither of whom play.

Index